COMPOSING
A TEACHER STUDY GROUP
Learning About Inquiry
in Primary Classrooms

✠ ✠ ✠

COMPOSING
A TEACHER STUDY GROUP
Learning About Inquiry
in Primary Classrooms

¤ ¤ ¤

Richard J. Meyer
Linda Brown
Elizabeth DeNino
Kimberly Larson
Mona McKenzie
Kimberly Ridder
Kimberly Zetterman

LEA LAWRENCE ERLBAUM ASSOCIATES, PUBLISHERS
1998 Mahwah, New Jersey   London

Lawrence Erlbaum Associates, Inc., Publishers
10 Industrial Avenue
Mahwah, New Jersey 07430

Cover mural designed by Nora Lorraine
Cover design by Kathryn Houghtaling

Library of Congress Cataloging-in-Publication Data

Composing a teacher study group : learning about inquiry in primary
classrooms / Richard J. Meyer ... [et al.].
        p.   cm.
    Includes bibliographical references (p.) and indexes.
    ISBN 0-8058-2699-8 (alk. paper). — ISBN 0-8058-2700-5 (pbk. : alk.
paper)
        1. Action research in education—United States—Case studies.
    2. Education, Primary—Research—United States—Case studies.
    3. Elementary school teachers—In-service training—United
    States—Case studies. I. Meyer, Richard J., 1949-   .
LB1028.24.C66   1997
372.24'1'072—dc21   97-31515
                                                            CIP

Books published by Lawrence Erlbaum Associates are printed on
acid-free paper, and their bindings are chosen for strength and
durability.

Printed in the United States of America
10   9   8   7   6   5   4   3   2   1

This book is dedicated to our families and friends for supporting us as we endeavored to have our voices heard.

And to the children of that very special school in which we learned so much during the years of our study group activity.

And to children, teachers, families, and schools facing the difficult questions with the spirit and enthusiasm of inquiring minds.

Contents

¤ ¤ ¤

PART II
SUSTAINED COMMITMENTS: CULTIVATING
THE GROUP, VOICE, POLITICS, AND ADVOCACY
by Richard J. Meyer

Preface

¤ ¤ ¤

If learning is not made public, it is a waste.

—Potok (1967, p. 142)

Our inquiry group began at Ridgeway Elementary School with many romantic notions of engaging in research that would change teachers, students,
grade-level teams, and the school. The group studied together for 1 year as
part of a district-funded research and development plan and continues to
work together 2 years later, long after funding has evaporated. Herein is the
story of the group, its individual members, the students in members' classrooms, and the many complexities of an inquiry group sustaining itself over
time.

In thinking about the organization of this book, I am reminded of some
old black-and-white movies that I once viewed in a history of film course.
Perhaps you recall scenes in such movies that begin with a completely
darkened screen. Then, the lens seems to open a bit and viewers can see a
tiny hole of light, making out a character or part of the setting. Slowly, the
lens progressively opens until the scene is revealed in its entirety. Film
makers refer to this strategy as "irising out" because it is similar to what
happens in your eyes as your pupils get larger and the iris gets smaller
(appears to move out) under certain lighting conditions. This book irises
out; in Part I, chapter 1 begins with a description of a lens and then focuses
at the center of the "screen" as teachers and students present their inquiry
in chapters 2 through 7. In Part II, the view progressively broadens in each
chapter as I move out from presentations by individual teachers, to a view
of issues across group members, and to broader contexts.

Chapter 1 is the lens through which the rest of the book is viewed. The
chapter has two parts: The first lays out a theory of staff development, and
the second presents the themes that emerged from the years of analysis of
the work of the study group, children, and staff at Ridgeway Elementary
School.

With the lens in place, irising out begins with views of and by teachers and children engaged in inquiry. In chapter 2, Kim Zetterman (hereafter referred to as Kim Z.) presents her second graders' work and her thinking about that work as her class studies the polar regions. Chapter 3 is Kim Ridder's (hereafter referred to as Kim R.) journey into inquiry with her first-grade class. The chapter consists of a section written by Kim R. and a section coauthored by Kim R. and some of her students in their study of rats. Kim Larson (hereafter referred to as Kim L.) wrote chapter 4 to present her dealing with the issue of individual first graders' interests. She was concerned that students might not be pursuing their own interests and addresses this with her students in this chapter.

Chapter 5, written by third-grade teachers Liz DeNino and Linda Brown, is their autobiographical account of becoming inquiry-based teachers. Both chapters 4 and 5 are also about relationships as readers are offered insights into the unique relationships that teachers cultivated as they engaged in their learning. Chapter 6 is Mona McKenzie's account of intertwining Montessori theory and method with contemporary research in written language development in her multiage primary classroom. It is also about spirituality and teaching and learning. In chapter 7, I describe my role as a university researcher and resource for the group.

Part II involves irising out further to a broader view of the impact and implications of this type of work. In chapter 8, I discuss themes and thoughts across the teachers' writing in the previous chapters and consider why some group members chose not to write. In chapter 9, I use the lens described in chapter 1, to move the focus outward to discuss how the group evolved into one of inquiry. Chapter 10 focuses on how group members sustained the group by responding to mutual and individual needs. In chapter 11, I iris out further to consider broader issues of teacher inquiry, specifically I address what occurs as teachers express their voices. This includes a discussion of the discomfort felt by nonmembers of the group who taught at the same school in which the group regularly met. I discuss the politics within the classroom, the school, the district, and broader contexts of this type of work.

The final chapter is a discussion of the implications of teachers and students as inquirers. I return to the lens presented in chapter 1 and offer possible ways of refining that lens in the future when considering the complexity of teacher and student inquiry.

Throughout the years that our group worked together making our stories public to each other, I learned what Allende (1989) means when she writes of the variety and intensity of telling our stories:

> There are all kinds of stories. Some are born with the telling; their substance is language, and before someone puts them into words they are but a hint of an emotion,

a caprice of mind, an image, or an intangible recollection. Others are manifest whole, like an apple, and can be repeated infinitely without risk of altering their meaning. Some are taken from reality and processed through inspiration, while others rise up from an instant of inspiration and become real after being told. And then there are secret stories that remain hidden in the shadows of the mind; they are like living organisms, they grow roots and tentacles, they become covered with excrescences and parasites, and with time are transformed into the matter of nightmares. To exorcise the demons of memory, it is sometimes necessary to tell them as a story. (p. 261)

It is my hope that the stories, curiosities, and passions of the students and teachers in this book will support and encourage other groups of inquirers as they initiate, sustain, and make public their work, and that university researchers involved with such groups will sense genuine support and respect for their commitment.

ACKNOWLEDGMENTS

We had quite a bit of help in making this book a reality. Lincoln Public Schools, Lincoln, Nebraska, provided funding for us during the first year of our group's work. Jane Erickson and Neal Cross were extremely supportive in allowing a year of research and development as part of the district's implementation of its early childhood curriculum. Jane and Pam Magdanz provided inspiration and reminded the group to think big and use our imaginations to uncover the many possibilities of ourselves and the students at Ridgeway.

Kathy Short helped me understand the many complexities of inquiry when it is viewed as contextualized work occurring within a school building and district. She, as always, was encouraging and thought provoking.

Naomi Silverman is a dream-come-true editor who listens very carefully and, when writers suffer the pain and loneliness of their work, offers care and nurturing.

During the analysis of 3 years worth of data, I was fortunate to have the help of colleagues such as Ruth Heaton, Steve Swidler, and Joan Rankin. And, as always, Hanna Fingeret was a friend and colleague who provided inspiration and feedback.

John Zetterman aided in the creation of a school climate that allowed and encouraged teachers to be different from their colleagues.

Thanks go to the children whose work is seen in the pages of this book. They are the reason we do this work, and they are the hope for the many possibilities ahead. We received outstanding and supportive feedback from Gail Burnaford of National-Louis University, Michael O'Loughlin of Hofstra University, and Gary Manning of the University of Alabama at Birmingham. We appreciate the time they invested and the encouragement they offered.

The mural on the cover of this book was designed by Nora Lorraine, art specialist and artist. Its theme complements curriculum about life cycles and living things. Students who worked on this mural came from many different countries, including Vietnam, Russia, Korea, Bosnia, Mexico, and the United States. The students reflect the international population of the school.

Children who worked on the mural:

Grade 1:
Addullah Al-Hajamy
Malak Al-Khaweldeh
Sonja Asllani
Tu Ha
Loi Le
Derek Lyne
Jackson McNeil
Aryelle Moore
Margot Nason
Kesha Nelson
Dana Nguyen
Anna Popov
Diana Ramos
Andrey Rybak
Oleg Titov
Alexandra Toftul
Hoang Vo
Julie Zwiebel

Grade 2:
Nash Bergman
Kimberlee Coil
Anastasia Crawford
Hun Choi
Alexander Derun
Sanja Fejzic
Teresa James
Hiep Le
Elizabeth Losh

Montessori:
Celeste Case-Ruchala
Chrissa Huss

Matthew Huss
Darko Kapetanovic
Eric Post
Kalisa Schweitzer

Grade 3:
Travis Beck
Ashley Flynn
Donovan Hilt
Taysha Krzhizhanovskaya
Amanda Loch
Loren Prasek
Andrew Sipple
Colby Woodson

—*Richard J. Meyer*

PART I

Teachers and Students Wandering and Wondering: Participatory Professional Development

¤ ¤ ¤

This book is about children's and teachers' learning at Ridgeway Elementary School.[1] It is about clearing the way for children's learning, which means getting a lot of stuff out of their way, getting it out of teachers' ways, and letting children and teachers wander and wonder together. Authentic learning involves making classroom, school, and community resources accessible to students. Such talk, when looked on as child-generated curriculum, is quite political because it unsettles many people in a school district. The years of work that the group of teachers in this book and I have invested in the children at Ridgeway have always had children's learning as the ultimate goal.

When we began meeting, we were not sure exactly how we would go about accomplishing the goal of enhancing children's learning. Eventually, the teachers found that when they listened to what their students wanted to learn, the teachers could support learning, far surpass district goals, and be surprised at the possibilities that were uncovered in their classrooms. Part I begins with a chapter on the theoretical and thematic justifications of inquiry-based study groups. It is followed by chapters on the inquiry activity of some of the group members and their students at Ridgeway.

---

[1] Although we use our own names and the real first names of most of our students throughout this book, "Ridgeway" is a pseudonym. Students whose confidentiality might be at risk are represented by an arbitrary first letter followed by a dash (e.g., L—).

Chapter 1

The School as a Place for Teachers' Learning

Richard J. Meyer
University of Nebraska–Lincoln

¤ ¤ ¤

The wise woman listened and laughed. "My dear child, you have found the secret."
Jenny was puzzled. "How can I have found it?"
"Because, you see, the secret of wisdom is to be curious—to take the time to look closely, to use all your senses to see and touch and taste and smell and hear. To keep on wandering and wondering."
"Wandering and wondering," Jenny repeated softly.
"And if you don't find all the answers, you will surely find more to marvel at in this curving, curling world that spins around and around amid the stars."

—Merriam (1991)

Teachers, as decision makers, are constantly wandering and wondering; they "marvel at this curving, curling world" as it unfolds within their schools and classrooms. They make decisions about who they want to be, their relationships with colleagues and students, and other parts of their personal and professional lives. They are involved in composing themselves.

Composing does not necessarily mean writing, as we might think when we recall composition classes. Composing may refer to thinking, moving, dancing, writing, talking, singing, improvising, or in some way taking the essence of who we are and reflecting on it, juggling it, mixing it up, facing it, questioning it, and, if we decide, transforming it. Composing is enacted through asking questions, squinting our eyes in thought, straining our minds, playing with our minds, engaging the minds of others; it can be as seemingly loose and flowing as jazz or as tight and structured as certain statistical analyses. Composing is enacted through inquiring minds.

As teachers ask questions piqued by their curiosity about who they are and who they are becoming, they make decisions. They may quietly acquiesce to the pressures of a district and teach in ways that they find disagreeable; they may quietly carry out sabotage against the district's required curriculum with few others aware of what they are doing; or they may engage actively as advocates for themselves, their colleagues, and their students as they construct curriculum that makes sense in the local contexts of their classrooms and their school. Any of these ways of engaging themselves as decision makers, or the infinite other possibilities of such engagement, are expressions of their composing. And there are feelings attached to composing. Teachers might feel the joy of learning with children and colleagues; they might feel the tension that rests in disagreeing with others; they might feel complicitous with activity that seems to hurt children's opportunities for success (O'Laughlin, Bierwiler, & Serra, 1996); all of these feelings, and a plethora of others, are parts of the disruption that accompanies teachers as they engage in composing who they are and how they want to be. Teachers' composing and disrupting activity may be reflected in classroom activity, thereby touching the lives of children who are composing and disrupting their understandings of themselves, their colleagues in learning, and their notions of schooling.

   Composing and *disrupting* are the themes of this book. Each chapter is saturated with these two themes, not because I imposed the themes on the work, but because the themes emerged from the work. Composing and disrupting are not dichotomous; they are mutually constructed and multifaceted. I continue the discussion of composing and disrupting after providing some background information.

   I have three purposes for this chapter. First, I briefly describe Ridgeway Elementary School and how our study group began; I refer to this as the context of our work. Second, I present a view of staff development that I have been conceptualizing and enacting with teachers in recent years (Meyer, 1995). Third, the remainder of the chapter focuses on the group's 3 years of being curious together. I discuss the two themes, composing and disrupting, that emerged from my analysis of the data that I collected at and with the staff and students at Ridgeway. The view of staff development and an explication of the themes are presented early in this book with the intention of having them serve as the lenses for viewing and understanding the influence that teacher and student inquiry had at Ridgeway.

RIDGEWAY ELEMENTARY SCHOOL

Ridgeway Elementary School is located in a medium-size city in a midwestern state; the school has various preschool programs and includes 590 children through sixth grade. Ridgeway is quite diverse with 9.01% African-

American, 16.5% Asian, 12.24% Hispanic, 1.7% Native American, and 60.54% White students. Twenty-six percent of the students are involved in the English as a second language (ESL) program. It is one of the city's five ESL schools with students from 15 different countries.More than 75% of the students attending Ridgeway receive free lunches, an indication of the socioeconomic status of the students. Of the 590 students in the school during the first year of this study, more than 100 moved to a different school and just about the same number arrived. The principal attributes this high mobility rate to issues and problems associated with poverty. A more complete description of the school is presented in Appendix A.

Our study group formed with the help of a 1-year grant awarded to Ridgeway following an in-district funding competition among the 32 elementary schools in the district. The grant money, originating from the district's early childhood consultant, Jane Erickson, was to be used to help the faculty incorporate the principles of developmentally appropriate practice (Bredekamp, 1987) into their classrooms. Although developmentally appropriate practice typically focuses on children 8 years of age and younger, all Ridgeway staff agreed to study the principles for 1 year. Different groups of teachers were involved in different activities and commitments over the course of the year. I was asked by Jane Erickson to participate in some capacity. Consistent with the view of staff development presented next, I offered to meet regularly with teachers to focus on issues they identified as important as they were trying to become increasingly developmentally appropriate in their practices. In Appendix A, I present more specific details about the formation of the group, including a discussion of incentives that were made available to the participants (in-district staff development credit or university credit).

The study group described in this book was made up of teachers from two first grades, one second grade, three third grades, a multiage/Montessori, and an early childhood special education program. The eight teachers and I met every Wednesday afternoon for the entire school year during the first year of our study group; Jane Erickson joined us twice each month. I was released from two courses at the university where I teach in order to spend considerable time at Ridgeway during the school week. I was at the school for a minimum of one full day each week. It usually took close to another full day to elaborate field notes, transcribe interviews and taped sessions, and engage in the ongoing constant comparative analysis (Glaser & Strauss, 1967; Spradley, 1980) that resulted in the themes presented here. During the years that followed, we met at least once each month, formally, and continue to do so at the time of this writing. With that brief overview of the context, I turn to an elaboration of the view of staff development that supported and cultivated the study group's growth.

A VIEW OF STAFF DEVELOPMENT

Wells (1986) explains how schools typically reach decisions about staff development:

> Traditionally, decisions about curriculum, pedagogy and school organization have been made by theorists, researchers and policy makers, based in universities or ministry offices. Plans for putting these decisions into effect are then drawn up by senior administrators in each jurisdiction, who transmit them to the school administrators who are responsible, in turn, for ensuring that they are implemented. In this hierarchical structure, expertise is equated with power and status, that is to say with those who, at the apex of the pyramid, are furthest removed from the actual sites of learning and teaching. (p. 1)

The approach I took in our study group is called *servicing-in* (Meyer, 1995) and is based on the idea that an outsider who approaches a school to do "in-servicing" does not understand the context sufficiently to make recommendations for teacher practice. Servicing-in requires the outsider (me, in this case) to learn about, be respectful of, and put some tension on the existing school culture. I worked at this relationship with group members by spending at least one full day each week at the school; I interviewed faculty and staff, worked with children, and was an active participant observer (Agar, 1980). Much in the way that Dyson (1993) discusses children's writing as an act performed within a community, servicing-in requires the outsider to learn about the community before engaging as a resource. It is a commitment over time and is steeped in the hope that Van Manen (1986) describes as that which "gives us patience, tolerance and belief in the possibilities for our children"(p. 27) and, I would add, possibilities for their teachers and those who work with their teachers.

Servicing-in supports teachers as individuals, consistent with Wideen's (1987) view that:

> ... collaboration, collegiality and mutual adaptation [are] necessary ingredients in any school improvement plan.à[this] views single-minded policy and managerial perspectives of school reform with skepticism. It rejects the notion that teachers and school principals can be manipulated through fiat and exhortation. (p. 5)

Servicing-in fundamentally rests in Vygotsky's (1978) notion of the zone of proximal development that suggests a tension between a learner and an *other* who acts as a mediator. The zone is an approach to problem solving that involves "collaboration with more capable peers" (Vygotsky, 1978, p. 86), the more capable being an *other*. In this servicing-in relationship with Ridgeway, the *other* (me, also called researcher, staff developer, or mediator) was a learner along with those who work at the school. Indeed, the role of more capable peer was variable in our group of teachers because each member had areas of expertise that were expressed during our time together, supporting any group member as an *other* who was more knowledgeable. This means that I was not, nor was any other member of the group, consistently and regularly the "more knowing other" that Vygotsky describes. This role changed as each member offered insights that were unique to their individual understanding of Ridgeway and as that understanding put tension on others' existing understanding.

Understanding and living a professional life in the school setting requires "social intelligence" (Dewey, 1938) so that individuals can create ideas, develop them, and maintain flexibility to fit what emerges within the context. Dewey expressed it this way:

> The plan, in other words, is a cooperative enterprise, not a dictation. The teacher's suggestion is not a mold for a cast-iron result but is a starting point to be developed into a plan through contributions from the experience of all engaged in the learning process. ...The essential point is that the purpose grow and take shape through the process of social intelligence. (Dewey, 1938, p. 72)

The foundational premises of servicing-in are that: teachers know the context well (Klassen & Short, 1992); they understand the institutional regularities (Sarason, 1971) with which they live; and that all changes are built upon their emerging change agendas. As I explained elsewhere (Meyer, 1995):

> Griffin (1983) defines staff development as "any systematic attempt to alter the professional practices, beliefs, and understandings of school persons toward an articulated end" (p. 2). In a servicing-in approach, the "articulated end" is constructed via negotiation with all present at the site. This means that the role of the outside individual changes from "developer" to mediator. Working together to articulate an end and develop vehicles for that articulation is much harder work than traditional transmission approaches to staff development because of the lack of predictability and the need to build a trusting and caring environment. (p. 4)

Servicing-in is an active approach to participatory staff development that views teachers as "meaning-makers" (Wells, 1986); Wells' discussion of children as meaning-makers whose meaning-making is often disregarded or offered low prestige in the school setting is applicable to teachers, too, because their professional thinking is overlooked when their professional development is prescriptive. Servicing-in is a democratic process in which agendas are mutually constructed. It involves supporting groups of teachers in "formulating their own alternatives, trying them out in practice, and selecting those that they judge to be successful" and is a commitment to "teachers in a process of learning" (Wells & Chang-Wells, 1992, p. 10). It is also a commitment to university researchers as being covoyagers on this learning journey.

Servicing-in is a sociocultural approach to staff development:

> [T]he goal of a sociocultural approach to mind is to explicate how human action is situated in cultural, historical, and institutional settings ... the key to such an explication is to use the notion of mediated action as a unit of analysis and the person(s) acting with mediational means as the relevant description of the agent of this action. From this perspective, any tendency to focus exclusively on the action, the person(s), or the mediational means in isolation is misleading. (Wertsch, 1991, p. 119)

And there is more to it, as well, because servicing-in may involve advocacy. Once members of a group increase their understanding of a situation, they might decide to initiate actions to change their own quality of life in the situation or the quality of life of those in their care—their students. Servicing-in is a form of social responsibility and social activism. Greene (1995) engenders this idea in her call for imagination as a facet of social change:

> Again, it may be the recovery of imagination that lessens the social paralysis we see around us and restores the sense that something can be done in the name of what is decent and humane. (p. 34)
> We need ... to recapture some of the experiences of coming together that occurred in the peace movement and the civil rights movement. We need to articulate what it signifies for some of us to support people with AIDS, to feed and house homeless persons in some dignified way, to offer day-long support to the very young in store-front schools, to bring into being teacher communities in our working spaces. (p. 197)

Of course, there already are "teacher communities in our working spaces," but these communities do not always support teacher development, student learning, or teacher activism.

A commitment to servicing-in is a commitment to uncertainty because we cannot predict what group members may identify as urgent, salient, or important and what actions they may want to initiate. As a literacy expert, I might offer suggestions for dealing with some issues within the extant school culture, and may help the group make connections to other agencies for help, if need be. But these actions always occur within our context at Ridgeway. Cohen (1996) suggests that "the school is the unit of change"; our work involves defining that unit less arbitrarily because the unit of change is the group that comes together as a thought collective that has initiating and sustaining change as one of its goals. There are no objective outside observers; everyone is a mediator, an other, and a participant.

Above all, servicing-in may be a rejuvenation of self, a return to self, or a discovery of self. It is a process of reenergizing; it is a return to self for those teachers and staff developers who found their voice, at one point in time, and then either let it go, lost it in the rush of living, or suppressed it. It is a discovery of self for those who were so *busy being good* that they never found a sense of individuality. It is a process that supports resistance because, as Walker (1993) so poignantly demonstrates, "Resistance is the secret of joy!" (p. 280). This is, then, political work because the work to support teachers in understanding their lived experience demands a shift in stance from regarding teachers as passive technicians (Shannon, 1989) to viewing them as active participants who engage in conversations. It is a shift from top–down transmission models (Freire, 1970a) of staff development to genuine conversations, as Hollingsworth (1992) describes:

> Politically, the move to the conversational format for support and research involved a shift in power from my previous role as the teachers' course instructor. I had to change my interactions so that I was no longer telling teachers what I knew (as the group's "expert" on the topic of reading instruction) and checking to see if they had learned it. I had to develop a process of working with them as a colearner and creator of evolving expertise through nonevaluative conversations. To accomplish this, I had to be still and listen. I also had to struggle publicly with what I was learning. Our change in relationship now required that I look at transformation in my own learning … as equally important in determining the success of teachers' knowledge transformations. (p. 375)

Servicing-in ultimately involves a journey into self, into self within a context (being a teacher in a school), into context (understanding the school), and into the lives of others (being a support for others' growth). Increasingly, it feels like a return to something old and wise, a journey similar to the one Momaday (1976) describes as "old and essential" (p. 4); it is "a quest, a going forth upon the way" (p. 88). It is a quest that leads across a variety of literatures and lived experiences. It is a quest that has themes for understanding change and areas of surprise and sometimes discomfort within self or the group.

Quite honestly, I imagined that our group would have "interwoven conversations" (Newman, 1991) about our lives and our literacy and that these conversations would be reflected in classroom strategies and activities that would support children's learning. Newman suggests that:

> … learning and teaching are distinct ventures…. Learning is constructing out of our individual experiences some sense of how the world works. Teaching involves intentionally helping to extend an other's knowledge or skill. Sometimes these two activities connect; frequently, however, they don't. (p. 14)

My goal was to support the connection between teacher learning and teaching. I hoped that our group would become a special branch of the literacy club (Smith, 1988) that would overflow into the teachers' classrooms. And we did that, but in much more complex ways than I ever imagined. As Hollingsworth (1994) explains, "Knowing through relationship to self and others is central to teaching the child" (p. 68). Our relationships became an important part of learning and teaching for the members of our group because of this view of staff development that supported teachers in naming the agendas for our studies.

INQUIRY IS ROOTED IN COMPOSING
AND DISRUPTING

The nature of servicing-in was transformative of ourselves (Hollingsworth, 1994), the curriculum in the participating teachers' classrooms at Ridgeway (Short & Burke, 1991), and of the ethos of the school. The two themes that operated as we learned and grew together, *composing* and *disrupting*, appeared consistently and concomitantly throughout the data. The themes are operational (processes) in that they describe activity that emanated from and affected the group. The themes are my notions; that is, they rest in my interpretation of our group's years together as I engaged in ongoing thematic analysis (Spradley, 1980) of our activity. Teasing these themes out of the transcripts of our meetings, the teachers' inquiries, and the children's inquiries was part of my role as a university-inquirer. I was involved in servicing-in and studying servicing-in, and the themes of composing and disrupting help explain the growth and tension that is presented in the rest of this book (teacher, student, and researcher growth and tension). The two themes and the categories that emerged within them are intended to serve as a frame for understanding the activity described in chapters 2 through 7.

Composing

Composing is not undertaken solely by teachers; it is undertaken by every individual in any setting. We make decisions about who we are, how we will act, and much more as we enter any new setting. These decisions are often made quickly and almost seem unconscious. For example, when you enter your doctor's office because your back is bothering you, you know (perhaps have even rehearsed) what you will say to the doctor. You have an idea of the language you will use, based on your relationship with the doctor, your personal history, your mood, and so on. When we stop to understand how and for what purposes we are composing ourselves, we gain insights into that composition that may be used to change, affirm, or adjust what we are doing. Teachers in schools are involved in composing themselves; so are their students. Indeed, every staff member in a school is involved in this process.

In the inquiry reported in the following chapters, you can see teachers involved in the process of composition. They are composing a view of self as a learner while supporting students in their learning; this is a process that is unique among teachers because many teachers do not see themselves as learners (Hendricks-Lee, Soled, & Yinger, 1995). The teachers' views of children's learning as a socially and mutually constructed event, in turn, supported the children's composition of themselves. The teachers' use of language (e.g., Kim R. calling children "budding scientists, doctors, and artists") and the structure of the classroom as a place in which learners compose themselves are consistent with the composing processes Wilcox (1988) describes:

> The structure and content of classroom interaction inevitably sets up within it certain images of the child. It subtly defines the child's present being and mode of becoming, as well as constructing an image of who the child will become. These images are likely to filter into the child's consciousness in various ways and contribute, along with the actions they bring into being, to the socialization and development of the child. (p. 293)

The teachers in this book support children who are cultivating themselves as artists, doctors, musicians, scientists, and more. Throughout this book, we offer more evidence of the ways in which children were supported in composing themselves as learners and thinkers.

As our group met, we came to understand that we were composing ourselves as writers, speakers, thinkers, advocates for a theoretical stance about learning, and as pliable learners. Members worked with their students to compose a learning environment in their classrooms and at composing a group culture that provided support. The members of our group relied on our group as an arena in which to compose themselves by being tentative, thoughtful, questioning, and curious together. I stress that I, too, was involved in composing, as suggested before in the discussion of staff development. We were all growing.

In the following sections, I present the categories of composing that emerged from my analysis of our years of work together. The categories are those areas of school life that were in some way influenced or changed as our composing progressed. Although I did much of the analysis and writing of this chapter, all of the members of our group read the initial and subsequent writings reflective of my analyses and discussed, debated, changed, suggested, and supported the analytical endeavor. These categories emerged from the members of our group and the students in their classrooms as they composed themselves as inquirers, learners, and creators of curriculum.

Composing Self. The group members found themselves in a variety of roles as the year progressed. We (when I use "we," I include myself) were thinkers and questioners early in the year. We had identified problems, areas of concern, or curiosities that we wanted to pursue by engaging in practical inquiry (Richardson, 1994). Our inquiry led to oral and written language activity, thus we composed ourselves as articulate and struggling (yes, both) readers and writers, too. Readers will see, in the following chapters, the many different types of speakers and writers the group members are becoming. Cochran-Smith and Lytle (1990) suggest that "current research on teaching … constrains, and at times even makes invisible, teachers' roles in the generation of knowledge about teaching and learning in classrooms" (p. 3). Individuals within the group became consumers and creators of knowledge about teaching and learning, similar to some of the (rare) groups that Cochran-Smith and Lytle (p. 4) cite as being involved in generating "knowledge about teaching and learning." The work made members visible to themselves by helping them to understand the school culture. We gained insights into our roles, our position in assumed power structures, and our willingness to address those roles and positions.

Group members' speaking, writing, and thinking developed over the course of our time together, and this led to a sense of voice. The study group's work reflected Brady's (1995) call for "the need for all voices to be equally privileged so that educators and students can locate themselves in history in order to function as the subject of history rather than simply the object" (p. 44). The group began to understand the need to put an end to "teachers … deskilling themselves" (p. 67) at the demand of district (and, therefore, corporate) directives. They understood their work as a call for liberatory staff development (Yonemura, 1982). It is a call for the work that needs to be done to let teachers be the substantive thinkers that Shannon (1989) describes. Although he is discussing the teaching of reading, Shannon's views on teacher and student liberation apply to what occurred in our group:

> Helping both teachers and students to develop their abilities to read their own histories and culture, to see their connections with the large social structure, and to act according to this new knowledge against external control will not only arrest the spread of rationalization of reading programs on a local level but can also lead to its defeat across the United States. (p. 147)

Teachers in our group, as is seen in the chapters to come, found their voices, expressed them, developed them over time, and risked speaking out about their own practice, practices within the school, and district policies. Thus, they composed themselves as advocates for themselves, their children, their work, each other, curriculum, and more. Each teacher found her self in these ways (as a researcher, a writer, a thinker, an orator, and, for some, an advocate); each grew because of what she found. The teachers, in turn, supported their students in becoming thoughtful, curious, and expressive. The following sections provide explanations of ways in which group members composed themselves, the group, and the group's actions as they and their students engaged in inquiry.

Composing Collegial Relationships.   The members of this group had not spoken significantly across grade levels. Ridgeway was organized into grade-level teams that did not often have the opportunity to talk across teams. By being part of our group, teachers initiated affiliations with other grade levels and gained insights into the thinking of teachers at other grade levels and the nature of the activities undertaken in their classrooms. These were new affiliations and tended to be threatening to nongroup members (a form of disrupting discussed later). There was, then, a composing of collegial relationships as individuals who were not previously regarded as those with whom one might associate professionally became active colleagues.

Students were also involved in developing collegial relationships in ways that were unique for them in school. Teachers supported their students in finding colleagues and composing worlds in which they could mutually construct themselves, relationships with each other, and curriculum. Composing collegial relationships, then, occurred within the study group and the classrooms. For example, two students who had not previously worked together both expressed interest in studying the human body. They spent considerable time studying diagrams of the heart and circulatory system. They asked each other questions, drew diagrams, and took copious notes. One of the students was identified (labeled) as a special education student and the other was one of the few identified gifted students at Ridgeway. Completing their dissection of a calf's heart, one turned to the other and said, "We're going to be doctors together, aren't we?" The other replied, "Yes, I think so." They were composing views of each other, possibilities for their futures, and their way of relating to each other as colleagues in learning.

Composing Curriculum.   Composing curriculum means that members of the group were actively involved in creating curriculum (Short & Burke, 1991) as teachers and students identified needs and interests of children. Inquiry (Short & Harste, with Burke, 1996) was the main vehicle for the composing of curriculum and the composition process was multifaceted. The students studied specific areas that they identified as significant for study; the teachers studied the students; the teachers also studied areas that interested them (literacy development, writing, and more); and the teachers studied themselves through their own and my ongoing research. This was curriculum for and by all learners.

There was considerable anxiety associated with the process of composing (or creating) curriculum as teachers wanted the children to meet with success, feared that the principal might disapprove, and were anxious about test results as the end of the year approached. This hints at some of the disruption, discussed later, that occurs with composition.

Composing a Forum for Teacher Expression.   Over the course of the year, our meetings became a forum in which teachers could express their needs. At times, we wanted to explore and make sense of what was happening in classrooms; other times the need to deal with schoolwide issues took precedence. And there were sessions devoted to personal lives as those lives overflowed into school. The public (i.e., within our group) expression of needs is not common to schools because the ethos of most schools (Lortie, 1975) forbids such activity. But our group was what Paley (1995) calls a "safe harbor" for our feelings and thoughts. In chapters 9 and 10, I elaborate on the development of our forum as a collective for reflection.

Composing Classrooms for Student Inquiry.   The members of the group developed kidwatching (Goodman, 1985) skills because of their thinking, interactions with each other, reading, talking, and writing. The sharing of ideas led to curiosities about the possibilities of what children might be able to do in classrooms. Such curiosity led to carefully listening to the expressed and implicit needs and interests of children, and the codevelopment, with the students, of curriculum that responded to those needs and interests. For example, Kim R. and Kim L. walked around their rooms with notebooks, capturing bits of conversations verbatim. They brought these language stories (Harste, Woodward, & Burke, 1984) with them to our meetings and described the contexts from which they were taken; then our group helped Kim R. and Kim L. to use their students' interests to think about inquiry groups. Kim R. and Kim L. returned to their classrooms and engaged their students in the same process.

A brief example demonstrates this process. Kim L. and Kim R. shared the large space that was formed when the accordion doors between their classrooms was left open for the entire year. Often, the children's writing time was preceded by discussions among groups of children scattered around the room. I found Kim L. and Kim R.'s classroom to be a place in which:

> [t]o be literate is to have the disposition to engage appropriately with texts of different types [including oral language] in order to empower action, thinking, and feeling in the context of purposeful social activity. (Wells & Chang-Wells, 1992, p. 147)

The children's discussions disposed them to write, to ask questions, and to inquire. As Halloween approached, the children discussed costumes, candy, and, more often, things that frightened them. This was a scary time of year, and places that were mysterious became increasingly fear-laden as the students invented what they did not yet understand.

"If you go down the basement of the school," one child suggested to a small group of his first-grade peers, "spiders will pee on you and [his body becomes rigid and his teeth clenched] you can't move!" His friends stared at him, awed.

The teachers, overhearing this discussion, bring it back to the large group at the afternoon meeting. They suggest that the children study things that are scary. The basement group (five children who chose to pursue this area of study) suggests that, if the principal accompanies them, they will venture down the eerie stairs and into the basement to make a video and book about the experience. Other students suggest ideas for scary topics they might want to study. The spider group will uncover the many marvels of arachnid life. The shark group, the dinosaur group, and the snake group will also face things that frighten them. These kids are brave, perhaps because they are in a group, together, with teachers who work at understanding and asking questions along with them.

The children's inquiry will eventually remove or alleviate the myths that sometimes generate and perpetuate fear; I call this *demythifying* their fears. The basement group will find empty computer boxes, plenty of overhead lighting, and one dead cockroach in the basement. It was once, they learn, the school cafeteria. Not all inquiry involves composing oneself to face fears; often interests, curiosity, an urgent need to know, or surprises provoke the inquiry process. The teachers in our group supported and cultivated inquiry, but this would not have been possible had they not been actively involved in composing themselves as inquirers along with their students. The teachers, too, asked questions, both of the children and within our group, because as they followed the students' inquiry they were engaging in their own. They, too, were demythifying their understanding of the possibilities and constraints of their teaching and learning in the school.

Soon, all of the teachers were bringing notes from their classrooms to our meetings; we were composing our group as a forum in which to analyze and stretch the composing of inquiry-based classrooms as forums in which students needs and interests were addressed.

Increasingly, our group became intrigued with inquiry. Members wanted to know how to help children compose and pursue a question or an interest. We wanted to understand the cognitive and social conditions that support children's engagement in inquiry. Inquiry assumed the status of a *student need* because we came to understand all that could be learned through this process.

Composing as Subjectification.   Subjectification is the process of taking ownership of self, voice, curriculum, questions, and needs. For the study group, it involved engaging in relationships that made teaching a very "human enterprise" (Lather, 1991, p. 105), one that was not objectively taught, learned, or enacted. It was an enterprise that was subjective, personal, and composed in the unique social (relational) contexts of a teacher's own classroom and explored and stretched in the study group. Subjectification is an active process of "teaching against the grain" (Cochran-Smith, 1991), of invention of self (or reinvention, in the case of Liz and Linda who felt they had learned much in the past, abandoned it, and were rediscovering their roots and beliefs), and of assuming ownership.

Discussions of the work that teachers do must also focus on issues such as putting an end to the objectification of teaching. Objectification focuses on teaching as objective work that can rely on curricular decisions made far from the site of curricular enactment. It implies neutrality and objectivity. The work of our group was not neutral and it was not objective; it could not be because:

> neutrality, objectivity, observable facts, transparent description, clean separation of the interpreter and the interpreted—all these concepts basic to positivist ways of knowing are called into question. Science as codified by conventional methods which marginalize value issues is being reformulated in a way that foregrounds science as a value-constituted and constituting enterprise, no more outside the power/knowledge nexus than any other human enterprise. (Lather, 1991, p. 105)

The teachers were working, many times, in the arena of "critical thought," because composing activity put tension on the status quo. I supported and struggled with them to find ways to turn critical thinking into "emancipatory action" (Lather, 1991, p. 109) in our group, in the classrooms, and in the school. Composing was emancipatory in that it liberated us (teachers, researcher, and students) to create ourselves, curriculum, relationships, and classrooms for inquirers. This is consistent with servicing-in because it involves mutually constructed conversations and agendas for action.

As is seen here, the teachers in this group subjectified their teaching lives by taking ownership; they worked at the subjectification of children's worlds by learning to honor and follow the children's cognitive interests and their social and emotional needs. This meant giving prestige to the "unofficial worlds" (Dyson, 1993) of children, those worlds typically not afforded recognition in school, as important grounds for building self, relationships, and curricular activity within the classroom. Children's study of rats or basements or spiders is consistent with what the children do when they are at play; they passionately invest themselves in finding things out and raising more questions. The teachers and I began to understand what Vygotsky (1978) meant when he wrote:

> ... play creates a zone of proximal development of the child. In play a child always behaves beyond his [or her] average age, above his [or her] daily behavior; in play it

is as though he [or she] were a head taller than himself [or herself]. As in the focus of a magnifying glass, play contains all developmental tendencies in a condensed form and is itself a major source of development. (p. 102)

When at play, children assume ownership of and responsibility for the activity in which they are engaged. When learners (of any age) are involved in subjectified learning, they are involved in thought collectives that are socially constructed and locally owned and operated. This is the true stuff of play.

Composing, as a process, both supported and created the categories previously discussed, including self, voice, collegial relationships in thought collectives, relationships between and among children in classroom thought collectives, curriculum, and subjectification. But composing did not exist without some tension.

Disrupting

The process of composing was not a smooth and easy process; it sent ripples through the school culture as relationships, curriculum, and institutional regularities (Sarason, 1971) were threatened. Each of the categories that constituted an emerging understanding of the process of composing were threatening and, therefore, disruptive of many of those same categories within the culture of Ridgeway School.

The difficulty of teacher change has been documented in the past (Sarason, 1971), as well as more recently (Griffin, 1995). Even as individual teachers might want to change, indeed actively pursue change:

[l]urking in the background are always the many-headed hydras of school culture, the barriers to deep and lasting changes in student–teacher interactions that remain hidden from most participants until their pervasive influence is felt.... Unfortunately, these conventions are not attended to, often because they simply are not obvious, change efforts founder, and, in the end, teachers are seen once again as foot-dragging impediments to school improvement. (Griffin, 1995, p. 44)

The "regularities" (Sarason, 1971) of the school are embedded within the culture of the school and make change difficult; Sarason (1990) refers to the many aspects of school culture that work to keep schools the same as "the intractability to reform." He discusses unlearning, relearning, and the necessity of a commitment of time (p. 146) as elements that are often overlooked by those involved in change. It seems that the culture of the school protects itself from any change and overlooks or silences teachers' voices that speak of change.

Teachers, staff, and students notice when someone in a school changes. If the principal suddenly seems moody or anxious, if another teacher seems teary or extremely happy, we notice. If a child changes in some way, we notice. Changes are moments in the composing and disrupting processes. Our relationship with someone, our understanding of who they are, and our expectations of what they might do are all bounded by our previous interactions with them. A change, something that is noticeable, disrupts the way things have been. Disrupting cannot easily be separated from composing. As Kim R. and Kim L. changed in their thinking and ways of being and talking about classroom activities and strategies, a teacher who was not in our group responded with curiosity, anger, and resentment.

Kim R.'s and Kim L.'s view of children was different from this colleague's view and this clear and articulated difference disrupted their professional relationship. The situation was exacerbated by the fact that Kim R. was the team leader, responsible for running the first-grade team meetings that this teacher attended. The atmosphere at those meetings was quite thick for a while because of the disruption that accompanied Kim R.'s and Kim L.'s composition of themselves as learners. They disrupted their colleague's view of herself as a teacher whose job was to teach, not to engage in inquiry (to learn). Hendricks-Lee, Soled, and Yinger (1995) suggest that "teachers who see themselves as learners create a supportive environment and are much better prepared for the massive challenges, for the continual setbacks, and the incremental successes that enduring education reform entails" (p. 289). Kim R.'s colleague viewed herself more as someone who enacted district-mandated curriculum and did not see a need to engage in inquiry because she was comfortable instituting that curriculum (basal readers, etc.). She was on leave when the school staff agreed to support the move toward developmentally appropriate practice and felt alienated from some of the changes that were occurring around her. We learned that a colleague can feel painfully excluded and that such feelings of exclusion are evidence of the disruption that a group of teachers such as ours can create within the school.

The process of disrupting is intriguing because it arose from the context of a hopeful setting, Ridgeway School. I do not intend to paint a rosy picture of a school in which everyone got along (they didn't), all kids were well behaved (they were not), and the teachers boasted of high test scores. It was not this way. Indeed, one typical day Mr. Z., the principal, dealt with many problems including a first grader whom he had left alone in the principal's office. The child urinated on the rug, on purpose, dropping his pants and urinating as the school counselor was approaching to talk to the child about the importance of not hitting his teacher. Ridgeway had a large proportion of children identified as behaviorally disordered; children did not always get along, nor did the faculty.

Disagreements were voiced publicly at faculty meetings and, more commonly, privately in smaller groups. But the ethos (Lortie, 1975) of the school was one of hope for the children's present and future. This was partly the doing of Mr. Z. because he was very respectful of teachers' stances. "I'm an administrator, like a hospital administrator," he said, "not a curriculum specialist. I rely on teachers to be smart about curriculum." He was honest and open about his concerns and directly confronted teachers who were not focused on helping children learn. Despite that, or because of it, or along with it, the presence and activity of our group contributed to a sense of disruption.

Disruption is unsettling because the usual context of the situation (Geertz, 1973) is made visible and, therefore, begins to seem unusual; the regularities are upset or, in the least, upsetting as they are brought into focus by group members. The group came to understand that their composing activity was also disrupting. As with the process of composing, disrupting is a process that has many categories. Each category became increasingly visible as group members engaged more in composing and as that composing led to increased disrupting. As I discussed this analysis with the group, we agreed that disrupting led to increased disrupting; composing led to increased disrupting; disrupting was a part of the composing process; composing provided initiative for further composing. I picture a rock being thrown into a pond. Suddenly the fish are aware of the medium in which they live because it is disrupted; they may change the way they swim (their reactions or responses) based on this present situation. Teachers and students feel composing and disrupting within a school because of the ripples. I would add to this metaphor that people learn better than fish; fish might forget their sense of disruption when the rock hits the water and the ripples affect them momentarily. Teachers often wait for ripples to disappear. Three years after our beginning, our group still seems to be at the root of ongoing composing and disrupting.

I turn now to the categories of disruption in order to present those ripples; the categories were the areas of school life that the group, in some way, influenced or changed over time. Recall that the categories emerged from my analysis; this particular use of language (e.g., "disrupting self") was not used by the group. The analysis is presented to help others understand what happened in, among, and because of our group.

Disrupting Self. The teachers in our group became unsettled within themselves. Originally, this seemed to reflect the initiation of conversations that, although not intended to cultivate competition, made individuals feel that others were meeting the needs of students with greater efficacy than they. The image of self as a teacher, doing her best, supporting students' learning, was shaken a bit. The teachers voiced this sense of uncertainty as the safety and willingness to take a risk within the group intensified. Often, disruption of self as an efficacious teacher was expressed by a call to understand what another teacher was doing. Group members wanted to know how the students did something, what the teacher's role was, how the teacher kept track, and how decisions were made in their colleague's classroom.

The desire to examine practice, to talk, to write, to express self, to find voice, to create curriculum, and to support inquiry within self and the classroom should, perhaps, seem more rooted in affirmation or composing of self than in uprooting (disrupting) of self. But we (including me as the researcher), as learners, experienced the tension within the zone of our learning; we felt disruption expressed as discomfort while we created or extended our learning.

The study group was a place in which members could cultivate and express their passions about teaching and learning; indeed, as Perrone (1991) points out, teachers who are passionate about learning want to study their practices, the curriculum, the learning environment, and themselves:

> Schools need to promote and support passion of this kind. Teachers need opportunities to reflect on their learning, on how they first came to the interests they possess and how to revitalize those interests. This suggests once more the need for schools to be settings where teachers share their learning with each other, read together, and have opportunities for writing and further study. The school needs to be a center of inquiry, an intellectually oriented place. (p. 117)

Perrone does not discuss the feelings of disruption that accompany such passion. Our group found that passion coincided with feelings of loss within self, much as Deal (1990) discusses certain aspects of staff development that lead to teachers experiencing grief as they let go of old practices. The teachers let go of old practices, explored new ideas, and explored self-as-teacher, -learner, -thinker, -speaker, -reader, -writer, -advocate, and more.

The teachers found that their students, even first graders, had notions of what was supposed to happen in school and these were disrupted as the children's interests were honored and pursued as part of the school agenda. I found that the children's and teachers' extant relationships and their understanding of curriculum were disrupted.

Disrupting Relationships.   After working together in the same school for a few years, it certainly seems natural that teachers expected each other to "be" together in predictable ways, based on relationships that emerged over the course of those years. A change in a single individual or in a group of individuals, such as some of the changes our group experienced and precipitated, disrupted existing relationships. The discomfort may have been a manifestation of a ripple effect of one person's learning and her subsequent challenging of team members and other staff about extant beliefs or practices within the school. Colleagues interacted differently with each other, disrupting expectations based on past experiences. Relationships were changing, views of school and schooling were changing, and tension mounted.

The group was a threat to relationships that were tentative as well as those that were firm. For example, Kim Z. was quite friendly with her team in ways that extended beyond cordial collegiality. She and the three other members of the second-grade team often met on weekends, Fridays after a week of school, and during school vacations. Their families were friendly as spouses got along well. One of Kim Z.'s second-grade colleagues began to change in her relationship to Kim Z., becoming pert, almost flippant, with her. She was upset because Kim Z. decided to allow her class to pursue a unit of study different from the other three second-grade classrooms (see chapter 2). Typically, the team did everything quite similarly, including themed unit studies. Kim Z.'s decision to allow her class to engage in inquiry caused stress in her relationship with her teammates, colleagues, and friends. Kim Z. said, "I feel like I'm hurting their feelings as a friend if I'm doing other things professionally" (personal interview, May 1995).

One of the most difficult things to face as teachers in our group began to change was the effect that change had on grade-level teams. Teams at Ridgeway were, previously, stable planning entities. Team members distributed labor as different individuals offered to teach or organize specific parts of the curriculum for all the children at a given grade level; other times they generated curricular activities that each taught, supposedly identically, in her own classroom. Historically, Kim Z.'s second-grade team planned together. For example, while planning for February, I observed as they sat around a table in the teachers lounge and formed piles, as each teacher donated ideas for certain topics. They had identical plastic tubs containing assorted manila folders, booklets, and worksheets; a topic was suggested and each teacher looked through her tub to find activities for that topic. The activities (covering topics such as Martin Luther King, Jr., Black History Month, Dental Health Month, presidents, and Valentines' Day) were then marked with a tag that instructed a paraprofessional to make sufficient copies for children in all four second-grade classrooms.

But Kim Z. was abandoning the team's planning strategies. She offered ideas to them, but also noted that her class would not be doing what the other second-grade classes would be doing. Her class had not satiated their interests on the polar region and she would not ignore the students' enthusiasm. Kim Z. reported to our study group:

You know? I mean it was like, "Oh Boy, well I've done it now." Let them [other team members] decide what to do so, you know, it was awful.... We [Kim Z. and her student teacher] felt really restricted and we felt like we had this whole tub of stuff that we had to get through and that the team was, you know, we were behind ... because we hadn't been doing what the team was doing, you know and so it was awful. We hated it, so, but now, they [Kim Z.'s second graders] are doing really interesting things now with this new stuff. It's completely different, it's not, you know, it's not anything like before. (Transcript from study group session)

Later, Kim Z. told us that she did, indeed, have all the materials that the group had piled up together and had duplicated for the children in all four second-grade classrooms: "... and I sat there and went along with that whole thing and that stack is still run off and we did nothing" (Transcript from study group session).

Kim Z. was very worried about this move away from her team's regular way of functioning. She was concerned on many levels, including the personal, because her team members were also her friends. Kim Z. was open to sharing her ideas, discussing what we did in our study group, sharing the readings, and working to include her other team members in her thinking, but she could not guarantee that all the team members' classrooms would eventually study the same things. The homogeneity of curriculum that was part of the second grade was now disrupted. By the end of the school year, Kim Z. had decided to move to the first-grade team, trading classrooms with a member of the first-grade team who was feeling excluded from the way that Kim R. and Kim L. planned. The second-grade team had been disrupted socially, curricularly, and, ultimately, in the personnel who constituted it.

There was disruption of relationships on the first-grade team, too. Kim L. and Kim R.'s colleague was angry and became somewhat resentful at the attention given to the inquiry-based classrooms by me, the district early childhood consultant, and other teachers in the district who visited Kim L. and Kim R.'s first-grade classrooms at Ridgeway. Their colleague was committed to teaching from the basal and maintaining a lot of control over the children. Kim R. and Kim L. were developing inquiry-based democratic classrooms. Relationally, the issue was not whether the children in the different first-grade classrooms were learning; the issue was that a team that formerly planned many activities together was disrupted by a split in the nature of classroom activity and the philosophical foundations for that activity.

Disruptions in relationships also occurred among students. The two first graders who dissected a calf's heart as they studied the parts of a body consulted the diagrams in plastic overlays from an encyclopedia and compared them to the heart in front of them, locating parts of the heart as one read complex words like "aorta" and both looked for that part on the specimen before them. The intensity of their study dissolved many boundaries that the school system created because their focus on learning, wandering, and wondering together was a personal and social expression of their passionate desire to know. Their own, their teachers', and some specialists' expectations were disrupted as the two scientists learned biology and discovered each other. The presentation of the teachers' and students' inquiry in chapters 2 through 7 bears this out further.

The students' participation in inquiry disrupted their relationships with their colleagues; teachers' relationships were similarly disrupted because of engagements in inquiry (both their own and their students' inquiry). The relational nature of inquiry-based curriculum makes it nearly impossible to separate disruption of relationship from disruption of curriculum.

Disrupting Curriculum. In the previous section, I gave some curricular examples but focused on the nature of relationships. It is also possible, of course, to focus on curricular disruption. Linda Brown experienced curricular disruption on the third-grade team. The team eventually decided to incorporate more individual child and teacher curricular decision making, a move away from the established regularities of the team. Linda said:

> Because even our team is different now, because when we first started everybody did the same thing at the same time on the same day. And now it's really changed, because, yeah, we still talk about the whole thing, like, okay right now we're doing the geometry and the architecture, and everybody has kind of gone off in their own little ... I mean, we're still together, but it's not the same day, the same time, the same thing. (Transcript from study group)

Curriculum as educative experiences has been described at length elsewhere (our group read Dewey, 1938; see also Short & Harste with Burke, 1996) and is not reiterated here. It became clear that the disruption of self and relationships was inextricably tied to the nature of classroom activity (i.e., the curriculum), and that the categories of self, relationships, and curriculum overflowed into one another.

Cohen (1995) suggests that the intersection of self, others, and curriculum is the point from which systemic change can be initiated. The teacher, as the individual responsible for the nature of the daily enactment of curriculum, is the key player in such change. Cohen submits that the move away from teaching as a technical career, focused on students' performance on standardized tests, is a move toward greater professionalism involving teachers as creators of curriculum. Our group's work suggests that teachers can be cocreators (composers) of curriculum with their students. What this means for schools is a change in the nature of curriculum; it is a move toward a renewed understanding of what it means to be a professional teacher. It means a disruption of self, relationships, and the curriculum.

> [S]ystemic reform envisions profound changes in teachers' professionalism, including steep elevation of professional knowledge and skill, extraordinary complication in teachers' roles, and radically new and demanding conceptions of professional conduct. (Cohen, 1995, p. 16)

Changes in self, curriculum, and relationships have an impact on the entire school. For example, the teachers asked for input into their schedules so they could create larger blocks of time during the school day when the students would not be interrupted and other blocks for teachers to work together (e.g., by having their special classes, such as physical education, immediately before or after lunch). The use of the physical space of the building was affected by changes in curriculum (moving toward inquiry) when the teachers allowed students into the hallway or teacher prep center (small rooms provided for teachers' desks at Ridgeway), areas previously not available for student use. And these changes caused tension because they disrupted institutional regularities (Sarason, 1971) that have long been in place.

Ginott (1972) suggests the difficulty of change when he offered advice to teachers for dealing with each other and with children:

> Improvement seldom occurs spontaneously. More often it is attained by deliberate effort. Every teacher can become aware of attitudes that alienate, words that insult, and acts that hurt. He [or she] can acquire competence and caution in communication, and become less abrasive and less provocative. (p. 63)

Sometimes curriculum activity hurts because of the disruption that accompanies it. Group members felt the pain and the joy of growth as that growth moved members away from some beliefs, practices, and colleagues and moved them toward others. They cultivated disruption and experienced disruption as they composed themselves and grew within the group.

Disruption, then, is not only a sign of growth, it is foundational to growth. We looked at, worked at understanding, and began to deal with the intensity of emotions that come with our composing, change, growth, risk-taking, and disrupting. Sarason (1990) suggests that, "[w]e have relatively few studies on what teaching in our schools does to teachers and other personnel" (p. 143). I would suggest that we have even fewer studies that help us understand what inquiring teachers and their students in our schools do to teachers, other students, and other personnel. Our work certainly suggests that they disrupt many aspects of life in school.

FACETS OF INQUIRY

At Ridgeway, there was much composing and disrupting going on at one time, all overlapping. I wondered if perhaps it was important to peel these processes back, one at a time as though they were *layers*. I originally thought of this as *layers of inquiry*. As I read some of the feminist literature and literature on pedagogies of liberation, I found the word *layers* to be distasteful because it implied a hierarchy with teachers and students near the bottom with little power, choice, or influence (as Wells described at the beginning of this chapter). The composing and disrupting of self, relationships, and curriculum are not layers that are separate, to be peeled back and understood as hierarchical pieces of teacher or student growth; they are, instead, phenomenological life processes, Van Manen's (1990) "essentials," that a teacher cultivates, with each essential affecting the others in composing and disrupting ways.

Composing and disrupting create the space for inquiry and make inquiry possible; it is the tension between the categories (self, relationships, curriculum) within composing and disrupting that opens zones of proximal development. These zones are tense, intense, and sometimes stressful places. Inquiry allows some resolution (via composing) and at the same time cultivates disruption, making inquiry, growth, and change exciting, passionate, frustrating, and intriguing.

I now refer to the many different individuals engaged in their inquiry from different perspectives or points of view as engaging in *facets of inquiry*. My purpose for using language this way is to put pressure on top–down views of teachers and teacher-inquirers and to support teacher and student inquiry as prestigious and important parts of school change. Of course, there are hierarchical layers of power within a school; I discuss these in Part II of this book, which focuses on the politics of teachers inquiring together in groups. (See the introduction to Part II for a brief overview.)

The inquiries within our study group and of the teachers' students are multiple facets of the same process, *not* a hierarchical structure in which university inquiry is given highest prestige, followed by teachers, with children at the bottom of some levels-based taxonomy of inquiry. The placement of the university member at the top of this type of a group, something I tried to avoid, is not unfamiliar:

> University standards for promotion and tenure typically require faculty to be experts (no matter how narrow the field of expertise) and to treat schools, teachers, and students as subjects, not partners. Despite real commitments from faculty to collaborate, the university milieu makes equal partnerships with teachers difficult. (Hendricks-Lee, Soled, & Yinger, 1995, p. 291)

I like the idea of *facets* of inquiry because it carries hope that each individual or group may enact inquiry from their point of view or stance, and each may sense prestige for their work. And, all the facets need each other to engage. It is the individuals' or groups' points of view that I refer to as *facets*. Not only is the word *facets* nonhierarchical, but it also suggests that there are *faces* within the inquiry. There are the individual faces of our students, teachers' faces, the faces within our group, and the faces within the school, district, the university, and the broader community (a facet I want to study much more). These points of view were facets of inquiring that were, indeed, temporary because they changed as the inquirers composed and disrupted various understandings and social regularities through inquiry; put more simply, groups changed as affiliations varied because of wandering and wondering expressed and addressed through inquiry. It is my intention to present the faceted view of inquiry throughout this entire book because it is how inquiry was enacted at Ridgeway.

Finally, I would add that the group's conversations were vehicles for expressing hope. Van Manen (1990) expresses the relationship between hope and teaching and learning:

> Through meditations, conversations, day dreams, inspirations, and other interpretive acts we assign meaning to the phenomena of lived life.... (p. 37) We might now turn to the phenomenon of teaching and ask if "having hope for children" is an essential theme of the experience of teaching. Can one imagine being a teacher without having hope for children? Is such a person still a teacher or would the meaning of teaching lose its fundamental meaning if it were not sustained by hope? (p. 109)

The study group was and remains saturated with hope. And that hope rested very much on democracy. Lester and Onore's (1990) discussion of the beliefs underlying a democratic classroom dovetails well with life in our group, where teachers who express "intention, commitment, and ownership" of their learning and their "experiences, feelings, beliefs, knowledge, and assumptions" are respected. It is within the spirit of voice, hope, democracy, and change that the work of the teachers and students of Ridgeway is presented in the following chapters.

Chapter 2

Children Assuming Control of Their Learning

Kimberly Zetterman
Lincoln Public Schools, Lincoln, NE

¤ ¤ ¤

BACKGROUND

... a curriculum is not a course to be run. Rather, curriculum is a meaning-making potential where knowledge is created, acted upon, and recreated at the point of experience. It provides opportunities for both teacher and students to experience themselves as learners, engaged together in inquiry in order to create, critique, and transcend their present realities.
—Harste (1993)

It has taken me 6 years of teaching to discover that I no longer have to run the "curriculum race." By providing a learning environment in which opportunities are available so that children will be encouraged to take risks, discover potential, and engage in learning, I will be able to experience learning with children as a teacher and a learner myself. My teaching philosophies have been further defined and critiqued through participation in our study group. The group empowered me to explore and implement a variety of teaching practices in my second-grade classroom. Because of the changes that have occurred in my classroom and the success I have experienced because of those changes, I am even more encouraged to pursue components of child-centered learning. I do not consider myself an expert in this field and therefore I want to research further to support my classroom practices. I firmly believe that all teaching practices need to be grounded in theory and research. I found myself being familiar with several leading researchers in the area of early childhood, learning and literacy (Calkins with Harwayne, 1991; Goodman, 1986; Graves, 1990; Harste, 1993; Vygotsky, 1978; Wells, 1986) but

I wanted to expand my knowledge base of what the research defined as successful components of learner-centered classrooms.

I hope my learning will serve as a guide for not only myself, but for others as I share my learning and my children's learning with them. Most importantly, I want my teaching experiences to exemplify that children are unique individuals, therefore the environment we provide for them must be a safe, nurturing, and stimulating place where they can grow as individual learners.

COMPONENTS OF MY CLASSROOM

The heart of this chapter is the extraordinary learning experience that occurred in my classroom through project work (Katz, 1994). But before one can completely understand that experience, it is important to understand what components make up the learning environment in my classroom, what teaching philosophies I carried into the classroom, and the role the children played in our learning environment. I explain several components of successful early childhood classrooms, including the physical, learning, and academic environments within the classroom, my basic belief in a whole language approach, and the role of children's choice in our classroom.

Physical Classroom Environment

When I began to explore successful components of early childhood classrooms, and more specifically those that are centered around the child-as-learner, I was drawn to the basics of the classroom. Where does the classroom begin? Child-centered classrooms have common physical characteristics; after exploring current literature, I found several of those characteristics that stand out and provide the basis for successful early childhood classrooms. Wasserman (1988) summarizes my view of the environment: "Like growing flowers, where certain specific conditions are provided to produce beautiful blossoms ... adults provide the conditions that establish the growing ground for empowered children" (p. 81).

The physical environment of the classroom can be critical to the success of the curriculum. Teachers and students alike need appropriate work spaces and accessible materials. Classrooms are usually set up at the beginning of the school year by the teachers. Fisher (1995) suggests that as the year progresses, teachers and students should feel empowered to make changes in the room to fit the needs of the learners. Most teachers of young children seem to arrange the classroom environment into a variety of learning areas. In Fig. 2.1, I present one classroom arrangement that worked for us for part of the year.

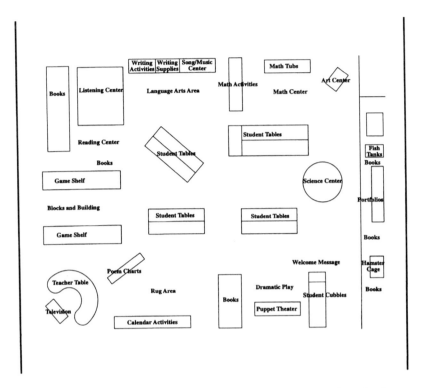

FIG. 2.1. One classroom arrangement used in Kim Z.'s second-grade classroom.

Learning Environment

The child-centered classroom stretches far beyond the physical aspects of the room. Most successful early childhood classrooms have a learning environment that is unique to their classroom community, and also seems to have similar characteristics woven throughout. The learning environment should not be confused with what might be called the *academic environment* that is discussed later. According to the *Primary Program* (Nebraska Department of Education, 1993):

> The learning environment is social in nature, providing a psychologically safe, secure and stimulating climate for all children. It provides time and opportunities for children to take appropriate risks, make choices and explore and investigate their world. (p. 9)

One of the most predominate characteristics of the learning environment is the social aspect. Avery (1993) refers to this as the "tone of the classroom" (p. 75). The social climate in early childhood classrooms needs to be one that allows for social interactions and the development of interpersonal skills. I encourage children to work and learn cooperatively throughout a variety of experiences. A second characteristic of the social environment is that it provides an opportunity for all children to be accepted and learn regardless of ability, ethnicity, or socioeconomic background. Children learn to value, respect and accept others through opportunities provided by the teacher. I use many of the ideas suggested by Fisher (1991), such as circle time or shared reading time, as events in which children can learn in a noncompetitive atmosphere that in turn results in strong community building for the classroom.

Academic Environment

Of the several distinct types of environments within one classroom setting, the last one I discuss is the academic environment. Avery (1993) describes that environment as follows:

> The decisions involving the academic environment include: time and scheduling, curriculum requirements, teaching strategies, record keeping—always taking into account each learner's needs. (p. 29)

Our group's reading and discussions led me to believe that scheduling and time management of an early childhood classroom is essential to the success of the classroom. Our days worked best when they were divided into large "chunks" or "blocks" of time. These blocks provided a balance between group time and individual time, and between active and nonactive times. It is important to note that such a schedule can be both stable and flexible depending on the needs of the teacher and children of each individual classroom.

Curriculum and teaching strategies have been redefined in early childhood classrooms over the past decade. I have concluded that the district-mandated curriculum is not abandoned, as many people perceive. The goals of most developmentally appropriate programs is to expand that curriculum (Kostelnik, 1992). It is the responsibility of the teacher to compile a list of skills considered appropriate for his or her classroom from the district's curriculum and then skillfully integrate those skills into daily reading, writing, projects, and other appropriate activities. As is seen here, I accomplished this task, while keeping the following in mind:

> The curriculum should begin from where the child is and build on the child's interests and natural sense of wonder. It should invite children to cooperate and collaborate with each other and be integrated wherever possible. (Nebraska Department of Education, 1993, p. 4)

The role of the teacher in the academic environment is to be a leader, a facilitator, and a learner. Teachers should be observers of children. By listening to individual children, I found I could more effectively guide and facilitate their learning. Kostelnik (1992) addresses the myth that teachers do not teach in developmentally appropriate classrooms. She concludes that many people still envision teaching in a very stereotypical way, very teacher-directed. She suggests that the teaching that occurs in many early childhood classrooms is not recognized because it does not fit this model. I tend to spend much time moving about the classroom working with individual students or with small groups. I teach children directly using a variety of instructional strategies.

This does not mean that teacher-directed lessons are never presented. Teacher-directed lessons play a valuable role in the instructional setting, but instead of consuming a large amount of instructional time, these lessons tend to be short, focused, and in response to a teacher-observed learning need of specific children (Avery, 1993).

Environments Within My Philosophy

The environments established in my classroom were based on my experiences, philosophies, and research-based theories. However, the belief I feel is most important to note is my overall philosophy of how children learn. This is best demonstrated by Goodman (1986):

> Whole language learning builds around whole learners learning whole language in whole situations. Whole language learning assumes respect for language, for the learner and for the teacher. The focus is on meaning and not on language itself, in authentic speech and literacy events. Learners are encouraged to take risks and invited to use language, in all its varieties, for their own purposes. In a whole language classroom, all the varied functions of oral and written language are appropriate and encouraged. (p. 40)

Baumann (1992) suggests that:

> ... a whole language philosophy presupposes that students assume considerable responsibility for their learning and that it is the teacher's role to promote, support and facilitate learning, not to govern or dominate it. (p. 2)

Goodman's and Baumann's philosophies and findings provided a strong foundation for whole language instruction in my learner-centered classroom. Baumann also describes three approaches to whole language instruction that might easily be incorporated into many early childhood classroom settings. The first is the *contract approach*, which is very flexible and requires the teacher and student to form agreements about what work will be done and when it will be done. The second is the *priorities list approach*, in which teachers rank the goals, tasks, or activities for the day and then reevaluate the schedule on a day-to-day or week-to-week basis. The third approach is the *blocked approach,* which involves scheduling large blocks of time in which activities take place (Baumann, 1992). The block approach worked best in my learner-centered classroom. This approach usually involves a themed approach including projects and activities integrating all subject areas of the curriculum. I have been most comfortable using the block approach while incorporating project work into my classroom. By using flexible blocks of time that can be combined for larger blocks of time, children can be engaged in meaningful activity for longer periods. My daily schedule allows for these large blocks of time throughout the morning during our literacy block (Fig. 2.2).

The Role of Children's Choices

According to Wasserman (1988), "Children who are allowed to make their own choices grow to see themselves as independent persons who can influence the environment in which they live. They learn to see themselves

```
8:10-8:20 Opening
          Attendance/Lunch Count
          Unfinished Work
          Personal Reading
          Journals

8:20-8:50 Togetherness Time
          Calendar
          Song of Week/Poem of Week/What's New? (Sharing)

8:50-10:00 Literacy Block
          Read Aloud
          Theme Study/Author Study
          Readers' Workshop
            Expert Book
            Literature Circles
            Conference with Teacher
            Skills Group

10:00 Recess & Break

10:00-11:00 Writers Workshop
          Read Aloud
          Mon.: Class Conference
          Wed.: Mini-Lessons
          Fri.: Author's Chair

11:00-11:35 Plan-Do-Review
          Children select and monitor self on activities that change
          weekly

11:35-11:45 Ready for Lunch

11:45-12:20 Lunch & Recess

12:20-12:45 Spelling

12:45-1:40 Specials

1:40-1:45 Break

1:45-2:25 Math Their Way

2:25-2:35 Kids Comments

2:35-2:45 Clean-up & Dismissal
```

FIG. 2.2. Daily schedule.

as persons of worth" (p. 67). Wasserman makes a strong argument for the importance of children being allowed to make choices about their learning. The children's thoughts, concerns, reflections, and questions become a more important element in the structure and instructional practices taking place in the classroom. Kohn (1993) describes some benefits of allowing children to make choices in their learning. The first benefit is the effect on general well-being. Elementary students have higher self-esteem and a greater feeling of academic competence when teachers allow for choice in classroom decisions. Another benefit is the effects on behavior and values. Kohn concludes that if adults want children to take responsibility for their own behavior, they must first be given responsibility. A child learns how to make decisions by making decisions. There is also an effect on academic achievement. Kohn sites the example of second graders who were given some choice about their learning, including the chance to decide which tasks they would work on. These second graders tended to complete more learning task in less time and, he states, a more recent study suggests that children who are allowed to make decisions about their schoolwork score higher on standardized tests.

Choice also effects teachers. My job became more interesting when it involved collaborating with students to decide what was going to happen in the classroom. I was freed from constant monitoring and was able to interact with the children as they worked. Kohn suggests that the final effect of choice is intrinsic because people value making decisions over being controlled by others.

The way in which children's choices are facilitated may look different in each classroom on any given day. Teachers and students may take turns deciding on something each day, such as what books to read. The teacher may offer guidance, suggestions, or even limitations, but ultimately the choice is left up to the children. I could not leave choices and decisions entirely up to the children. Instead, we negotiated, providing a powerful demonstration of cooperation and collaboration.

Children are allowed to make choices in my classroom for many reasons, including many of the benefits just discussed. My feelings about the role of children's choice in the classroom are best summarized by Fisher (1991): "I believe that when encouraged to choose activities that are whole, meaningful, and functional to their lives, children naturally engage in activities that meet their intellectual, social, emotional and physical needs" (p. 11).

THE DAY IT SNOWED PENGUINS
AND POLAR BEARS

Upon entering Room 138 in mid-January, one might think it was snowing penguins and polar bears. Our classroom was being taken over by "polar" research, writing, and projects. Everywhere you turned, children were discussing the height of the Rockhopper penguin or the length of a caribou, or asking questions such as, "What does a musk ox eat?" Why would second graders be discussing such topics? Well, you might say it's a thematic unit that has "gone to the children!".

It all began shortly after the first of the year when, like many teachers, I had a wonderful themed unit planned about penguins. But, as we know, children come to us with their own learning agendas (Wells, 1986). In the past, those agendas sounded like this statement from Donovan: "Mrs. Z., do you know if vampire bats really suck your blood?" Or it sounded like Amanda's constant curiosity about seashells as she visited with a friend, "Ashley, do you think something lived in this one?" Nor was it uncommon to hear a discussion unfolding between Cory and Nhat about how to say this or that in Vietnamese. Amanda, Donovan, Cory, and Nhat are all second graders in my very diverse heterogeneous classroom at Ridgeway Elementary. These brief journeys into student-led learning began to intrigue me. What would happen if we pursued children's questions with greater intensity?

Classroom activity reflected the students' typical curiosity, but they had many more questions about penguins than I had anticipated; they also began formulating questions about other polar animals: "Where do they live?" "What do they eat?" "Mrs. Z., did you know polar bears don't live with penguins?"

Taking the time to explore and answer these questions would provide rich learning opportunities and, rather than limiting ourselves to teacher- or district-directed objectives, we would discover new and different areas of learning though the children's questions. With the philosophy (Nebraska Department of Education, 1993) that, "The curriculum begins from where the child is and builds on the child's interest and natural sense of wonder" (p. 14), I decided to put other plans on hold. The organized lesson plans that were coordinated with my three other team members included pre-planned lessons, laminated file folder games, penguin vocabulary words to learn, and polar bear measurement activities to complete. Visions of my preplanned lessons slowly began to fade as a persistent voice in the back of my mind pushed me to listen to the children. I wondered: "What was my role? What should I do?" In my heart and in my mind I knew. "The teacher invites children to participate in planning and creating a rich, stimulating environment which encourages interaction, exploration, and investigation" (Nebraska Department of Education, 1993, p. 14).

As my student teacher looked on, I put away the binder with the organized lesson plans, set the file folders in a basket for the children to choose during an independent choice time, and carefully tucked away the polar bear measurement activities for another day; we had more important questions to explore.

On reflection of these beginnings, I realize now that I was developing an inquiry-based classroom in which knowledge is created, questions are encouraged, and all members of the classroom value each other as learners (Boyd, 1993). Four components have been identified in good inquiry-based classrooms: values, focus, opportunities, and assessment (Reimer, Stephens, & Smith, 1993). Throughout our polar project, these components were evident in our classroom.

Valuing Learning and Learners

Boyd (1993) suggests that values in an inquiry-based classroom tend to guide and inform a classroom regardless of the curriculum. Values that guided our classroom came from myself as a teacher/learner and from the children. One area valued in our classroom was learning opportunities: providing time, space, and multiple resources for children's learning. Learning opportunities look different in our classroom as compared to more traditionally structured classrooms.

Our morning began with togetherness time (calendar, poems, songs, sharing, and planning for the day); then we worked within a 2-hour time period called a literacy block, which included, but was never limited to, readers workshop, writers workshop and project work. At the beginning of our school year, these three blocks of time seemed to be more defined, but by second semester it just seemed natural to let everything flow together into project time. Reading, writing, and learning all together as one process made more sense to both the children and me. Through project work, I was able to meet each child's individual needs in a way that provided academic growth and opportunities for them to share their learning and be valued by their peers.

Finally, our classroom had a strong value of community. Children saw themselves as both learners and teachers. They saw themselves and me as a team working and learning together to discover answers, feelings, strengths, and more questions. I view learning as a socially constructed process among all members, teachers and students alike. Children are also encouraged to be risk takers, to ask questions, and to discover information. Conversations are critical to the learning process, and students soon learned that their voice had value in our classroom.

When they encountered questions we were unable to answer in our classroom, the students knew where to seek the answers. "Lets go to the library and ask Ms. Kenney [library-media specialist]," suggested Amanda. So they went upstairs to the media center, a daily ritual. For days, with the help of Melody Kenney, our Chapter I teacher (E'Lise Stump), myself, and a student teacher (Kevin Chavez), the students pored over books, charts, magazines, and CD-ROM programs on the computers.

"Let's make a list," said Charity.

"Write down all the animals that live on land in Antarctica," suggested Cory. Soon the tables were covered with charts listing different categories of information: *Land Animals of the Arctic, Animals that Live in the Antarctic Water,* and *Plants of the Tundra.* The charts were surrounded by piles of books and second graders struggling to read words like "caribou," … "Oh, its like a reindeer!" smiled Ashley.

"Muss,… Muck, … Musk Ox," sighed Jennifer as she untangled her tongue. And, giggling with delight, Amanda said, "Macaroni? … Macaroni! … like we eat, Mrs. Z., a penguin is named Macaroni!"

"Macaroni!" I said, while thinking surely she must be mispronouncing a somewhat scientific name for the penguin, but there it was in a book she had found. Amanda quickly began formulating question after question about her polar animal: "Why does it have feathers that look like hair?" "Don't you think it looks like the Rockhopper penguin?" "I think … is it shorter than Donovan's penguin?"

As students became researchers, they needed an organized way to collect data other than random notes of information. As teachers, Kevin and I needed a means of keeping track of the data the children collected. That data would be used later for assessment of individual learning and to evaluate which of our district objectives were covered throughout the project. We developed a form, and the children were encouraged to use it (Fig. 2.3) because it allowed them to collect information about their animal's characteristics.

Ongoing records of students' progress, which the students helped to maintain, aided us in planning between the Chapter I teacher, the media specialist, and me as we worked daily with small groups of children on their research questions. For about 2½ weeks, we worked for 1 to 1½ hours daily, sometimes more if our schedule allowed, reading, writing, listening, talking, and learning. The students learned vocabulary, information, library skills, and reading/writing skills as we explored the polar regions both in the library-media center and in our classroom. Although the specific skills (vocabulary, animal characteristics, geography, and measurement skills) that were learned by individual students during this experience are important, what is truly significant is the learning environment that was formed.

Glover (1993) suggests that classrooms are made up of conversations, and that everyone's voice, both teachers and students, should be heard in that conversation. Many voices were heard in our learning environment. Donovan's voice was heard as he became our expert on how to construct three-dimensional penguins. He helped Amanda construct a stand for her penguin with the use of a discarded wrapping paper tube.

Ben's voice was heard as, for the first time this year, he showed an interest in a topic and truly saw himself as a writer when he could locate and use important information from a library book. Daily, I observed children as they

My Polar Animal

_____

By:_____

Characteristics:_____

_____

Food: _____

_____

Water: _____

_____

Shelter: _____

_____

Space: _____

_____

The most interesting thing about this animal is_____

_____

_____

FIG. 2.3. Form used by children to record information on their polar animals.

exceeded my highest expectations for them, but none so clear as the day Charity, a less confident reader, went to seek out and read information on the harp seal, alone, in the library-media center. Triumphantly, she returned thirty minutes later with several sentences she could proudly read as interested classmates applauded her accomplishment. These are just a few examples of events that helped formulate, redefine, and establish our learning environment. It is the beliefs, ideas, and values of the learners and learning that grew from this environment that guided and focused the polar project from this point onward.

Focusing Beyond District Curriculum

The second component of an inquiry-based classroom is the focus.

> ... [I]n any academic endeavor, teachers have both explicit and implicit ideas about where the endeavor is headed and about what the potential for learning will be along the way. (Reimer, Stephens, & Smith, 1993, p. 29)

Focus can mean different things to each teacher or learner depending on where they are in the learning experience. My focus changed many times over those first 2 weeks from just a themed unit on penguins, to researching polar animals, to a complete project approach, to learning about the polar regions as guided by my children's questions rather than by my teacher-directed learning agenda. This did not mean however that my focus as a teacher was lost; it only meant that the focus on particular learning activities would look different depending on how I would weave them into the daily learning experiences of the children.

I think it is hard for many teachers, myself included, not to get caught up in the curriculum race. I wanted a balanced curriculum that focused on providing learning opportunities that allowed children to inquire, explore, create and learn at a level that would go above and beyond the district curriculum.

Because my focus had now become more project-centered, I tried to keep in mind what Katz (1994) says:

> The key feature of a project is that it is a research effort deliberately focused on finding answers to questions about a topic posed either by the children, the teacher, or the teacher working with the children. The goal of a project is to learn more about the topic rather than to seek right answers to questions posed by the teacher. (p. 1)

Therefore, as I set up the learning environment with the children, my focus was on the research process, valuing children's questions, and helping them seek answers to their questions. The answers to those questions were not always easy as I had a wide range of learners, including a learning disabled student, a speech-language impaired student, several English as a second language students, behaviorally impaired students, children served in Chapter I, and several gifted students. The most difficult task we had to overcome was being able to read all the information we were finding. The children's focus seemed to be on discovering the strategies they needed to read all of the new information they were locating. These strategies began to look like buddy reading, using the CD-ROM (it reads to you), seeking help from the Chapter I teacher or media specialist, and using some basic reading skills and strategies to learn the new words or concepts.

Soon, however, both my focus and the children's focus took a different direction. I wanted to encourage the children to share their research with each other and possibly to share their experiences with their parents, too. As we continued to work in the library-media center, Ms. Kenney and I began to discuss how students could share their learning. The children wanted to know what their research looked like. They wanted to "see" the emperor penguin, the snowshoe hare, and the polar bear. Their writing was not sufficient for them. They wanted something more concrete. I could see more and more ideas formulating in their minds as they examined illustrations and really began thinking about how their writing was telling about their animal. But what would show how it looked?

Thus began the creation of the Learning Bubble. Earlier in the year Ms. Kenney attended a library-media specialists' workshop at which she learned how to create a bubble out of a plastic painter's tarp, electrical tape, and a fan. With a little persuasion, I was sold on the idea of using the bubble as a way to make our learning visible. I did hesitate momentarily for several reasons: Could I take on a project so big? Would I be able to meet the "required" curriculum through this project? Would the children learn?

After a discussion with my student teacher, discussions in the study group, and some self-evaluation, I knew this would be right for the children, and, of course, when I suggested it to the kids they were excited about trying it out. Ms. Kenney, Ms. Stump, Kevin (student teacher), and I spent several hours the next afternoon crawling around the floor of the media center using electrical tape to seal the painter's tarp around a fan to form our Arctic bubble. Because this was our first attempt at a bubble, the children were not included in this part of the construction process, not because we didn't want them to see our struggles, but as an effort to save valuable class time. The bubble was an "L" shape, about 10 feet long, 4 feet wide, and close to 5 feet tall when inflated by the fan (Figs. 2.4 and 2.5).

The next morning the children couldn't wait to see our creation.

"Wow! It's cool!" exclaimed Ben after seeing the plastic dome for the first time.

FIG. 2.4. View of the learning bubble from the outside.

FIG. 2.5 View of the learning bubble from the inside.

"Can we go in?" asked the rest of the class almost in unison. After collectively deciding on some basic rules, such as "Take your shoes off" and "Don't poke the bubble," we ventured inside. It felt like we had stepped into another world as the fan blew a cool breeze around us. The children began discussing ideas for using their research information to create projects to fill the inside, to change it from just a plastic bubble into a Polar Learning Bubble. The students took ownership of the project and from this point on it was all theirs.

Opportunities to Learn and Express Meaning

Over the next few weeks we tried to successfully facilitate the third component of an inquiry-based classroom: opportunity.

> ... all we can do is provide children with rich opportunities to learn—opportunities made rich by the conceptual framework of the teacher as well as by the teacher's skill in helping children successfully negotiate and express meaning. (Reimer, Stephens, & Smith, 1993, p. 29)

The children were given many more opportunities to explore and gain knowledge through a variety of materials. They acquired additional information they needed from books, magazines, newspaper, videos, filmstrips, tapes, and computers. After gathering information about their animal or land form on their polar animal sheet, students began to reorganize and rewrite their information for a published piece to be typed by either the student or the teacher. The students took great pride in being able to read their information, including many new "big" words, into a tape recorder for a recorded class tape to be played for visitors to the Learning Bubble. Let's look a little more closely at two students.

Beverly. As Beverly bravely sat in the small study room in the library-media center ready to read her published piece for the tape recorder, I could not help but notice the circled and underlined words in the various shades of colored pencil and the well worn sticky notes around the page of her research (Fig. 2.6). Beverly was a shy, quiet girl, small for her age, who showed little self-confidence. Her round face was dwarfed by the large, thick eyeglasses that were forever smudged and sliding down the bridge of her nose. Beverly rarely talked and usually had a furrow between her brow as if she was always in deep thought about something. She was also one of my less proficient readers (Goodman, 1986), who chose to diligently research her favorite polar animal, the blue whale, no matter how difficult it was for her. Her eyes absolutely sparkled the first time she told me it was the *biggest* animal in the world, biggest being one of the few words she was able to read independently. From that day on, Beverly was known in our classroom as the blue whale expert.

Finally, the day Beverly had been waiting for: Her turn to read into the tape player. She had practiced and practiced and assured me she was ready.

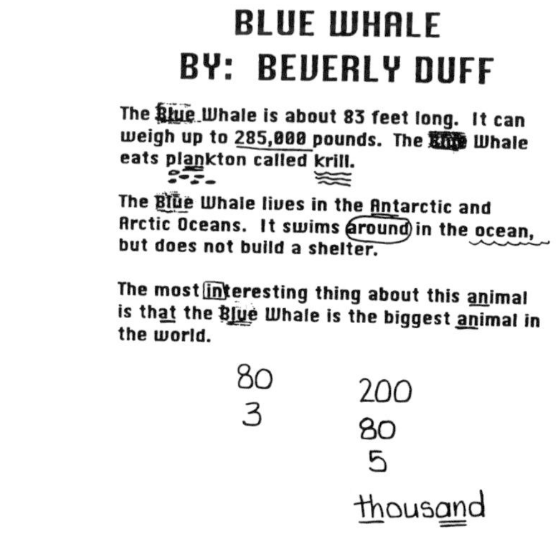

FIG. 2.6. Beverly's report with markings she added to facilitate her reading.

I simultaneously pushed the play and record buttons and slowly she began. As she came to the numbers 83 (the length of the whale) and 285,000 (the weight of the blue whale), she quickly referred to the sticky notes where each part of the number was written in a special color to help her remember it. Then it was on to the next sentence with that troublesome word "around," but not for Beverly as her finger traced *around* the red circle that enclosed the word she pronounced perfectly. The word *blue* was highlighted with a blue crayon; the *an* in *plankton* was underlined to help her focus on the sounds she knew in order to successfully predict the remainder of the word. She used a wavy line to remind herself of the word *ocean* and underlined *an* and *at* to help her say longer words with these chunks in them. The box around *in* in *interesting* helped her recall that word. And so she continued confidently down the page, until the "stop" button was pressed at the end of her piece and her rarely seen smile signaled a big accomplishment for an emerging reader.

As I look back on Beverly's learning experience during the polar project, I wonder if Beverly was truly an inefficient reader or if it was just that she was undervalued as a reader by myself and her peers. I believe that Beverly had little idea of what reading is supposed to be until she was exposed to nonfiction. Through this experience, she saw reading as meaning-making; the project and the reading became so important to her that she began to see reading as a way to acquire knowledge and construct her own learning. For Beverly, the polar project was an opportunity for her to take ownership of her learning and to become a reader in our community. Her use of extra cues (including colors, chunking words, and more) to mediate her reading was her own way of gaining access to written language.

> In an inquiry-based classroom children are encouraged to express themselves and their learning in many ways.... [T]here are multiple ways of knowing and expressing ourselves in the world and [these are] essential to the creation of multiple perspectives and deeper understandings. (Reimer, Stephens, & Smith, 1993, p. 29)

Ashley.   Many of the children chose to take their knowledge of polar animals and create that polar animal into a life-sized model to be displayed inside our bubble and so continued many opportunities for learning through choosing the materials, problem solving the construction and placement of the animals, and measuring, measuring, and more measuring.

Measuring is the one word that comes to my mind so vividly because of Ashley's study of caribou. Ashley was fascinated with that animal from the moment she found out it was related to the reindeer, so much so that she decided to go home and tell her father this piece of extraordinary information. As she entered the classroom the next day, with computer paper in hand, she stated, "Mrs. Z., my dad didn't believe me that the caribou was related to the reindeer, so we looked it up on our computer and here's the information and now he believes me!"

After researching the animal so thoroughly, Ashley decided that the Learning Bubble should contain a life-sized caribou. Having seen me put an image on our classroom overhead projector and then project it larger onto the wall, she decided this would be a good way to make the outline of the caribou. After some careful consultation with the encyclopedia, Ashley had her overhead ready, and she also made a trip down the hallway to collect a large piece of butcher paper. She gathered three yard sticks, and, after referring to her research several times, the measuring began. I have never seen a second grader work so seriously at a measuring activity. She must have moved the overhead back and forth 20 times until she got the correct length and height for the caribou. But the measuring was not over.

"Mrs. Z., my caribou needs cardboard to make him stiff so he can stand up," she said. This meant we were off to the basement in search of cardboard boxes (which is a whole other story) so the measuring could continue until Ashley had successfully created a life-sized 7 ½-foot long by 4 ½-foot tall caribou for our bubble. She typed her report (Fig. 2.7) and it went into the learning bubble next to the caribou.

Katz (1994) suggests that there are three phases to project work: getting started, field work, and culminating and debriefing events. By this time we

CARIBOU
BY: ASHLEY FLYNN

A Caribou is a very large animal. The body can be 4-7 1/2 feet long and 4 1/2 feet tall. It weighs 200-600 pounds. A Caribou has a thick fur. It has wide hooves and is a strong swimmer. It swims in rivers throughout the tundra. The Caribou eats lichens.

Caribou do not have shelters because they live out in the open. They live in the Arctic on the tundra of forest habitat.

Adult Caribou shed velvet coverings from their antlers. Caribou also have furry noses to keep them warm. Young Caribou are born during the summer. Caribou hooves are broad and flat. Their hooves click when they walk.

FIG. 2.7. Ashley's report on the caribou.

had definitely gotten started and were well along in our field work, so it was time to embark on our culminating event. Culminating events might include "... preparing and presenting reports of results in the form of displays of findings and artifacts, talks, dramatic presentations, or guided tours of their construction" (p. 1).

It was hard to believe that the day finally came when the last Rockhopper penguin was on its iceberg and the polar bear was appropriately placed away from the snowshoe hare. The Learning Bubble was ready for its first visitors. The children had written a special invitation to family and friends to join them for an Arctic/Antarctic exploration of the bubble.

As sure as the highlight for me was watching these second graders grow as learners over the past 6 weeks, the highlight for them was touring friends and family through the polar world they had created. The tour day began with much excitement and anticipation. Every student had at least one family member or special guest attending the afternoon tour. Our morning was spent making last minute preparations, such as one more piece of tape to secure the polar bear, or a few more pieces of styrofoam strung together for a snowier effect in the Arctic. We also prepared our room, setting up displays of books used for research, setting out our writing, and choosing a favorite video of penguins to show on our television. During togetherness time that day, we had quite a lengthy etiquette discussion, inspired by questions the children had about tour procedures. We discussed how to properly introduce our families or special guests and decided on some table manners for our refreshment time afterward. The children were quite serious about every little detail. Those who experienced the Learning Bubble that day and in the weeks that followed, as we continued to give guided tours, also experienced children as passionate learners.

Assessing Learning

We took some time to reflect on our learning while the Learning Bubble remained in the library-media center for others to explore. With this final step, we came to focus on the fourth component of an inquiry-based classroom: assessment.

Assessment during projects should demonstrate children's overall strengths, knowledge, and progress. Therefore, assessment does not occur as a single measurement at the end of a project. Throughout the project, I was constantly evaluating students with a variety of strategies, such as anecdotal notes on children as they were working. I usually carried a clipboard with computer labels on which to take notes. Documentation on children throughout the project included comments about their reading skills, writing skills, and math concepts introduced. I also noted problem-solving strategies, social skills, and conversations with me or their peers.

Having these notes on sticky computer labels made it easy for me to place them in my student documentation notebook at the end of the day.

Assessment during projects also meant collecting student work samples for student portfolios, a practice strongly recommended by most advocates of project work (Hartman & Eckerty, 1995). One sample of work I chose to collect from students was the form used for their research (Fig. 2.3). This document was not only a sample of student writing and research, but it was also an evaluation of several of our science objectives for animal habitats. Many students also chose their research report, pictures of their animals, or journal writing (Fig. 2.8) about the projects to include in their portfolios.

Portfolios included reading (audiotapes), writing, art, and math samples chosen by the children and me from work saved over 2-week time periods. Each document also included a reflective evaluation sheet filled out by the students, explaining why the work was chosen for inclusion in their portfolio.

Student writing throughout the polar project served as a valuable assessment tool during the project. Many students chose to write reflective pieces about their progress on the project in their personal journals, while others wrote creative stories about penguins during writers workshop. I relied on the district's reading and writing objectives as the minimum point of reference of the students' growth. As students began choosing polar books to read during readers workshop and personal reading time, I found that the minimum was exceeded by many of the students.

PENguins   ThE Rockhoppe pinguin
2-3-95
The rock hopper penguin is about 22 inches tall.
The rock hopper pinguin eat fish, squid, and krill.
It is call the creasted pinguin beacause
it is has spiky gobden faethier above his
eyes. The most interesting thing abouti this
anomil is that it hopps from rock to rock.
The rock hopper pinguin lives in the Artica.
There wings are for swimming Not for flying.

FIG. 2.8. A student's journal entry about an animal being studied for inclusion in the Learning Bubble.

Some things I learned while making our learning bubble....

_____

_____

_____

_____

_____

_____

_____

The best thing about it was_____

_____

_____

The most challenging thing about it was_____

_____

_____

If we made a learning bubble again I would like to learn about

_____

FIG. 2.9. Evaluation form completed by the students.

Throughout the polar project, every aspect of the project was established and facilitated through our classroom community. The children had taken an active role in deciding what to study, how to facilitate that learning, and what the final product of their learning would be. Therefore, I wanted the assessment and evaluation to be reflective of this process, also.

The children in my classroom had experience with self-evaluation prior to the polar project. They were asked to evaluate their reading and writing growth as they completed a book in readers workshop or a written piece in writers workshop. They also had opportunities to explore self-evaluation through portfolios and by completing student report cards or leading their parent conference each quarter. Because of this background experience, and from doing reflective journal writing throughout the polar project, self-evaluation was second nature for the children. I chose to develop a some-what open-ended form for the students to use, one that was similar to other evaluations they had completed (Fig. 2.9). Their ideas, thoughts, and feelings were very surprising and insightful and at times evoked emotions of such pride that I was overwhelmed. The following quotes were taken from students' self-evaluation sheets; their spelling has been changed to conventional spelling.

Some things I learned while making the Learning Bubble:
"I learned that not all caribou babies are born at the same time. I learned that they are born in the summer. "—Ashley
"I learned a lot more. I learned about my harp seal and about polar bears and other animals. "—Charity
"They stand on their nests and wave their heads at each other."—Amanda
"We learned about penguins. Chinstrap penguins fight more than any other penguin. Penguins eat fish and squid. King penguins are better in water than on land."—Cory

The best thing about it was:
"Writing the research."—Donovan
"Seeing the Learning Bubble—it was so cool!"—Ben
"My mom came to school and came in the bubble."—Jennifer
"That we got taped by Ms. Kenny and that we got to invite our friends in, too."—Mayte

The most challenging thing about it was:
"Getting the research done."—Charity
"Reading hard books."—Mayte
"Making the emperor penguin."—Donovan
"Making the blue whale. It was 83-feet long. I made half of a whale and spout. "—Beverly

The final piece of evaluation came from the parents. I wanted their impressions and feedback in order to fully evaluate the success of this type of learning. As a teacher with nontraditional practices, I have found that parent support of programs and curriculum is invaluable. Therefore, before I attempt any new practice in the classroom, it is important to inform parents, providing information and background theory about such practices. I followed this format from the very beginning of the Learning Bubble: sending home notes, making phone calls, doing informal visits with parents and students after school, and having a variety of articles available about the project approach for parent reading. With this background knowledge, and feeling comfortable with our prior communications, most of the parents returned the evaluation with enthusiasm (Fig. 2.10). The following quotes were taken from the parent evaluation forms.

Did your child share information with you about our polar project?
"He not only spoke about his report but also about the reports and projects of his classmates."—Ben's mom
"Everyday while working on the project."—Ashley's parents

Did your child seem more excited about this project as compared to other teacher-directed topic this year?
"Very excited, everyday she would come home with more information."—Mayte's mom

February 1995

Dear Parents,

As you know we have recently completed a project on the polar regions, our "Learning Bubble." The approach to this project was somewhat different in terms of "traditional" teaching. Although I did introduce the unit on penguins, I never intended to take it so far. The polar learning bubble was very much child initiated. Although Mr. Chavez and myself facilitated, guided, and provided input, the learning was very much guided by the children's needs and interests. I was amazed at the learning experiences that occurred, and the knowledge the children have gained by approaching learning in this way. In educational terms it is sometimes called the "Project Approach." As I continue to grow as an educator, I am constantly looking for ways to improve student learning. As I watched children take charge of their learning, be excited to read and write, and curious about new topics, I am convinced that taking this approach to learning is something to be explored.

Therefore, I am asking for your input and reactions to this approach.

•Did your child share information with you about our polar project?

•Did your child seem more excited about this project as compared to other teacher directed topics this year?

•If you were able to visit our Learning Bubble, what did you think?

•Other comments?

Thank you,
Kimberly Zetterman

FIG. 2.10. Evaluation form completed by families following their visit to the Learning Bubble.

"Ben spoke often about the Learning Bubble, he usually does not discuss school projects with me unless I directly ask him about them."—Ben's mom
"She was very excited about the idea and what it would look like—this really motivated her and increased her curiosity about the project."—Amanda's parents

If you were able to visit our Learning Bubble, what did you think?
"I thought it was real nice, it gave me a chance to learn something new."—Mayte's mom
"One of the best hands-on displays I've ever seen. We were very excited to come visit it and Dad was impressed, too."—Donovan's parents

Other comments:
"Excellent learning opportunity. We noticed a lot of excitement about learning and heard about the progress of the bubble and facts about the animals along the way."—Amanda's parents
"This was an excellent example of cooperative learning. I am in agreement that cooperation in education works better than competition in the classroom."—Ben's mom
"This was such a fun learning project for all the children. It mixed learning and playing and cooperation all into a wonderful experience for all the second graders."—Donovan's parents

BEYOND THE BUBBLE

After completing the Learning Bubble, I was confused about where we should go next with our learning. In order to have time to think and reflect, I decided to present a preplanned unit about dental health to my class. It did not take long to realize my mistake. The students were not interested in their teeth. They were less and less attentive. I began to hear comments like: "This is boring!" "Do we have to color this?" "Can't we learn about sharks' teeth instead?"

What was I doing? Only a few short days ago I had a roomful of enthusiastic learners; now I was trying to force them back into a teacher-directed learning style just because I needed to reflect. Well, enough reflecting! I knew we needed to move forward and I knew the children would show me the direction. The next day I announced that we were done with teeth. I was greeted with smiles, astonished looks, and an exuberant question from Cory, "Do we get to do another Learning Bubble?" I told him I wasn't sure, but that was what we were going to decide together.

The next few days seemed to fly by as the children compiled lists of topics they wanted to study next. After several discussions the topic was narrowed down to the zoo. More discussion and reading about the zoo led to three subgroups: zoo people, zoo animals, and zoo places. Needless to say, we were off on a whole new inquiry adventure, together, as teachers, students, and learners.

REFLECTIONS

The research, theories, practices, and personal thoughts I have explored give me and other classroom teachers much to think about before the first bell rings in August. Hopefully, it also provides us with a springboard to begin developing or redesigning our early childhood programs to focus on the child. If there is one thing I have learned through research and practice, it is the fact that change is hard. It requires a whole new way of looking at children. Kohn (1993) makes a powerful statement in regard to change: "Parting with power is not easy, if only because the results are less predictable without control" (p. 18).

Teachers need to make the decision to release some of the control before change can occur and the focus can then become the child. It is important to remember that change does not happen overnight. Teachers must choose practices that are best for themselves and their students. Teaching young children is an on-going process involving many decisions daily. And, with a commitment to learner-centered philosophy, a love for learning, and a love for children, it is a process that returns countless wonders of discovery every day.

Chapter 3

Learning With Children What It Means to be a Teacher

Kimberly Ridder

Lincoln Public Schools, Lincoln, NE

◻ ◻ ◻

What is a Teacher?
A guide, not a guard.
What is learning?
A journey, not a destination.
What is discovery?
Questioning the answers, not answering the questions.
What is the process?
Discovering the ideas, not covering the content.
What is the goal?
Open minds, not closed issues.
What is the text?
Being and becoming, not remembering and reviewing.
What is a school?
Whatever we choose to make it.

—Glatthorn (1990)

Five years ago, this poem would have raised many question in my mind: "What do you mean, a guide?" "How can teachers be effective if they don't answer students' questions?" "How can this prepare students for standardized tests in March?" But today when I read it, I am better able to understand the deep meaning of the author's words.

During the past 5 years, Kim L. and I strove to make our first-grade classrooms into an environment similar to the one described in the poem. We keep the accordion doors open between our two adjoining rooms. We have spent many hours reading research articles, attending workshops, and taking graduate courses. Bits and pieces from each of the different sources have been used to help change our classroom into an environment we now consider to be more developmentally appropriate for our young students.

THE MOVE TOWARD PROJECTS

Today, someone entering our classroom may see small groups of students setting up field trips, signed out to work collaboratively in the media center, or disassembling a variety of machines to see how they work. A visitor may also observe children sharing hypotheses, interviewing experts, or leading group discussions. But the one thing that anyone entering our classroom is sure to notice is the energy generated by the students working in their project groups.

Katz (1994) suggests that:

> A project is an in-depth investigation of a topic worth learning more about. The investigation is usually undertaken by a small group of children within a class, sometimes by a whole class, and occasionally by an individual child. The key feature of a project is that it is a research effort deliberately focused on finding answers to questions about a topic posed by the children. The goal of a project is to learn more about a topic rather that to seek right answers to questions posed by the teacher. (p. 1)

We became interested in the project approach while attending a summer workshop. One of the guest speakers was Judy Graves (1994), an educator and consultant from Portland, Oregon. She presented information about the young children in Reggio Emillia, a town in Italy that provides preschoolers with many opportunities to learn by pursuing projects of interest. Judy also showed how sixth graders engaged in projects to pursue interests. She explained that the project approach is based on an integrated model, tying children's experiences together. She helped us understand how building connections and relationships within the children's worlds helps them make sense of the environment.

Judy's presentation inspired us to believe that the project approach could greatly benefit the students in our classrooms. We spent the remainder of the summer immersed in literature. The *Primary Program* (Nebraska Department of Education, 1993) was one of the pieces that helped us make many connections. It focuses on developmentally appropriate practices and supports a project approach to learning. The *Primary Program* states:

> The project approach is firmly grounded in the principles and ideology of the *Primary Program* ... [it] should be part of a balanced curriculum. The skills, knowledge, and attitudes acquired by formal instruction are better learned and remembered when applied in a real context. Using projects with children is an opportunity for application and consolidation of the learning we value. (Integrated Studies section, p. 27)

Project groups are an exciting addition to any classroom, but with any such addition comes change. In the following sections, I discuss the changes that occurred in my classroom due to the use of project groups; the roles of teachers and students was dramatically recomposed as we began our inquiry via students' projects. (In chapter 8, I describe some of the roller-coaster feelings that accompany such work.) The final part of this chapter is the presentation of one project group's inquiry.

TEACHERS AS FACILITATORS

Kim L. and I worked hard to compose new roles for ourselves. This involved disrupting some old beliefs and moving our practice to being more consistent with our newer, emerging beliefs. We wanted to guide learning experiences through strategies that encourage children to problem solve, think creatively, make decisions, and expand their thinking skills. We wanted to help children become aware and accepting of the different talents and abilities that each possesses. We wanted to help children communicate in symbolic ways with water colors, computers, clay, drawing, culture, and other forms of expression.

In previous years, Kim L. and I developed theme-based learning centers for our students. Because we were so accustomed to planning each day in its entirety, we found ourselves knee deep in questions: "How do we move from a very teacher-centered curriculum to a more student-centered curriculum?" "What is the first step in the relinquishment of control?" We played with these questions for some time before finally deciding on a plan of action.

We had read Wasserman (1988), whose thinking became instrumental in our pursuit of a more student-centered classroom. This helped us focus on the first change: altering the physical make-up of our room. Throughout our study-filled summer, we noticed one theme recurring in article after article: the importance of the learning environment when working with young children in project groups.

> The learning environment is social in nature, providing a psychologically safe, secure and stimulating climate for all children. It provides time and opportunities for children to take appropriate risks, make choices, and explore and investigate their world. It offers children experiences which encourage them to interact with others, to develop interpersonal skills and to work and learn cooperatively and collaboratively. (Nebraska Department of Education, 1993, p. 9)

To begin our "makeover" everything was pulled from our dust-covered shelves. Learning areas were set up throughout the room and all the books, manipulatives, and learning materials were placed at appropriate centers. The discovery center was packed full of wonderful items to explore. Seeds, bones, a cow's tooth, and living plants were all displayed for small eager hands to manipulate. In previous years, these items had been left in their dark storage places to be pulled out when they fit into a unit of study that we designed without the children.

The art center was also "chalk-full" of wonderful media for children to experiment with. Painting easels were put up, and we pictured them as always full of activity as children took turns creating works of art. Clay-covered fingers would work intensely to create intricately designed sculptures. Paint, chalk, markers, and glue would always be in stock and finished pieces allowed to rest on the back shelf until taken home at the end of the day.

I remember the gut-wrenching nausea that settled in as we scanned the classroom; it looked cluttered and busy, a far cry from the tidy and organized classroom we had once worked hard to maintain. We felt vulnerable seeing all of our theme materials spread around the classroom. Thoughts began to fill our minds: "What if the projects don't work and we have to return to preplanned themes?" "All of the theme materials have already been exposed to the children." We cringed as we looked at the easel set up permanently in the art center; visions of paint-stained carpet danced in our heads.

To help the children become accustomed to this new environment, we added a 30-minute exploration time to our daily schedule. During this time, the children were encouraged to explore the classroom. They used the time to investigate the different learning areas, construct knowledge, and interact with each other.

As the children interacted with each other during this time, Kim L. and I listened to their conversations and questions as they used the materials they encountered. We took notes on the things they found intriguing, the things they went back to day after day. It was through this "eavesdropping" that we were able to identify areas of interest and possible project group topics. Some of the topics that emerged included the human body, snakes, machines, and bats. The creation of the spider group was discussed in chapter 1.

THE RAT PACK

The Rat Pack, as they later became known, was a group of children thoroughly fascinated and somewhat frightened by Snowball, the classroom rat. Daily, the group would gather around the finger smeared aquarium that was Snowball's home. Questioning eyes would take in Snowball's every movement. Notes on Snowball weren't taken down on paper, but were being sorted in the students' inquisitive minds. No one was willing to handle Snowball; in fact, the metal screen covering the cage went untouched. Words such as "dirty," "scaly," "beady," and "yucky " were heard as the students expressed their thoughts and feelings regarding the white ro-dent. When asked why they considered Snowball to be dirty, interesting stories surfaced. "I saw rats in the garbage cans in the alley," or, " My dad killed a rat in the garage," were some of the memories shared by students.

The *Primary Program* explains that all children interact with information and experiences by moving through a learning cycle. The learning cycle includes the movement from awareness, to exploration, to inquiry, and finally to utilization. Our students were aware of rats and were exploring as they observed. This seemed like the time to move to inquiry. We noticed a change in this group over the period of 1 week. They went from individually exploring the rodent to the next stage of the cycle, inquiry. They were no longer content with observation of the animal; they now wanted to directly examine it. As a group, they asked to remove the screen, allowing them to directly investigate the rat. They had formed a project group with a clear focus on one small thing: a white rat.

It was interesting to observe the children involved in their inquiry. Snowball could frequently be found in the center of a circle, enclosed by the legs of the students. One day Snowball was reunited with her sister, Snow-flake. The children were intent on understanding how the two communi-cated. Cassie was appointed as the note-taker, in charge of documenting any exciting observations. It was thrilling to hear them discuss their findings with one another, comparing their observations and thoughts. Nothing Kim L. and I could have planned would have proved more engaging to this project group. Because rats were common occurrences in their lives, the subject was relevant and meaningful to them, keeping them interested and connected to their everyday lives. Perrone (1991) supports this, noting, "To draw students into the depth and complexity of a subject, we must look for topics that relate to students' lives " (p. 21).

The final stage of the learning cycle is utilization, "the application or transfer of what has been learned about events, concepts, people, and objects " (Nebraska Department of Education, 1992, p. 23). We weren't able to witness this until later in the school year when a student brought in a hamster for show and tell. As we discussed the small animal, it became evident that most of the information being shared was being provided by members of the Rat Pack.

One child explained that the hamster was a rodent because of his two incisors. Cassie then offered information on the hamster's nocturnal habits. Teresa also joined in with her in-depth description of a mammal and all the reasons a pet hamster fit into this category. Even though the rat was studied the semester before, the students were able to recall and apply the information to a new situation with accuracy and expertise. More of their learnings are presented later in this chapter.

Other project groups emerged from the 30-minute exploration time, too. It was clear that these groups needed large blocks of uninterrupted time to interact, experiment, communicate, and reflect. We moved to a schedule that allowed the children 30 to 45 minutes of time to invest in their inquiry.

We changed the way we planned. Instead of sitting down during our planning period, without the children, we sat down to collaborate with the children. We met daily with project groups to discuss their plans and ideas. As a group, we listed the materials and resources they would need to carry out their plans. Together, we worked to locate these items for the following day. The students were also aided by the speech pathologist, Chapter I teacher, media specialist, and occasionally the art and music teachers.

CHILDREN'S ROLES AS DECISION MAKERS

Malaguzzi (cited in Edwards, Gandini, & Forman, 1993) says that, "We must catch the ball that children throw us and return it in such a way that makes them want to continue playing the game, perhaps inventing their own games along the way" (p. 5). An important characteristic of the developmentally appropriate classroom is the personal investment of the students in the learning process. Hartman and Eckerty (1995) explain that when children have personal investment in the learning process, they remain motivated over time. Our students remained interested because they had a considerable amount of influence on the topic, direction, depth, audience, and presentation of their projects.

Our projects lasted from 1 to 6 weeks, at the children's discretion. They usually chose concrete topics, directly related to places, people, events, or objects familiar to them. Buses, homes, school, and machines seemed to be popular choices because of the direct relation to the children and their worlds. Projects must be something that children can investigate directly so that they are able to draw from observations, construct models, observe and record findings, explore, predict, discuss, and present their new understandings (Katz, 1994).

Kim L. and I observed this to be true while watching a group of children undertake a project on simple machines. In addition to reading about simple machines, children were involved in exploring machines daily. As a group, they disassembled old record players, vacuum cleaners, and tape recorders, carefully sorting and categorizing each of the salvaged parts. The children also worked daily to construct machines of their own. It was not uncommon to see children scurrying through the room in search of that one important piece that would be added to their project. They were avid record keepers, insisting on keeping track of their organized and sorted machine parts.

The inquiry base of a project group seemed to carry over throughout the day as children continually noticed things in their daily lives that were constructed using simple machines. Students pointed out simple machines on the playground, in the cafeteria, and even came to school excited after sighting a simple machine in their own home. After a 3-day weekend, Heather came bursting into the room with her discovery that the roof on her house was an inclined plane!

Not only did the machine group continue for 6 weeks, it did so with an overall enthusiasm from each of its members. Group members asked daily to be excluded from recess so they could continue to work on a project, and many students gave up their free choice time to write about a machine they had invented.

Although we honored their interests and helped them pursue those interests as best we could, we found that topics that are inaccessible to children limit opportunities for hands-on observation, an important component for successful projects. Inaccessibility is demonstrated by an example of a project group focusing on caves. Although the children exhibited initial excitement over the topic, enthusiasm faded quickly due to the children's inability to directly examine their subject. The group members were never able to personally experience the sounds, smells, or sights of a real cave. Everything they learned came from secondary sources including books, pamphlets, and letters. None of these resources could re-create the feel of a cave's cool, damp air as it clings to the skin. The eerie sound of the water hitting the ground as it drips from a 4-foot stalactite or the dirty musty smell that fills the nasal passages could not be experienced. The group learned a lot about caves, but the excitement they exhibited in previous projects seemed to be missing.

The use of project groups and an increased understanding of how we learn has changed the anatomy of our classroom. A classroom now able to offer its students the opportunity to engage in inquiry is one that supports the creation (Rick Meyer would say composing) of engaged and dedicated learners. The Rat Pack illustrates my point.

STUDYING ONE INQUIRY GROUP IN DEPTH

The pages that follow this section are an actual book, The Rat Pack, that I made with the support of the group of children who came to refer to themselves as the Rat Pack. This group of children, mentioned previously, was doing much more than learning about rats. They were confronting their fears, changing their beliefs about rats, forming a community of learners, learning to read and write while they used reading and writing to learn, and helping other class members learn about rats. They are scientists, artists, diplomats, and philosophers.

I chose this group, arbitrarily, to study one group in depth in order to get a fuller sense of what the children were learning and how that learning occurred during project time. I made copies of everything they wrote while they inquired. I kept track of books they read and roles they played in terms of relationships, leadership, and helpfulness.

After discussing this data in the study group, I decided to write *The Rat Pack* as a way of showing how the students and I learned as inquirers. *The Rat Pack* is an interesting genre because it is a book by a teacher (me), that contains the book (in photographed form) that the children wrote to present their learning. The children's inquiry is presented within and as the subject of my inquiry. This is another way that you can see Rick Meyer's idea of facets, discussed in chapter 1.

I included, in *The Rat Pack*, photos of the other groups that were inquiring at the same time. These give readers an indication of the variety of the students' interests and their final projects, reflective of the children's discussions of what to present and how to present it. The spider group made a web representative of one type that spiders spin. The snake group made a full-length (life-size) python. The dinosaur group wrote a book, and the owl group presented a poster session with their findings. Kim L. assisted the spider group; the speech pathologist worked in my room during this time and used her time there to support the dinosaur group. The families' comments do, indeed, speak for themselves. Many more parents (75) attended this presentation of projects by our two classrooms than attended a whole-school parent–teacher organization meeting held a few weeks prior (3 parents attended that meeting).

The Rat Pack requires some help in reading for those not familiar with invented spelling and, also, because some of the photos did not reproduce the children's writing that well. The following conventional spellings of their writing are provided for increased clarity.

On page 2, the questions the children wrote are:

1. What do they eat?
2. How do they have babies?
3. How long are their lives?
4. Can they see different colors?
5. How do you know if they are pregnant?
6. How are they born?
7. Do rats talk to each other?
8. When they are born, do they eat?
9. How do you know if they are a boy or a girl?
10. Are they endangered?

On page 4, the children wrote to three outside experts: the science teacher (Mr. S—), a veterinarian, and a pet store owner.

On page 6, the children wrote questions for their ongoing inquiry, having located two rats and placed them together:

- Did they communicate? Yes.
- Did they go through the maze? Yes. (Their reading revealed the rats' ability to learn to run through mazes and they wanted to try this.)
- Did they go through the maze again? Yes.
- Did they communicate again? Yes
- Have they been fighting? Yes.

On page 7, note that the children used yarn, markers, glue, and other materials to express their findings. The final book was quite thick because of the variety of materials included to make the illustrations look like real rats.

On page 10, note that the students presented in costumes they made; the costumes reflect the three categories of rats about which they learned: hooded, white, and brown. The pages that follow are a reproduction of *The Rat Pack*.

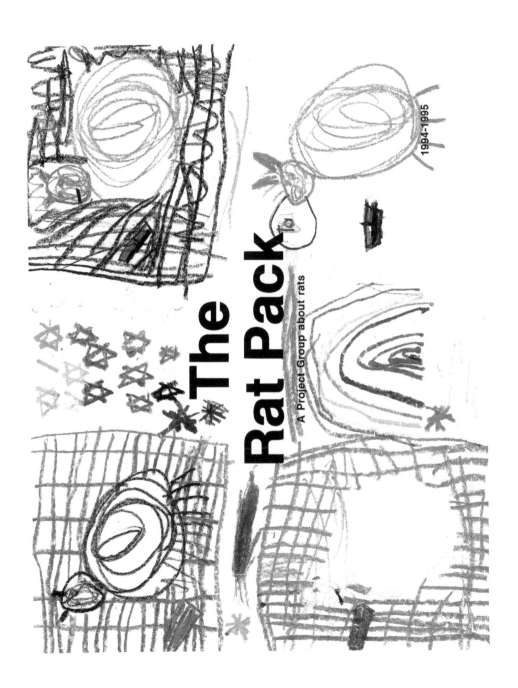

The
Rat Pack

A Project Group about rats

1994-1995

59

The study of rats emerged as a subtopic of the class chosen unit, "Scary Animals." Students were frequently heard discussing different "scary animals" throughout the day. At recess groups of children would stand next to the the building and try to catch spiders as they scurried by. One of the students checked out many books on sharks and even found a book that helped him learn how to draw sharks. Cassie became fascinated with our classroom pet rat,Snowball. Although she enjoyed looking at him she was not willing to touch him as were any of the other children. Cassie insisted that she liked Snowball but was afraid of him because of his ugly tail. Documentation of happenings similar to the ones described above continued until six possible project groups surfaced. The six groups followed the theme of "scary animals" and included rats, spiders, snakes, owls, dinosaurs, and sharks. The following is a collection of some of the research done by the students referred to as the "Rat Group."

1

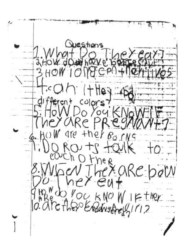

The first meeting of the "rat group" consisted of brainstorming questions and observations the students had about rats. The chosen student recorder documented the questions asked by the group. Brandon commented on the "squiggly mark" at the end of each sentence, thus a mini-lesson on question marks was born! The meeting concluded with the question, "How will we find the answers to the questions asked today?" The suggestion was made to do "homework" on this question and bring the answers to project group the next day.

2

Cassie's homework on how to find
the answers to the questions they had
about rats.

The students came back with many ideas on how to find out the answers to their
questions. Cassie drew pictures of her ideas at home. She suggested that they
"read books, use the computer and study snowball. " Teresa felt we should talk to
Mr. Sibert, the fifth grade science teacher. Kimi thought it would be fun to visit a
pet store and Brandon decided we needed to call a "vet."

3

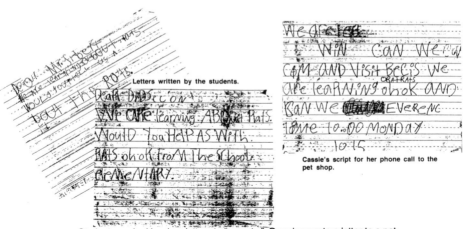

Letters written by the students.

Cassie's script for her phone call to the
pet shop.

Students worked hard on letters to "experts." Brandon wrote a letter to a pet
shop. Teresa and Kimi wrote Mr. Sibert and Cassie wrote to Dr. Secon, a
veterinarian. The group also decided to call the neighborhood pet shop and
schedule a field trip. Together they wrote a script for Cassie to follow during the
phone call.

The call went perfectly and a field trip was arranged for the following Monday at
10:00 A.M..

4

The children enjoyed the pet shop and were able to witness the live birth of baby rats. Many of their questions had been answered through the viewing of this exciting event.

The pet store owner did a nice job of answering their question on how to tell the difference between a male rat and a female rat. He explained that the male rat has two holes and a lump by its tail.

The kids were so excited by the trip that they couldn't stop talking about it on the walk back to school.

5

Students observing Snowball.

Notes taken on how rats communicate.

Cassie, Kimi, and Teresa asked to borrow Mrs. Lloyd's rat, Snowflake. The girls put Snowball and Snowflake together to see how they would communicate. They made many scientific discoveries and even took notes on what they observed taking place between the two rats.

6

Kimi paints her page on how rats communicate.

Cassie and Teresa Work on a page in their book.

The group decided to share their newly acquired knowledge in the form of a big book. Each member wrote about something they had learned during their study of rats and then illustrated it with the media of their choice. Even though the students were given group time to work on their book, many of them chose to continue their work during their free time.

7

WHEN: WEDNESDAY
NOV. 16

TIME: 10:00 - 11:00

WHERE: MULTI-PURPOSE
ROOM

PLEASE RSVP BY
TUESDAY, NOV. 15 BY
RETURNING THE SLIP OF
PAPER.

FROM: ROOMS 114 & 116

PLEASE COME TO
OUR PROJECT
PRESENTATION
ON ANIMALS THAT
ARE SCARY

As the students' knowledge continued to grow they began to express a desire to share their expertise with others. The suggestion was made to present what had been learned with families and friends and thus the "project presentation" idea came to be.

Together the class charted things that needed to be done to prepare for the presentation. The list included; invitations, posters, signs, snacks, and placemats. Each group then committed to completing one of the preparations. The rat group chose to do the invitations.

8

I love rats! But...

My rat died on December 4. I was sad yep, yep. I was sad all right.

When the rat died I was at my friend Pam's house, and I was so sad.

3

book about rats.

I felt so bad and sad.

4

When I got back, we had a funeral, it was sad.

5

Help me, I'm sad, Ahhhhhh!

6

Enthusiasm was high among group members. They ate, drank and slept rats! Teresa and Cassie wrote books about rats, Kimi spent every spare moment with Snowball and Brandon brought a staple remover to school to show as a model of a rat's incisors!

9

The "Rat Group"

With the presentation day came many jitters. The students had rehearsed their parts many times and felt confident with their abilities to present.

Pride was an emotion experienced by each group member during the presentation of rats in front of an audience of around 75. Without any help from adults, the students shared their expertise on rats with friends and families.

Students were also able to celebrate their learnings with families in the room after the presentation. Cake and punch were enjoyed as the students chattered excitedly with their visitors. The "scary animal" project groups ended leaving everyone involved with a feeling of overall happiness and total success.

10

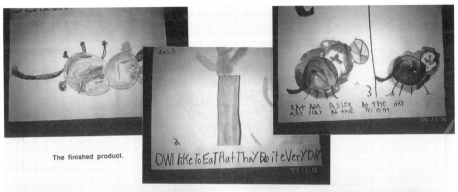

The finished product.

CaSSie

2

OWl liKe To EaT RaT ThaY Do it eVeRY DaY

RAt ARe ASlee At the dAy RAT PLAY At the NioHt

3

'94 11 15

TheIp TAIL is As LoNg As the BoDe.

4

Rats eat vegetables, do9 food, fruit, and nuts.

5

'94 11 15

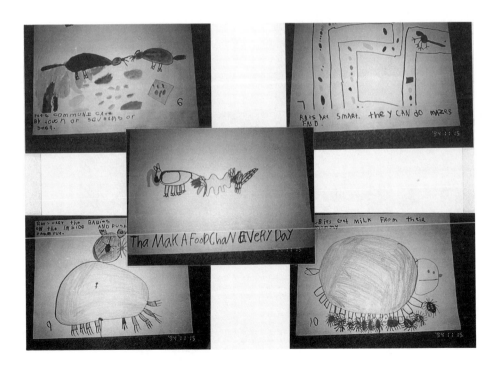

res commune cate By touch or savesns or snen.

6

Rats ARe SMART. the Y CAN do mAZes FND.

7

'94 11 15

Tha MaK A FooD ChaN EVeRY DaY

Res cary the BABies oN the INsIde AND push thom out.

BaBies Get MiLK FRom their mommy

9

10

'94 11 15

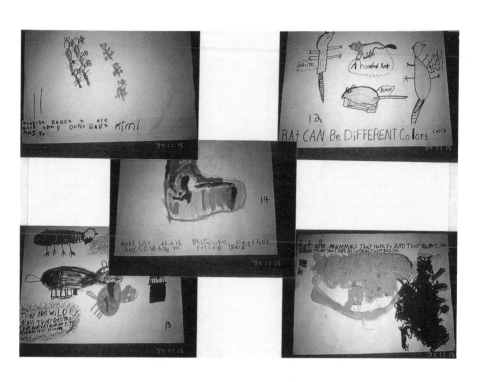

The "Spider Group"

The "Snake Group"

The "Owl Group"

The "Dinosaur Group"

66

"The presentation party!

FiRsT gRaDe PrOjEct PRESENTATIONS

PLEASE TELL US WHAT YOU THINK!!

November 16, 1994

Thank you for coming to our presentation today.
Please take a minute and write your thoughts about the children as learners and presenters. We really appreciate your time and support.

Follow-up questionnaires were sent home with students and the reactions were wonderful! Everyone involved seemed to overwhelmingly agree on the success of project groups.

11

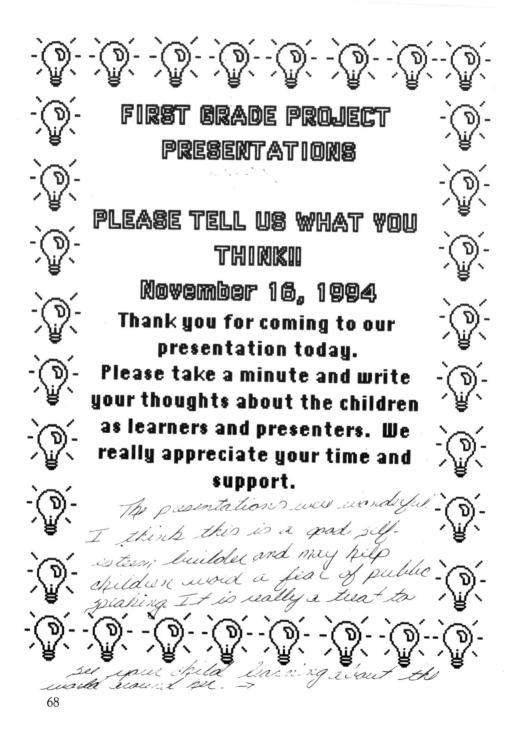

FIRST GRADE PROJECT PRESENTATIONS

PLEASE TELL US WHAT YOU THINK!!

November 16, 1994

Thank you for coming to our presentation today.
Please take a minute and write your thoughts about the children as learners and presenters. We really appreciate your time and support.

The presentations were wonderful. I think this is a good self-esteem builder and may help children avoid a fear of public speaking. It is really a treat to see your child learning about the world around her. →

68

The first graders present thoughtful & well-researched project. They were articulate and interesting. I was thrilled to watch!!!

I thought the children did a very good job on their researching for their particular project. I also feel they all did a good job of presenting. I was very pleased with the whole program. Diane Girdner

I thought that the children knew alot about the animals. and that they are learning very well in school.

The children seemed to do very well in speaking infront of the group. They seemed very interested in and to understand well, the subject in which they learned. + had a lot of fun!

They did very good. Pat James
I liked it   Joe James
It was delightful and good research.
Melinda James   They were good. Kim Summerill
I thought it WAS GREAT!

It was so exciting to see this project grow over the weeks. The children were motivated to find out answers to their own questions, not contrived questions. As learners and presenters they seemed proud of their accomplishments, they had power and control of their learning. The projects you class did and their presentation is such a good example of what can happen when we let go of the idea that children are empty vessels that we fill with information.

We thought the children did an excellent job. you could tell they did alot of research for there presentation. They also did a great job speaking in front of everyone. Thank you for inviting us. Also congratulations!!! Denise Corl, Gloria Corl, William Spicklesmire & Natalie Mason.

Chapter 4

Refining Projects: Making the Leap Toward Individual Interests

Kimberly Larson
Lincoln Public Schools, Lincoln, NE

¤ ¤ ¤

Welcome to our first-grade classrooms, where Kim R. and I have been helping the kids engage in learning through inquiry projects. It is no coincidence that comments such as these could be overheard from some of the children:

> **Abdullah** [to a parent helper, after receiving the gift of a toy motorcycle from his dad earlier in the week]: "Terrence, would you help me write about motorcycles?"
>
> **Ryan** [after finding a bug on our classroom floor, discovering with the help of our library media specialist that it was a cockroach, and planning to take his bug home to live with him]: "I want to go to the library and get a book about my cockroach! Margot and Aryelle, do you want to go with me?"
>
> **Andrey** [as a result of attending a track meet over the weekend at which he saw a college student involved in a practicum in our classroom]: "Ms. Larson, would you read to me about track meets?"

The children were anxious to learn about a variety of topics, and they did not hesitate to ask to visit the library or read a book in order to gain new information. The projects that were going on now, many months and a summer break after we and the students had first initiated them, were somewhat different from our first attempts. We moved toward an even greater expression of individuality by allowing students more control in choosing and carrying out their projects. This chapter describes some of the changes we made and the reasons for those changes. These changes took place during the second year of our study group. We weren't meeting weekly, but Kim R. and I still relied on each other and on members of the group to help us think out what we were planning.

Kim R. and I were proud of the way project group studies went in the classrooms we shared at Ridgeway Elementary School. The idea of letting the children choose their own topics of study and guiding the direction of their studies was new to us and seemed like an exciting way to teach many of our first-grade objectives. What we did not realize at that time was that the excitement of the students and parents, and the incredible amounts of learning that all of us experienced during that first year of having children do projects, would far exceed any expectations that we had. It was that excitement that led us to support the students in extending the possibilities of inquiry projects.

Kim R. and I worked together for many years, sharing ideas and inspirations, and each year we looked forward to the challenge of improving the way we taught the required curriculum objectives. During the first year, we decided to jump right in, allowing children to sign up for study topics that were based on our observations of their interest areas. The children were allowed to be in groups of five or six, and we tried to influence them to sign up for the topics that truly interested them rather than the topics that their favorite classmates chose to study. We also learned that sometimes friends can take a topic and make it very interesting to each other; there is definitely a social side to all of this.

PROBLEMS WITH PROJECTS

We began asking ourselves, "How could we build on our successes to improve this part of the children's school day?" We were feeling that we needed more time for project studies, that 30 minutes a day was not nearly enough. Often, it seemed that we just got started and it was time to stop.

How could we create a longer work time for the children in a day that was already too short for all that we wanted to do? We sometimes wondered if, as teachers, we were guiding too much of the children's studies, their projects, and the topics that they chose. I suppose that our responsibility to meet our district's curriculum demands might have influenced the direction of the groups as we guided them. We felt a constant pull between our obligation to teach required curriculum and our desire to allow children to guide the direction of their learning by giving them choices throughout the day. It was important to us that the children felt ownership in their project work, so they could be better engaged in their work and, as a result, important learning could occur. The freedom to choose the direction of their learning provided our students this opportunity for engagement. But would we teach every objective expected of us as first-grade teachers utilizing this approach? Our dilemma was this: "How do we support more freedom while dealing with the demands of the district?" We learned that we more than surpassed district and our own expectations. Not only did the children learn to read and write, they learned that these tools and others serve them in their quest for information and understanding.

The 1995–1996 school year (the second year of our study group) began, and we allowed several weeks of school to pass before starting our first project studies. As we had done the previous year, we spent a lot of time listening to the conversations of the children before talking with them about what they would like to study. We charted all of their ideas, and then we, as the teachers and organizers of the classroom, chose six of these topics for the children to choose from. The topics were all practical and allowed for a lot of hands-on exploration. The children studied rabbits and chinchillas, to name two (we had a pet rabbit and chinchilla in the classroom), and project group work basically followed the same routines and procedures as our groups had the year before. We continued to ask ourselves the same questions, especially about individuals' interests, with no answers yet discovered.

In January, when we charted possible topics for the most recent project study groups, several children suggested predictable topics such as food and snakes. It did surprise me to hear one child suggest that we study writing as a project study topic. I was thrilled because teaching writing had become a passion of mine since participating in the state writing project the previous summer. Kim R. and I had reorganized our classroom schedule to accommodate daily writing time. I imagined that a writing project group would be a joy to join, observe, and guide. I was anxious for our first meeting, which would be held the following morning.

The writing project group, consisting of six children, met daily beginning on January 12. Coincidentally, I was meeting with a writing group of which I am a member on the same day and had my notebook of writing with me. I shared it with the group, showing them drafts of papers in progress, a computer disk crammed with my current projects, copies of other group members' writing that had been shared with me previously, and a list of topic ideas that I refer to when I need a new idea for writing. I also had a copy of the recent *neblab* (*Nebraska Language Arts Bulletin*; Larson, 1996) that had a copy of my first published piece of writing.

"You wrote that?" they asked, perhaps thinking that they too might be able to write something and have others read it in a publication of some sort.

"Yes," I said, "It's the first piece I've ever had published."

It was also of great interest to them that other teachers they knew had articles published in the same journal. The children recognized the members of our group who contributed to the issue that had teacher research as its theme.

Perhaps inspired by the poem that I had written, Zach told the group, "I wrote a poem. I'll go get it!" He returned a short time later with a several-sentence piece of writing about cardinals that he had written the day before during the class' journal writing time.

> This is a cardinal.
> It is red.
> It lives in a nest.
> They are red.
> They sing good.

Zach read his poem to the group, his pride in his work evident in his eyes and his smile.

The writing group, which began with this conversation about the publishing of writing, evolved into a group that felt like I was reliving my summer experiences in the writing project. Eventually, this group affected the very structure of the entire first-grade classroom. It magically transformed the nature of project work time, turning it into many inquiry studies, with the excitement of learning everywhere. But that is getting ahead of myself. It wasn't all that easy; and it wasn't really magic, either.

I should not have been surprised when, during our next scheduled work time, the first thing the children wanted to do was organize a notebook for their writing supplies. They had seen mine and wanted one of their own. We went to the school's basement and retrieved abandoned notebooks (hardly noticing the dust and unknown words printed on the binders). Zach wanted one with a clip inside the front cover for his special papers; other children checked out the size of the rings or how easily the notebooks opened and closed. After choosing what we needed, we headed back up the stairs to our classroom and talked about what would go into these newly acquired treasures.

This was all going quite well. Then, on the second day of our writing project group, Michael expressed that the newness and excitement was wearing off.

"This is stupid," he said. "I don't want to be in this dumb group. You can't make me write anything."

Then, as we looked at the copies I made of Zach's cardinal poem, Michael said, "That's a stupid poem."

He was one member of the group who seemed determined to have my undivided attention through negative comments and nonparticipation. He had been in a project study group of mine previously and had been challenging to work with, to say the least. On this particular day, I chose to ignore

Michael, mostly because the rest of the group was happy and enthusiastic, and I hoped that their attitudes would be contagious.

They weren't. Michael ended up making up some work time with me while his classmates were outside at recess later that day. I was concerned about Michael and his expressed lack of interest in what we were doing. Should he be forced into a study group that he wasn't interested in? Thinking back on the day that group members were organized, I remembered that Michael had really wanted to be in the food study group. (Who didn't? I was hungry when we were signing up for groups, too, and probably would have enjoyed this area of study if I had the chance!)

After about a week of meeting, the group that had originally wanted to study writing had turned into a group of serious writers truly reminiscent of the writing project. They were writing every day and were choosing the kinds of writing they wanted to do, from research to poetry. They shared their work with each other, made copies of their writing for others in the group to read and keep, talked about what they noticed about each other's work, and pointed out what they liked about each other's writing as well.

Abdullah wrote a story about his mom. He wrote: "I love my mom. She is sick sometimes." When he couldn't think anything else to write, I asked him about his mom.

"What does she look like? Is she beautiful?" I was thinking that this question would spark an idea in this sweet, sensitive child's mind. He looked at me for a minute and kindly said, "Sometimes!" After a little more reflection he said aloud, and then added to his story: "She looks like my dad " (see Fig. 4.1).

By the time the group met on January 22, a little over a week after we started, Michael's lack of interest was no longer an issue. Michael had

FIG. 4.1. Abdullah's story about his mom. "I love my mom. She is sick sometimes. My mom looks like my dad."

expressed an interest in studying about Mississippi earlier in the school year, but he was the only one interested in this topic and so a study group had never formed. When Michael discovered that he could write about anything, he decided to write about Mississippi. This was an important shift in our inquiry groups. The way this group was set up allowed Michael to pursue a very individual interest.

"How can you learn more about Mississippi?" I asked him. He knew that his grandma could teach him about the state because she lived there. He also knew that he could learn through reading books. Michael had identified both primary and secondary sources to satiate his interest.

Michael visited the library with one of the adults in the room. He did not want to stop working that morning when it was time to get ready for lunch. During our scheduled writing time later that day, Michael found an adult to help him continue reading his books and seemed anxious to be able to get back to them the following day. He was excited and engaged in his work because he was able to choose his own topic for study, and it did not matter to me or to him at this point that he was the only one with this particular area of interest.

Because the children were such eager participants in this project group, I noticed the contrast with the other project group that I was supervising; they were studying snow. It had been very snowy and icy this midwestern January and perhaps, as teachers, we pushed (maybe picked) this topic for the children. Rather than sharing ideas, asking questions, and writing about their learning, the children sat and looked at me the majority of our meeting times. When we went outside to explore the snow I heard, "It's cold. Can we go back in now?" I offered suggestions for studies that I thought the children would be eager to explore: snowmen, ice skating, where snow comes from. But I received little more than stares and smiles. It was to the point I realized that I was not looking forward to our meetings, and I'm sure the children felt the same way.

After noticing the increased engagement in the writing group's project studies, as compared to the snow group, I began to rethink the way that we managed projects for all of the children. I thought about the successful elements of the writing group that could possibly be incorporated into the entire classroom of children. I thought a lot about the two groups, especially the contrast in interest and enthusiasm.

I liked that the children were all engaged in writing about topics that they had chosen completely on their own. Some of the children chose to write alone, some of them worked with others as they wrote. Some of the writing required research, and the children were going to the library on their own to find books that provided information they needed. Some of the children were writing about topics that they were already experts in, such as Aryelle, who wrote about her mom one day and her doll "Callyna" the next. These mini inquiries allowed her to focus her interests in a variety of areas.

The children were beginning to plan projects that would utilize a variety of learning skills to complete. Michael began to construct a project that went along with his study of Mississippi, building a replica of the state's capital building using boxes and popsicle sticks. Just the organizing of needed materials involved using his knowledge of math, problem-solving strategies, and letter writing. He wrote a letter to his mom to see if she would get boxes for him from her place of business, as well as a note to the cooking group for popsicle sticks (Fig. 4.2).

I spent the better part of a weekend in early February thinking through the impact of changing our daily schedule, and reorganizing how we worked with project groups so that all of the children could possibly experience this freedom and enthusiasm in their studies.

Was it worth the time and energy that would be required for making changes in our school day? Could we manage more groups of children that were all involved in researching and creating projects in varying stages of development and completion? Would Kim R. think I had gone crazy? Didn't we have enough to do without making changes in a program that was going well for most of the children at the present time?

After returning to school on Monday I spoke with Kim R. about the possibility of reorganizing our school day. Typical of what happens between us, the spark of an idea that can renew enthusiasm for teaching and improve the amount of learning for the children took over; pretty soon we were both busy questioning and planning.

How could we supervise so many groups of children at once?

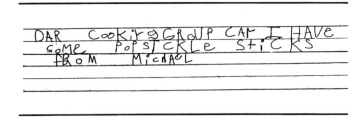

FIG. 4.2. Michael's written request to another group for supplies. "Dear Cookie Group, Can I have some popsicle sticks? From Michael."

What if every child in our two classrooms chose a different topic? We did not feel that our time could be divided between that many children needing help finding books, reading books, writing about what they had learned, and guiding their studies through questions and discussions.

Could the students manage more responsibilities themselves, keeping track of their daily work and letting us know of their needs on a day-to-day basis?

In the end, anticipating potential problems ahead of time and planning for their possibility led to the successful transition to our new project group studies.

PROJECTS MORE REFLECTIVE OF INTERESTS

The first thing we decided to do was to share the enthusiasm of the writing project group with the entire class. What better way to do this than to have the children themselves explain what they had been doing? On February 9, 1996, Zach was the first member of the group to share his notebook and his work. He explained to our first graders: "This is my notebook and it opens like this. It has a clip here and I keep my papers in it like this."

The children in the class watched carefully, an unusual silence filling the room except for the sound of Zach's voice. Zach carefully turned each page of his notebook and told about his writing. He talked about the dividers that he had placed in strategic locations throughout his book and read aloud some of his writing about bats. Zach had copies of illustrations from a bat book he had found in the library, and he showed them as he told his friends what he had learned about bats. He read, "Bats hang upside down to sleep. They sleep during the day and hunt for food at night."

Zach's classmates listened eagerly about his work—especially interested in his notebook and his bat pictures. I decided to have one member of my writing group share each day in order to introduce the rest of the first graders to our group's way of managing the project research that we were involved in. The library-media specialist would let our children visit the library as much as possible. Things were falling into place.

Kim R. and I both felt that it was important for the children to share the work that they were doing because they learn so much from seeing and talking about each other's work. The excitement after Zach's presentation confirmed the importance of this, and so we also made a calendar for "Project Sharing." These were 10-minute time periods for the students to share anything that they had been working on, talk about their questions, and get important feedback from their peers. We somehow managed to squeeze two 10-minute periods that were for this purpose into our morning schedule.

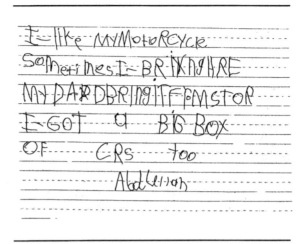

FIG. 4.3. One of Abdullah's treasures from his notebook. "I like my motorcycle. Sometimes I bring it here. My dad brings it from the store. I got a big box of cars, too."

On February 12, it was Abdullah's turn to share the treasures that he had collected in his notebook. He read his motorcycle story to the class after walking his friends through the initial pages of his notebook: "I like my motorcycle. Sometimes I bring it here. My dad bring it from the store. I got a big box of cars, too " (Fig. 4.3).

Abdullah was a beautiful child from Iraq, who was beginning to make sense of letters, sounds, sentences, and stories. He was also interested in learning more about motorcycles. We talked as a group about how Abdullah might accomplish this goal. We talked about the books that were available at our school library. Several children also said that they had relatives who had motorcycles, and they eagerly volunteered these people as resources for Abdullah's research.

Something exciting happened in the class as we were discussing Abdullah's area of interest. I overheard one normally quiet child in the back of the room having a conversation with a friend about a topic that she was interested in studying:

"Do you know what I want to study?" She paused for a moment and looked at her friend. "Mermaids. My mom told me that mermaids only lived a long time ago."

Her friend responded: "There's not really such a thing as mermaids."

The children were beginning to see the possibilities for themselves of the unlimited topics for their research and exploration. This little girl, Cassie, said that she wanted to study mermaids in order to learn whether mermaids really existed. Several other children in the class expressed an interest in the study of mermaids as well, and the mermaid group was officially formed. The children's individual interests, it seemed, quite often did not mean that they worked alone. However, we had more project groups going at one time than ever before; we did not necessarily see each group each day, but we became confident that individuals were studying their primary interests and could help keep track of their progress.

We discussed with the children the changes we were making in the structure of our school day, allowing more time for projects. It was exciting to hear the children planning what they would like to study. As we discussed their ideas for study topics, children naturally formed groups that truly centered around their individual interests. We gathered notebooks for the children's use for collecting their work, just as the writing group had done. They, too, experimented with the rings, pockets, and clips; they labeled their notebooks with their names and stickers that identified them as project work. They chose paper to put into their notebooks and selected some dividers from the remnants that we gathered from our cupboards. They began making lists of things to study. They already were assuming more control of their learning by controlling the way they would use the tools for that learning. It would certainly have been simpler to assemble the notebooks ahead of time for the children. However, we saw that when the students were involved in this process, they felt pride of ownership and used materials thoughtfully.

Several days later, I gave the children a page to put into their notebooks for their reflections about their daily work. This included spaces for the children to respond to three prompts: (a) What did you do today? (b) How did your work time go? (c) Comments. The intent was to give the children a direction and a focus for their work time, and a way to help them to become accountable for their time. Student developed their own systems of organizing papers so that they were able to find whatever was needed on any particular day.

We began each work period with a Status of the Class check (Atwell, 1987). The children gathered on the rug area and planned with their groups the work that was to be done each day. The children wrote what they would be doing in their notebooks, and Kim R. and I quickly asked each student for a brief verbal report of his or her plan. We kept a daily record of the students' plans in our notebooks; we referred to this when checking to see if the students were participating in a variety of learning activities as they completed their project work. This took no more than 5 minutes to complete, yet proved to be an effective tool for accounting for the children's time during this hour of our school day. Once the Status of the Class form was completed, the children set off to carry out their work plans. In the examples that follow, you'll get a sense of the increased individuality that developed in the students' projects.

EXAMPLES OF PROJECT GROUPS IN ACTION

The following is a summary of the work of five of the project groups. I have included the expectations, the surprises, and the areas of excitement and of learning for me as the classroom teacher. Cambourne (1995)summarizes quite accurately some of what I found in my classroom, even though he is referencing his own study:

> My classroom data show that the process of transformation is enormously enhanced through discussion with others. Such discussion allows the exchange and interchange of interpretations, constructed meanings, and understandings. Furthermore, these data support the claim that learning that has a mandatory social dimension to it is usually successful. Just as toddlers can learn to control the oral language of the culture into which they're born only by socially interacting with others, older learners also need a myriad of opportunities to interact with others in order to clarify, extend, refocus, and modify their own learning. (p. 187)

The Cat Group

The cat group organized itself on the first day of project studies. It's members—Rick, Bud, Anna, and Araceli—were anxious and excited to begin their work.

As with any project group, I expected that they would be engaged in meaningful reading and writing activities, learn some research skills, develop some skills that would enable them to function productively as a group, and learn something about the topic they chose to study, cats. I also expected that I would have to be with this group in order for them to work productively together and to get along with each other as they participated in their learning activities. My concern was that the group did not have a member who was an independent reader or writer. Two of its members were participating in the English as a second language program, one received speech and language services, and one student was a young first grader who was not yet able to write or read any words other than his name.

Questions filled my mind: "How would this group function when an adult wasn't there to guide their discussion or help with reading or writing activities?" "Why did these children get together and form a group?" "Would it make more sense that a child with limited language, reading, and writing abilities would want to be with others that were stronger in these areas?"

Some of my questions were answered in the weeks following; others remain unanswered.

One of the university students from Rick Meyer's class helped this group in its initial stages of study by assisting them when they wanted to find nonfiction books about cats at our school media center. She read some of these books with the children and talked with them about cats. I met with them on a few occasions as well, trying to lead a discussion about the purpose of their studies. I asked, "Why did you choose to study cats?" "What do you want to learn about cats?" All four children in the group had a difficult time verbalizing the questions that they had regarding their study topic, but they could all explain to me why they wanted to be a member of this group.

Araceli said that she wanted to be in the cat group because, "I used to have a cat when I lived in Mexico." Anna, whose first language is Russian, wanted to be a member of the group simply because she liked cats. Rick had a cat at his house and was willing to talk with the others about what he knew about his cat. Bud was unable to verbalize any reason for choosing this group or any questions he had about cats. He listened attentively to the others as they shared their reasons for being there.

There were a few days of this group's study that were particularly meaningful for them, and for me. Breanna, another child in the class, wanted to bring in her pet cat to share with the class. All of the children were invited to participate in this presentation, but the cat group prepared for the visit by planning questions for Breanna and her mom.

"Does a cat feel soft?" Anna wondered.

"How do you hold a cat?" Rick asked. "How do they play?"

"Why do cats scratch?" Araceli wondered.

Their questions reflected the first-hand experiences that the children had with animals, rather than the desire to learn why cats were mammals, the length of a typical cat, or other information that might take the students to a different level of learning as far as content.

When the cat came for its visit, the cat group was excited and actively involved in learning about the cat by touching it, looking at it, and talking about the cat with its owners—Breanna and her mom. I recorded the answers to their questions as I made sure they were asked intermittently during the visit. I wanted to ensure that we could discuss the answers together in a follow-up conversation, when the cat's presence was no longer a distraction. This hands-on experience of having a cat come to the classroom for study provided an opportunity to learn answers to questions using the five senses and by talking together.

There were two other periods in the cat group's studies when I noticed that this group of children was engaged in their activities relating to cats and learning about cats through oral language. One of these occasions was when they wanted to make cats and decided to use clay as a medium. One student wrote a note to the art teacher asking to borrow some of her clay. For the next 2 days during study time, the children sat together and formed and reformed clay cats. As they worked, they looked at pictures of cats and talked together about a cat's body parts and what they knew about cats. I observed them sharing as they divided up the balls of multicolored clay that they had obtained on their own. I watched them help each other with the parts of their cats that they were having difficulty forming. They attended to the task at hand until they each had a product they were proud of. Each cat had a head, a body, four legs, and a tail; some had ears and whiskers. The children encouraged each other and made sure that each cat model contained the critical elements of a cat's body. I was impressed that group members worked together cooperatively and worked to complete the task at hand. The group had bonded, and the dynamics of the group were positive and productive.

The other period of time during the cat group's study that I noticed that they were particularly engaged in their work and working together cooperatively was when they wanted to make cat costumes. I encouraged this activity, thinking that if they made costumes they might write and perform a play about cats during which they would wear their costumes The play would reflect their learning about their chosen study topic. The children wanted large sheets of paper for the cats' bodies and wanted to make masks to wear on their heads. They worked for several days cutting, coloring, and assembling their costumes and attended to their work for long periods of time, again incorporating what they knew about cats into their costumes. They assisted each other with the parts of the construction that were difficult for some of the group members.

They never did write their play, although I attempted to lead them in this direction on several occasions. I did insist, however, that they do some writing as part of their project. Writing is important because it helps children organize their thoughts about a topic as they relate their learning to another audience. I tried to honor meaning-making through clay and paper but also paid attention to the fact that I was obligated to teach the children to read and write.

My expectations of the writing each child completed was based on what I knew of each individual student. Because two group members (Bud and Rick) received extra help through Title 1 services on a daily basis, I asked their Title 1 teacher to help them write their stories. Bud and Rick dictated their sentences to the teacher, and then copied them onto writing paper. Anna chose to copy some sentences that a university student had written with the children's help on a previous day; Araceli wrote her story independently, using her knowledge of letter-sounds and known sight words. All of the children pasted their reports onto large pieces of manila paper and illustrated them with pictures of cats made with crayon.

FIG. 4.4. The cat group's report. "We learned about cats. Cats are soft. Dogs want to chase cats. Cats like to eat mice. Cats like to eat fish. Cats take a bath with their tongues. They scratch. Cats climb trees. We learned this by computer."

We held a project fair in the hallway outside our classrooms when all children had completed a culminating project to show their learning, about 6 weeks from the beginning of our inquiry. The children organized the set-up of booths for their displays, sent out invitations, and explained their work to guests as they visited the children's fair. Hundreds of visitors walked our first-grade hallway, talking with the children and providing them with an audience for their learning projects. Among the visitors were other students from our school, parents, grandparents, brothers and sisters, teachers, and administrators from within our school and outside of our school. As is seen in the discussions that follow, the fair was a celebration of learning presented in a wide variety of media (clay, murals, paintings, books, posters, and more). The cat group had clay cat models, costumes, and written reports about cats. They had functioned in a positive, productive way as a group as they engaged in discussions and used art as a medium for learning. Their writing surprised me and reminded me to keep an open mind about the possibilities when engaging children in inquiry (Fig. 4.4). Each student's work was both part of the whole group's mission and an individual expression.

Fish Group

The fish group helped me to understand what Avery (1993) mean when she says:

I came to understand that integration is not something I as a teacher plan and implement, but rather something that occurs within learners. When curricular units are broadly framed and begin with the children, building on what they know, connections between all the disciplines occur. Reading and writing and talking and listening really are tools for learning, regardless of the topic (p. 465)

This group organized itself with an immediate intensity about learning; they requested a visit to the library so they could check out books about fish. They spent the first week of their studies finding books, independently reading, or having an adult read with them about fish. The dynamics of this group were different from the cat group because this group had two children, Julie and Aryelle, who were independent readers and were able to write several sustained stories that reflected their knowledge of a chosen subject matter. Breanna was also an independent worker, a curious first grader learning to read and write. She joined our class in the middle of the school year and was beginning to form friendships within the class. Ryan was an emergent reader and writer, understanding what books are all about and beginning to find them useful for learning and enjoying independently.

These children had personality traits in common; all four children were confident in their abilities, very verbal, and had the dispositions to be leaders within the classroom. It was interesting to me that these four ended up together in a group. Did this happen intentionally or was it a matter of coincidence? Either way, it turned out to be a powerful combination of inquirers.

Once again, my expectation of what would happen was different from what actually occurred during this group's study of fish. I expected that they would write detailed reports that reflected what they learned about fish, make fancy models of fish (perhaps to scale), or create an aquarium as a home for fish that they would obtain through their own creative resources.

This group did learn a lot of facts about fish, but decided that they wanted to create a "fish center" for our two first-grade classrooms as their project. They worked for several weeks planning many activities that would be present for the children to do at this center: an art activity, games, fish painting, the opportunity to make a clay model of a fish, and books to read about fish. They also wanted to perform a puppet show that the students could watch and listen to. Julie wrote directions for the center on 3x5-inch cards which explained the fish group's expectations:

Painting: You got to paint a fish. That's all.
Clay: Make a model of a fish. That's all.
Book Center: You read the books. That's all.
Puppet Show Center: We will play the puppet show. If you don't want to hear it that's fine, but if you do want to listen you have to sit quietly.
Art: Markers, crayons, and paper. You draw a fish.

Game Center: You got to play nice with the games because they are breakable. (Transcribed from directions written by Julie)

The group spent several class periods writing a play about fish, but it was never completed. This might have been because instead of writing one play together, they decided to each write one, and then to vote on one play for the group to perform. The actual performance of the play must not have been a priority for the group. They could never agree on which play to perform, but they did collect puppets from a variety of resources that the children could use at their center for doing their own puppet shows.

The group made center sign-ups for our classroom doors when they had all of their activities ready. They also signed the calendar for a project talk when they were ready to share center directions with all of the students in the class. The group explained each center, showed the materials they had collected, and all participated in sharing directions with the class. Each day, at least two members of the fish group were present at their center for helping children who chose to visit the area. The most popular activity seemed to be painting; each time a student painted a picture of a fish, a group member moved it to our classroom display case. The display case turned into a giant fish tank, with sand and shells in the bottom, and a wide variety of painted fish hanging, pinned, or taped inside.

For our project fair, fish group membners decided to set their fish center up in the hall. They set up several tables. On one table, they displayed books about fish. On another table, they displayed the art activities that the class had previously completed. They set their display up in front of their window and explained all of the activities to the visitors as they passed by. Each group member also wrote about fish as part of his or her completed project. All of the children's writing was on display for sharing with the many visitors to our project fair. Group members, again, expressed their individuality within their group's work.

The Shark Group

My view of projects is that when learners are involved in groups, learning is affected by the group. This may seem obvious, but I was confused as to why certain types of children seemed to find each other and form a group. The fish group was made up of very creative kids who gravitated together; the cat group had struggling readers; the shark group concerned me because the children who had trouble staying focused had found each other and decided on a topic of study, sharks. The students in this study group—Michael R., Steven, Abdullah, and Andrey—were all very capable, but three of the four members needed reminders about rules and had some trouble staying on task unless I was close at hand. I was determined not to intervene in the

group by separating some of the children because I was anticipating management problems within the group. I did think about doing this, but wanted
to see if the children could learn to work as a team in a cooperative way.
The students in this group were independent and often chose to break
classroom rules, rather than follow them. Would I have to be there daily to
prevent fighting or disruptive behavior? Would behavior problems interfere
with the learning process? I remembered Michael M.'s engagement in his
topic of study (Mississippi) as a member of my original writing study group,
and how his being able to choose this area to study and his desire to learn
about his chosen topic had alleviated many of the behavior problems that
he frequently exhibited. I was hopeful that the same thing would occur with
the shark group, and for the most part, these boys did end up working
together cooperatively and enthusiastically.

This group of children loved going to the library (to get away from my
watchful eye?) and spent many class periods there finding books, using
computers for locating information about sharks, and finding a different
place to sit and read together. A university student who was helping in our
classroom on a regular basis met with this group during her visits. She read
to them and talked with them, discussing what they found interesting in
their studies. I noticed that the boys were particularly attentive to their
books when they found a picture of a shark attacking a person or another
animal in the ocean. They went back to the pages with graphic illustrations
and shared them enthusiastically with me and with others in the class. They
even marked these pages with sticky notes so they could find them easily on
future visits to the book.

The boys decided to make a mural of sharks and spent two class periods
making a list of materials that they would need: colors of paper, sizes of sheets
of paper, and how many of each color they might need. They worked for
many days drawing sharks, cutting them out, and gluing them to a large
piece of blue paper that represented the ocean.

Andrey, a sometimes quiet student from Russia, formed a deep bond with
Ms. Lorraine, our school's art teacher, because of his study of sharks. While
working on the group's mural, Andrey wrote a letter to Ms. Lorraine asking
her to help him draw a shark. She scheduled a special time for this, and
together they looked at shark books and sketched a shark that Andrey later
colored and placed on the group's mural. The next week, Andrey asked me
if Ms. Lorraine could help him write about sharks, as well. Because Ms.
Lorraine is an art teacher, I did not initially understand the request and tried
to steer Andrey into a different direction for help in the area of writing.
Andrey was insistent and wrote another note to Ms. Lorraine, asking her if
she would write with him. I spoke with her over lunch one day, and she
agreed to spend some time with Andrey but was not sure how to help him. On
the day of their meeting, Andrey dictated to her what he had learned about

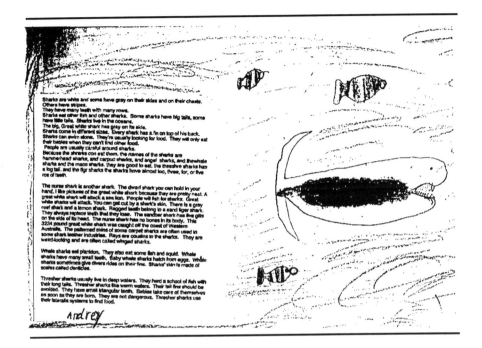

FIG. 4.5. Andrey's report on sharks.

sharks. Andrey later finished his report with a university student who helped with the typing of Andrey's draft. Ms. Lorraine was Andrey's special guest when we had our project fair. He wrote and illustrated a special invitation for her, and she attended the fair, spending some special time with Andrey as he shared books he had read, his writing, and his completed art work.

The other members of the group decided to use their mural for their project for the project fair and, like the cat group, they were resisting the writing aspect of their work. Eventually, with the help of Mr. Seibert, a library teacher, the boys typed copies of reports on sharks. They read their reports (Andrey's is shown in Fig. 4.5) and discussed their mural at the project fair.

The group members ended up working cooperatively most of the time, even when unattended by an adult. They were engaged in their work throughout the weeks of their studies, developed the ability to work as a group to complete a mural, and were able to verbalize, and later read, the reports that contained the information learned as members of this study group. I was learning that ownership (Atwell, 1986) was an important part of all this. Students who may have gravitated toward one another in an effort to avoid work and to misbehave were sucked into their projects by their own interests. Respecting their individual interests was making this work quite well.

The Kid Group

> There are only two lasting bequests we can hope to give our children. One of these is roots ... the other wings. (Hodding Carter from *Peter's Quotations: Ideas for Our Time*, 1977, reprinted in *The Primary Program*, Nebraska Department of Education, 1993)

In a first-grade classroom, there are those children who seem to have wings all day long. They enjoy flying, either gently swooping or quickly flitting, from one thing to another. Lack of commitment may be the issue, or it may be a genuine curiosity about what everyone else is doing, a curiosity that can only be satiated by moving. Members of the kid group were often winged. Margot decided early on that she wanted to read and write about kids. She had two other children, Kesha and Karryssa, join her periodically as well. Karryssa also visited the cat group and the fish group on a regular basis, changing her mind almost daily about which group she wished to become a permanent member of. Eventually Karryssa decided to study with Margot, about kids. Kesha wanted to focus her studies on her grandma, but often sat with the kid group members as they worked while she wrote and drew about her Grandma Willa. She liked to be rooted near others while following her own agenda. I was willing to give these three children the time they needed to locate their individual and shared interests.

The kid group was almost completely independent in their studies. Margot spent most of her study time reading books about kids, books like *Best Friends* by Patricia Riley Giff (1988), and learning about kids from other countries from study prints that she found at our library-media center. She found the reading of these difficult and sought adult help. She spent some of her time reading to Karryssa, whose reading skills were not as developed as Margot's. They were helping each other, really, as Margot learned about oral reading and Karryssa learned many reading skills listening to Margot and taking the occasional risk by reading some with Margot's help.

Margot and Karryssa would have been content to only read books together, but I explained the importance of sharing what they were learning. They began making posters about kids and colored for many days until their posters were just the way they wanted them. I continued to encourage their writing, and eventually they both spent several days preparing written reports about kids (Fig. 4.6). We put their artwork and writing together and

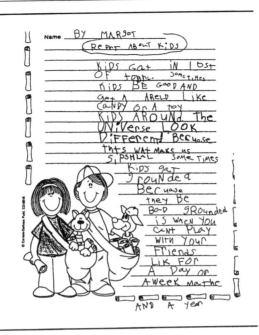

FIG. 4.6. The report about kids by the kid group. "Report about kids. Kids get in lots of trouble. Sometimes kids be good and get a reward like candy or a toy. Kids around the universe look different because that's what makes us special. Sometimes kids get grounded because they be bad. Grounded is when you can't play with your friends like for a day or a week, month and a year."

their work was displayed proudly as the two girls sat side by side at the project fair. Although they still had wings, they certainly had rooted for a while as they studied kids.

Grandma Willa

Kesha set roots quickly when we began to provide children with the opportunity to pursue individual projects. Katz and Chard (1989) helped me understand just how important it is to allow children to be alone, if that is what they need, when they are studying something dear to them:

> The criterion of social competence does not require that all children be social butterflies. It is not a source of concern if a child chooses to work or play alone, as long as he or she is capable of interacting productively and successfully with another when social interaction is desired, appropriate, or necessary. (Reprinted in Nebraska Department of Education, 1993, p. 58)

Kesha's Grandma Willa died suddenly of a stroke in February 1996. Kesha and Willa spent a lot of time together, and the death of her grandmother was difficult for both Kesha and Kesha's mom, Sherri. Kesha chose to write several journal entries during our daily writing time about her grandmother and she asked to share this writing with our class and with her own mother.

When it was time to choose project study topics, Kesha knew from the start that she wanted to do a project about her grandma. I discouraged this topic. After all, she couldn't research her grandma at the library and she would be working alone. Fortunately, Kesha was insistent on this topic of study. Her project turned out to be very touching and meaningful for Kesha and for me.

Things changed so much for Kesha after her arrival at our school in November; at that time, she stated emphatically that she could not write. In a few months, as a member of our class, she developed confidence as a writer and had the ability to express her thoughts in writing using her knowledge of letter sounds, her willingness to invent some spellings, and the traditional spellings she knew.

When Kesha returned to school after her grandma's death, she wrote this story about her Grandma Willa in her journal:

> She always babysitted me for a long time.
> I am going to miss my grandma for a long time.
> I love my grandma. from Kesha. (Spellings made conventional for ease of reading.)

The next day she wrote a similar story about her grandpa, William, who had died a few years earlier:

> He always babysitted me for a long time.
> I am going to miss my William for a long time.
> I love my William. from Kesha Dawn. (Spellings made conventional for ease of reading.; see Fig. 4.7)

FIG. 4.7. One of Kesha's ongoing reports on her grandparents. "William. He was baby sitting me for a long time. I am going to miss my William for a long time. I love my William."

Kesha was sad about the deaths of her grandparents but seemed to take some comfort in writing about them. She shared her writing with her mom and her cousin Ricky, a Ridgeway sixth grader, during our spring parent–teacher conference. The four of us sat together with tears in our eyes, but smiles on our faces, as she proudly read her writing.

It was shortly after this time that we were choosing project topics and Kesha began to study about her grandma as a project. She worked on her own, day after day, sitting near her colleagues. She wrote many stories about her grandma, and spoke about her often during conversations with me.

The day she committed herself to a project on her grandma was the same day that the cat group was making clay models of cats; Kesha decided that she wanted to make a clay model of her grandma. Kesha wrote a note to the art teacher, requesting clay for her model. She was so anxious to get started that she began her work at the art room immediately and returned to our classroom 45 minutes later with a finished clay figure of her grandma.

Kesha decided to type a story about her grandma on the computer. She wrote the first draft of her grandma story on April 10.

> my grandma was very
> very sitck sitck and very
> because she was sitck I
> miss she was very very
> very sitck sitck sitck (Invented spellings not changed)

On April 11, a parent volunteer helped her add memories about her grandma to her story. She wrote them by hand, intending to type them on the computer at a later time. Throughout the month of April, Kesha spent every minute she could typing on the computer. She added to her original story until it was just the way she wanted it:

> She had a stroke. She died in Feb.
> William died 3 years ago.
> He was my grandpa.
> He said something to my mommy.
> "I will always be with you."
> She said, "Thank you."
> Grandpa said, "Thank you."
> Mommy said, "I love you."

She then decided to make a poster about her grandparents. She included illustrations of herself with her grandparents, grandma's favorite chair, her bathtub, the waterbed that she loved, her grandparents watching the football game on TV, her grandmother's car, her house, her favorite color—green, another picture of Kesha because "she really loved Kesha, too," and pictures of the caskets in which her grandparents were buried.

(a)

(b)

(c)

(d)

(e)

FIG. 4.8. (a): Kesha working on a draft. (b): a draft being typed into the computer. (c): reading a draft to colleagues. (d) and (e): Kesha and her mother presenting at the learning fair.

While at home, Kesha and her mother made a collage of family photos. Grandma Willa and Grandpa William were in the center, surrounded by photos of their children and their grandchildren. Kesha proudly told the class about her pictures during a project sharing time. She told us how she and her mom made the collage together. After Kesha shared her pictures, one of the children, Margot, asked Kesha, "Are you sad because you miss your grandma?" Kesha said that she was. Margot then asked, "Why did you do a project about your grandma if it made you feel sad?" Kesha maturely explained that sometimes it made her sad to think about her grandma. Then she said, "Sometimes it makes me feel good to think about her, too. That is why I did the project about her." Kesha had discovered the power of writing as a way to work through her grief and as a way to preserve the memories of someone that she loved.

The day of our project fair, Kesha surprised the class by bringing a report that she had dictated to her mom the night before; she wanted to read it to the visitors at our project fair that afternoon. She sat and studied her report throughout the morning. She proudly sat in the rocking chair and read it to all of the students in our classroom at our morning meeting. That afternoon, she held this report in her hands and proudly read it to the visitors at her table as she sat with her mom. In Fig. 4.8, you can see her illustrations, her poster hanging behind her, and the clay model of her grandma displayed in front of her.

As the only member of the "grandma" project group, Kesha had written reports, read her own and her mom's writing, done research at home through her collage, and created several pieces of art and writing that I know she and her mom will treasure for the rest of their lives. I could not have set higher goals for any child as a member of a project study group; Kesha guided her own learning as she reached each goal she set for herself.

ASSESSMENT

I knew that I needed to be accountable for the children's progress during their inquiry. I kept many anecdotal notes, saved copies of all their written work, took many photos, and have video footage of the groups as they worked and presented. Our Status of the Class forms are another record of progress and development. The actual completed projects show a variety of media, growth over time in reading and writing, and much learning about the areas of study. For the kid group, the students did not seem to incorporate their learning into their writing, but much happened during that group that I have documented. Their conversations were intense and their discussions of what and how to write were lofty.

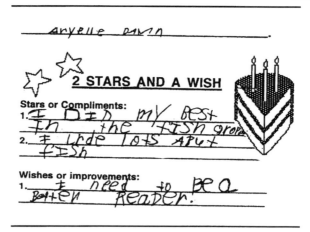

FIG. 4.9. Aryelle's student feedback form. "I did my best in the fish group. I learned lots about fish. I need to be a better reader."

The children filled out a feedback form (Fig. 4.9) and guests were also asked to provide feedback (Fig. 4.10). These forms also showed how thoughtful the children were in their endeavors and that adults noticed that thoughtfulness. There were, honestly, surprises. Children were doing things that we did not know they could do. They pushed themselves, as evidenced by their projects. The feedback that we received from our visitors indicated that the work that was completed by the children was impressive and appreciated.

MY GOALS AND MY LEARNING

Calkins (1994) suggests that:

> ... in the end, our teaching needs to grow out of our beliefs. We need to know these beliefs in order to articulate them, and we need to reconsider them often. The process of discovering what we believe, of thinking critically about these beliefs, of putting them into practice—this to me is curriculum development. (p. 181)

When we began having the students participate in project groups in the fall of 1994, my beliefs as a teacher were quite different from what they are today. Originally, my most important goal was to have the children learn lots of information about the topic that they were studying. Of course, this would happen while they were working together in a developmentally appropriate way, as they completed some type of project together.

After working with several groups of children over a 2-year period, because of talking to the members of our group, and because of the reading that I have done, my goals have changed in many ways. Of course, I still think it is important that children are learning as much as possible about a topic of their choice, but this is no longer my most important goal for them.

My goals for children participating in project group studies are now as follows:

- Children will come to understand that they have choices regarding what they study at school, and the choices that they make will determine what they learn and how they will go about learning it.
- Children will learn the skills necessary for participating in a group for the purpose of learning.
- Children will learn that they can find answers to questions that they have regarding any topic, if they learn to locate the appropriate resources.

Thank you for coming to our project fair.

We are proud of our hard work and enjoy sharing what we have learned with you.

Please take a minute to write a note to your child about his/her participation in this 1st grade project. Your feedback is very important to us.

Kesha   what a wonderful job you did! If grandma could talk she would say " Oh Kesha, you did that? What a big growing' smart girl". But in my heart I know a part of grandma was there every single day when you worked on a project about her and you can bet she's doing nothing but smiling. It is important for all who love someone they love to keep some part of that memory alive, thank-you to all of her teachers and thank-you Kesha for doing just that! This will remain in my memory forever.
You did great Kesha!!!!

signature   date

I LOVE YOU;
YOUR MOM xoxoxo

FIG. 4.10. Family and guest feedback form.

- Children will improve their ability to read and write because of their engagement in these activities during project work.
- Children will love to learn and will discover that their world is constantly providing them with exciting opportunities for learning.

Because of the changes we made this school year in the way we handle our student project groups, my learning about children and the ways that they learn continued to develop. Some of the most important things that I learned as a teacher are:

- My expectation of what would happen in a project group usually did not match what really happened as the children participated in their chosen learning journeys. It was difficult for me to give up control of the groups, but as I did, the children's projects were more student generated and their ideas for projects were truly their own.
- The students' interest in their work was at a higher level because they had more choices as far as the topics that they could study. By enabling them to choose from any topic of study, interest was higher, which led to increased engagement in their work.
- The projects created by the children seemed more meaningful to them, and were not limited by our prescribed curriculum objectives. Kesha's project about Grandma Willa comes to mind as an example of work that will be remembered and treasured by her, her friends, and me. It also provided therapy for her in her time of loss, and began to teach her the importance of writing as a tool for working through grief. She taught this concept to others in the class, as well, by sharing her work and her thinking. Projects really do teach the learner and his or her friends.
- The children became very independent in their studies. They learned to keep records of their work by completing forms for planning and evaluation on a daily basis. They went to the library to find books or to use the computers for research. We expected that children would be responsible for their learning, and they lived up to that expectation.
- The *product* doesn't seem to be the most important part of the project work completed by the children. The choices that they made along the way that guided their learning, as they went through the *process* of completing their projects, provided them with the truly meaningful opportunities for growth and learning.

PARENT PARTICIPATION

Parent participation this past school year far exceeded my expectations. On occasions when parents were invited to participate as audience members while the children shared completed projects, the majority of the students had at least one special guest attend. The children who did not have the opportunity to have a parent in attendance instead invited a sibling or special teacher (in one case, the school nurse).

Parents attended school as volunteers in order to listen to children read and to help children with their writing. Two parents came to school two afternoons each week to assist children with researching and organizing their projects. Parents began stopping in to have lunch with their children on many occasions, which indicated to me that these parents felt comfortable with the environment of our classroom and the school. It seems that each school year brings more opportunities for parents to be included in their children's school day. Project work seems to safely welcome parents into the classroom in a unique way. It lets them work with a small group-whose members are excited about what they are doing.

CLOSING THOUGHTS

As I wrote this chapter about my experiences during the past school year, I repeatedly found myself asking questions, and seeking answers to those questions. I certainly learned that individuals can get their interests met in a group or alone, as needed. But, for every question for which I learned an answer, there were many more on which I will continue to reflect. During the upcoming school year, I plan to search for answers to new questions. I am wondering:

- Is there a way to combine writing project time and project work time, providing meaningful learning opportunities for children, and keeping the critical elements of both of these programs? It seems hard to separate the two periods of the afternoon, so maybe I shouldn't. Indeed, maybe they are already combined!
- Why do children need to stay with one learning topic for an extended period of time? Is this an important element of inquiry, or can I be more flexible? How much should they fly and how much should they stay rooted?
- What is the children's learning agenda compared to my learning agenda for them?
- What are the children *really* learning?
- Am I really able to teach them anything, or is it only possible for me to provide learning opportunities for them throughout the school day?

It is my nature to question and seek answers to my questions, as I grow to become a better teacher. I am excited to see what the next school year provides me in my travels as a learner and a teacher in my first-grade classroom.

Chapter 5

A Relationship That Supported Mutual Change

Linda Brown
Liz DeNino
Lincoln Public Schools, Lincoln, NE

¤ ¤ ¤

The process of engaging in change, especially when it requires a major alteration of a system of beliefs and assumptions which have developed over many years, is difficult and demanding. We have to provide the opportunity for that change to come from within rather than trying to impose it from without.

—Doake (1994)

We have taught third grade at Ridgeway as members of the third-grade team since 1991; we have had one or two other team members each year since then, depending on the number of students in third grade. Our teacher training was very traditional, relying on teacher-directed activities that support a district-mandated curriculum. In this chapter, we tell our stories, including some of the struggles and celebrations we experienced along our journey. First, we each tell some of what we experienced before our study group formed and then we present some of what has happened to us because we had each other and our study group for support. This chapter is about a collegial and personal friendship; it is meant to describe two journeys coming together as the travelers join hands.

Before beginning those parts of the chapter, we know we would not be honest if we did not tell readers how difficult the process of writing this chapter has been. As Rick Meyer wrote in beginning of this book, we all approached the study group with romantic notions about change. When our group decided to write about the things that we were changing, we both wanted our voices included. Liz is extremely busy with family life, and writing essentially became a second job—one that she did not have time for. Writing created increased tension in her life. For Linda, writing felt forced and stilted. The thoughts were there and Linda felt like a good speaker, but putting things on paper was quite difficult. The two of us spent many hours together, straining over sentences. We would read ongoing drafts to our group and not feel satisfied, even though the feedback from the group was positive.

It is just not that easy to write! We wrote our separate stories and read them to each other. Then we wrote our story together. They did not fit well. The children did not seem to be in the pages. Where were the children? We would go back and write some more ... now we weren't there; it seemed like a collection of children's work. We'd go back and write some more and wound up with a sort of boring chronology. Weekends, evenings, and all of the extra time we previously had, evaporated as we wrote and wrote and wrote. And still we were not happy.

Rick Meyer took the chapter and moved some parts of it around for clarity. He read the transcripts of our meetings and reviewed his field notes and suggested things to add, stories we had forgotten that we had discussed during our group time. He was like an editor who was also someone who knew us; was this acceptable? We read the changes he suggested and found ourselves saying, "Yeah, that's what we do and how we do it," and, "No, that part's got to go." Understand that we wrote this chapter, but were relieved to have a colleague, who was a friendly editor, to help us. We needed this; we had reached our limits with the chapter and were too frustrated to enjoy any further revising. We tell this to be honest; we tell this so you know that this chapter is still ours, very much so. And when you write your own chapter or article or book, you'll know that the struggling that you feel is real and that it is okay to have help. We want other teachers to know that it is not easy to face yourself as a writer. We'd read about that in Graves (1990), but until we lived it, we had no idea how hard writing is. So, even though we had read about how hard it was, it just hadn't sunk in.

Quite honestly, writing is both rewarding and scary. It is frightening, in some ways, because we have taken the risk and put ourselves out here for readers to see and criticize and evaluate. It is rewarding because we hope readers feel like they have something in common with us and see places they might want to change or grow in their own professional development.

Doake (1994) says that, "Our teachers have come up through a school system that has tended to tell them what to learn, when to learn, how to learn, and even how much to learn" (p. 132). As we read that statement, it reminded us of the fact that we taught a lot like our teachers taught us. Why did we? Doake speaks of the difficulty of changing our teaching practices because of psychological barriers. One barrier is the feeling of not being able to make decisions about the curriculum that we teach. We had always been presented with a district curriculum in the form of textbooks and objectives to be met. We taught the objectives without question. We used textbooks to teach subject areas and we covered the required material. You will see that as we began to look at other ways of instructing, we struggled with the idea of getting away from the district curriculum and textbooks we were expected to cover.

We changed for two reasons. First, we are learners. Both of us are curious, we like to read, and we like to try new things with our students. Second, we enjoy having a relationship such as ours. We tend to ask each other questions, challenge existing curricula, and challenge ideas about change, too. We like to have our new ideas well-baked before we bring them to our students. We hope that you will, as you read, see both our need for ongoing learning and our relationship as the two parts that helped us do what we did. We also know that we are not done; we have new questions even as we write this chapter.

Our love of learning and our friendship has helped us put into practice the ideas that we have been reading and studying in our study group. We are teaching kids, not covering material; we are focusing on individuals more than looking at our classroom as one group. Before our year in the study group, we did not feel confident to take on the responsibility of planning for individual students and preferred group instruction. This was because it was easier to overlook individual problems when they were dissolved in a whole group. It is not easy to admit that, but we know that we just went on teaching the material, regardless of specific children's reactions or responses. Throughout our time with the study group, we took more time to be together and to interact professionally with the other members of the group.

Through study and dialogue in our study group, we have taken risks that we never thought we would take. The changes we made were brewing for many years, but we needed more contact with each other and with other teachers to stretch our thinking more and to give us the support to try new ideas. Our group gave us the necessary support to risk some changes. Rick's interest in autobiography (Meyer, 1996a), as he read drafts of his book to us before it was published, made us wonder how we got to be at the point we were when our group came together. We began to think of our professional autobiographies. We start with brief autobiographies as a way of setting the stage for a discussion of our work together in our third-grade classrooms.

LIZ'S TEACHING PAST

I have been in the teaching business for 23 years. I received my first degree from the land grant university in our state in 1972. I've taught every grade from second through sixth, but most of my teaching experience is with 8-

and 9-year-olds. Throughout these years, I have also been very busy raising my family.

During the first 7 years of my teaching career, I took university classes and workshops to bring new ideas into my classroom. One workshop I took focused on teaching thinking skills. In 1977, the district consultant in gifted education told us to teach these skills to the academically gifted students in the district. I thought these skills could be used by all students. When I questioned the consultant about this, I was told that the educational program for the gifted student had to look different from the program for the rest of the students. I did not pursue the issue much with that person, although I did use the skills with all my students. Privately, I questioned authority quite a bit and reacted by quietly doing what I felt, within my classroom, without telling others. I developed learning centers for my students and made these available to all of the students in my classes over the years.

I was also influenced by the open classroom concept. I spent 2 years teaching on a third-grade team with a friend from college. We were in a building that was more than 50 years old; the walls were removed to be consistent with the openness that the district wanted. We shared a double-sized classroom with our desks together in the middle. She was in this situation longer than I and she explained how things would run. We spent some of each Thursday and Friday planning for the next week. We felt so good when we walked out of the building on Fridays, having planned for the following week. Centers were arranged, page numbers of teachers manuals were written in our plan books, and the worksheet packets were run off. We were efficient. Perhaps we were too efficient.

One day, near midyear, a student's mother came to talk to me after school. She told me that it was difficult for her son to come to school. He had severe stomach aches and wanted to stay home. I found it hard to believe that one of my students was unhappy. She asked me if I knew of any problems he was having. I didn't. When I tried to talk to the boy, he was silent. As the weeks went by, I tried to give more attention to that child, trying to help him feel good about himself and learning; but I never reached him. He moved away over the summer, but I still think about him today.

Our classroom was an open space, but it was not open to the children's thinking and feelings. I was covering materials by planning all the activities, but I was not teaching children. My teammate had created a safe environment for me to learn, but I had failed to create a safe one for the students.

There was such tension and sadness in the feelings that I had about this child. Teaching had become too easy—weeks planned by creating centers, page numbers in textbooks and teachers' guides. There had to be more to it. So, after 2 years in the open classroom and because my second child was born, I decided to take a leave of absence. I returned to the university and took two classes on gifted education and one on reading strategies. The latter taught me about theories of reading; I found my practices challenged and questioned by the materials we were reading and by the instructor's presentations. I had taught many students to read using the basal approach. What was wrong with it? The instructor demonstrated the use of trade books to teach reading. She revealed some facts about basal readers that made me question using them. The controlled vocabulary and the ridiculously small amount of time that children got to read were quite upsetting once I began paying attention to those details in my teaching. Students waited for long periods of time to read short passages. This just did not make sense. But, what made the most impact on me was the fact that the students in the low reading group usually stayed in that group for their entire elementary school careers. They focused on drill work and didn't get much time to read. My reading since then (such as Goodman, 1986) supports this even more.

As part of this course, I was required to interview a child to find out her thoughts on reading and writing in school. It was very insightful, as I found that Ginny, a first grader, thought that reading was "knowing the words." She described the turn-taking involved in the reading of a story with her teacher. When asked what the most important thing about reading was, Ginny said, "Saying the words right." She said nothing about reading for meaning, or reading to learn something about the world in which she lived. This bothered me because she was a girl who has important and useful reading habits at home. She went to the library with her mom or dad or brother every week; she was read to every night at bedtime and also read alone. But her beliefs and understanding of reading at school were different. School reading was work; it was workbooks and worksheets and reading a story in a small group with the teacher asking questions.

Ginny told me that a good writer is one who can make the letters perfectly. Wow! That started me thinking about the important things that I could teach children about reading and writing. When I returned from my leave, I focused on having children understand that reading is the construction of meaning by the reader. People can learn things when they read. People can read just for fun. Stories are great entertainment. Writing is a means of expressing yourself and of communicating your ideas with others.

Through reading and discussing with fellow teachers, I began to see how my role would change as I taught children to read using trade books. I could individualize, give choices, and support kids as they enriched their lives (and their vocabulary, proficiency as readers, and more) by reading good literature.

This was the beginning of a change for me as a teacher of reading. One of the first changes I made was to give the students time to read. Half of the reading period would now be used for reading books of their own choosing. They also read aloud to me each week so that I could see the strategies they used as readers. Enthusiasm soared. They literally raced to the room to see if reading was the first option of the day. During individual time, I taught them strategies to improve their comprehension. We also discussed plot, characters, setting, and word meanings. I saw struggling readers learn to read better. They smiled when they finished reading a good book. One student asked me if the author of a book that he had just finished reading had written any other books. This was the kind of proof I needed to convince myself that I was taking a journey that was worth continuing.

Over the course of the 23-year journey, I have earned a master's degree in education. I have raised three children, and I continue to grow as a learner and as a teacher. In 1991, my life was made richer because I joined the third-grade team as a classroom teacher and became partners with Linda. Following her story, we write together about how we have changed with each other's help and as members of the study group.

LINDA'S TEACHING PAST

As an educator for many years, I always thought that my theory for educating children was really simple. I would receive the children from the previous grade level and take them from wherever they had been the year before to as far as they could go with me as their teacher. This theory was influenced by my own past experiences, my college courses, student teaching, and the writings that I read. Facing that theory meant that I had to discover as much as I could about myself as a teacher. I studied my teaching and my students' learning and the relationships between those. I was lucky to have some wonderful experiences along the way to help me in my growth.

I taught in the Follow Through Program in my first years. This federally funded program's philosophy of educating young children related to the government's push to help economically and socially "disadvantaged" (the language at that time) children to achieve to their potential. Follow Through was expected to continue the practices of the successful Head Start program. There were six different education models developed throughout the United States; our local one was guided by the Tucson Early Education Model (TEEM). Locally, TEEM teachers were treated to ongoing presentations by Ken and Yetta Goodman, Alice Paul, and Roach Van Allen. We were living the roots of whole language teaching as those roots were growing.

The cornerstone of the Follow Through mode was the use of centers built around the academic areas of reading, math, language arts, and discovery (science, social studies, and health). The children were given choices to accomplish learning objectives. We relied on Bloom's taxonomy (1956) to create different developmental levels of choices. I worked with a paraeducator who helped me full-time in my classroom. I usually worked at the reading center in order to teach needed skills, but I also spent time at the other centers whenever skill work was needed. My paraeducator also helped at centers to provide support and assistance for the children. The children rotated through the centers during the day. Developing centers for the children helped me to understand different learning styles and the importance of allowing children some choice during the school day. I also had the children involved in whole-group discussions of literature.

When federal funding ceased in 1980, the many facets of Follow Through that were cut included the paraeducator, my relationship with other Follow Through teachers in the district, and the far-reaching relationships that the program supported with research experts who were involved with us on a monthly basis. I tried to continue teaching from all that I had learned, but the system made it difficult. I was placed in a very small classroom and given 30 or more kids. We barely had room for chairs and desks, so centers were relegated to the window sill or just did not occur at all. I went back to the comfortable and convenient whole-group instruction that was typical for me before Follow Through. I used teachers' manuals and followed the district curriculum guides. I never questioned any of the curriculum manuals or the objectives in that curriculum. As I look back on that period of time (from 1981 to 1987), I realize that what I did with my students was almost robotic. I covered the curriculum and textbooks on a timeline. If I couldn't get a particular subject completely covered by the end of a school year, I worried that I had short-changed my students. What I should have worried about was that I was shutting off any enthusiasm that my students had for learning. What I never thought about or questioned was how children learn best and what my role should be in that process. I lost myself as a teacher, not an easy thing to admit.

Beginning in 1987, and I am not sure why, I entered a thoughtful period about my teaching. I was becoming aware of how bored the kids were and sensed that my teaching was not making the difference that I had felt during Follow Through. I began reading articles and books and talking to my colleagues in the district more. Our district was increasing its staff development activities, and we were required to attend different sessions. Perhaps the district was responding to the teachers' desires to learn more. A colleague invited me to the first Whole Language Umbrella Conference in St. Louis in 1990. I was able to listen to and absorb from many of the people I was reading and some folks whom I had never read, but was excited to find: Bess Altwerger, Nancie Atwell, Yetta Goodman, Brian Cambourne, Jerome Harste, Jan Turbill, and Andrea Butler. I was also fortunate to hear Dorothy Watson, Ken Goodman, Bill Martin, Jr., and Patricia McKissack.

I found myself reenergized by the Whole Language Umbrella experience. Teachers were teaching the way I wanted to teach. It could be done. I learned of the importance of language to human learning and that learning is both personal and social. This means that classrooms need to be communities and that I needed to have a positive view of learners. Learning needed to be joyous and fulfilling. My teaching life was changed at that conference. By the beginning of the following school year (1991–1992), Liz was a member of my team.

What can I say about meeting a teaching colleague who is a friend, a caring ear, a challenger of ideas, and a thinker? I was lucky to have found her. We have been through much together. We know each others' families and the joys and sad times of those families. When my husband died of cancer, Liz helped me. We have known the tragedies and the successes.

We now turn to our story, the portion of this chapter that we wrote very much together. We retrace some of our mutual teaching past and how we work to push each other. We know that relationships can not be duplicated and hope that you see our ideas as coming out of our trust, willingness to risk, and caring for each other and the students at Ridgeway.

OUR RELATIONSHIP AND OUR STUDENTS

We admit that we are a strong power in the third-grade team. As a twosome, we can be intimidating but usually do not mean to be so. We have influenced other members of the third-grade team as they joined us. Most either thought that our ideas were worthy of use in their own classrooms or decided to do things differently. We are open to discussing and planning with our whole team and, at the same time, open to the idea of individuality expressed by each team member. Team planning is an integral part of life at Ridgeway. Mr. Z., our principal, suggests that teams plan together. We follow that mandate, but we also honor all members of the team. We are discussing this idea here because it has not always been easy. Sometimes we have made a team member feel excluded, althoughthis was not our intention. Other times, we know that a team member has struggled because of a desire to go on his or her own journey with his or her children; we supported that but acknowledge here that we have seen that such journeys are lonely and not always easy.

When we were assigned to the third-grade team in 1991, we began planning together; we shared ideas with each other and seemed to just fit together. We knew something good was happening for us and, through our thinking together, for our students, too. Before school opened that year, we talked about our beliefs about children and teaching and learning and decided that we would change our writing program first. We had read Calkins (1986) and thought that writing would be inexpensive to change; there was no need to purchase many books or other student materials. We did what Calkins said; we gave students the time to write. They wrote daily, using story maps and webs when necessary. We saw that we could teach the district language arts objectives through writing workshop. Using the children's writing, we taught specific skills during conferences. But we were not yet confident enough to teach entirely without using the English textbook. Looking back, as we think of the wonderful writing that our students did, we know that we had to feel secure with each change we made. Letting go of the book was something we would do the following year.

We learned from our students' feedback and activity. They pretty much told us that they were frustrated when 20 minutes of writing time had passed and they had to shift to math. As we evolved in teaching writing, we realized that students needed more time: to reflect, to organize, to edit, to publish, and to share. We changed our writing to 45 minutes per day. The students knew they could count on that chunk of time for writing, and we found ourselves with more time to focus on individuals.

The following school year, each child had a personal writing folder that included information about writing, an edit checklist, a peer conference guide, and a special form for attempting spellings if they wanted to use it (blank columns in which they and colleagues in the room attempted the spelling before approaching the teacher.) We taught minilessons about important parts of the writing process and made sure that we saw each student at least once each week. Our discussions with each other were focused on what our students were doing and our feelings about that activity, as well as what we might try next.

Our confidence in focusing on specific needs that children expressed was growing. We did not need to teach some prescribed curriculum because our students were indicating what was needed. For example, Linda was having a weekly conference with Alli about publishing a story she had written. Linda noticed that Alli was ready to include quotation marks in her writing because the insertion of dialogue would make the story more visible to the reader.

> **Linda:** Alli, would you like to make your story more exciting?
> **Alli:** Yes, but how would I do that?
> **Linda:** You can use quotation marks in your story to show real conversations between your characters. When readers get to hear the characters speak, the story feels more alive.
> **Alli:** Show me how to do that.
> [Nicole, Glenna, and Megan overhear the conference.]
> **Nicole:** Ms. Brown, could we see how you use quotation marks?
> **Linda:** I thought that you [Megan] and Glenna were already using them in your stories.
> **Megan:** We are but we're not sure about them. We haven't used them enough.
> **Glenna:** Could you show us again?

So Linda taught the minilesson to this small group who were interested and quotation marks began to appear in their stories. Other important parts of writing were taught this way, too.

During the 1992–1993 school year, the district adopted a new reading series to address the district's reading objectives. This new basal series was a topic of intense conversations over many lunches during the school year. We thought that most third graders would be interested in the themes that the book laid out. The series suggested reading the story with the entire class, as a whole group. This was a change for us and for our students because we were organized into ability groups for reading in the old basal series. We know that this does not fit whole language philosophy, but we were changing gradually and with much thought to each detail of our move.

We began teaching the series as recommended in the teacher's guide and found it was a lot of work to keep the students' attention during the reading of the story. This was round robin reading with a whole class. Supposedly, this was to help the low reader and challenge the more proficient readers. It was not working. The passages were frustrating for the struggling readers because they couldn't read for meaning; the more capable readers seemed to hate it because they had to wait so long for a turn to read or discuss. As teachers, we became watchdogs, making sure that students were following along in the story. We knew that some of the students didn't like reading from the textbook. They didn't understand, nor did they want to, the notion of an anthology as a collection of stories and excerpts from longer books. They wanted to read real books. We gathered all this information and talked and talked. Actually, we complained: about kids, about the contents of the book, about the idea of one required reading book, and more.

We decided to take a break from the new basal by teaching a unit on fairy tales. We had been reading some of these to our classes, and they enjoyed hearing and discussing them. We would use a variety of library books and allow the students to read the fairy tale they chose. There was a dramatic change in attitude toward reading. The students read for longer periods of time, and we could teach strategies in a more natural and individualized way, consistent with the way we were teaching writing. For example, a group discussed the fairy tales they were reading and discovered the similarities and differences in plot, characters, and the use of magic in the stories. Other groups also had intense discussions. All of the children wanted to participate. As we reflect on this unit, we know that the reasons that things changed for the better were that the students were given choices, the sense of community grew among the students as they read and reported on those choices, and the students saw that reading was more than what they had experienced previously.

Soon, we moved to having the students engage in research in the library. They used books and the CD-ROM system along with encyclopedias and other sources to find information. We planned with the Chapter I reading teacher and the library-media specialist. They helped because their work with groups allowed all of the groups of researchers to be smaller.

During our second year together, we learned more about collaborating with each other and about paying attention to students' enthusiasm by planning activities that took their enthusiasm into consideration. We eventually moved out of the basal completely and into using trade books, becoming whole-language classrooms that supported readers and writers in their development. We were getting used to taking risks together. Mr. Z. requested that we make the third grade even more developmentally appropriate by becoming part of the year of study that a district grant would support. We would develop our classrooms even further during the coming year (1994–1995) by joining the study group.

JOINING THE STUDY GROUP
FOR CONTINUED GROWTH

During the summer of 1994, we studied together to become familiar with the developmentally appropriate practice. We attended the summer workshop that Rick and Jane ran and then decided to meet weekly throughout the summer to plan for the coming year. We decided to change the environments of our classrooms so that they were more child-centered. We also were interested in integrating the curriculum and using portfolios for assessment. Our weekly summer meetings were exciting because we were making many decisions.

We spent the summer transforming ourselves and our teaching practices. Many hours of discussing our beliefs helped us to realize that we were moving toward more child-centered classrooms. We changed our schedule to allow the children more time to read and write without interruptions. This would also allow the children to make more choices about their literacy activity.

A difficult part of making so many decisions during the summer was that our entire team could not attend. One member of the team had an accident and needed surgery, and the other member of the team would be a new teacher, not yet hired; she became an active member of our group once the new school year started, but we had made many decisions without her or our other team member. Both seemed fairly agreeable to going along with our thinking and planning when we filled them in at a meeting before school began in the fall. They seemed willing to try the daily schedules that we had constructed, the move toward more learning centers, and the increased use of math manipulatives.

We started the school year with each student having three folders: one for writer's workshop, one for record keeping, and one for spelling. Each child also had a notebook that would be used as a journal. The record keeping folder was the new addition from the previous year; it contained a blank calendar and record sheets for students to keep track of personal reading goals, books they read, and stories they wrote. We also put a small student dictionary in that folder.

As the year progressed and we felt more secure in what we were doing, we shifted the time blocks to fit the needs of the students. We allowed reading time to increase and the time spent at centers to decrease when we saw that the kids wanted to finish books and write responses in their record keeping folder. We let the schedule become flexible and allowed time slots to become blurred as children read during writers workshop or engaged in research projects during reading time.

We paid careful attention to what the students' actions were telling us. For example, at the beginning of the year, Liz began her reading program with an author study as it was outlined by the district office. She had four literature groups for which she chose books by a given author. She quickly learned that the books were enjoyed by some children and not by others. Some could not read them and others didn't want to read them. We were reliving what had happened with the basal because of the nature of the reading material. We keep learning the same lesson: let the curriculum develop with input from the kids.

A few of the children enjoyed the choices Liz made and read their assigned books. Liz paid attention to the students' frustration and allowed them to read books of their own choosing. She abandoned the idea of forced author study and encouraged children to read what they wanted to read. She suggested that children who liked a certain book might enjoy others by that same author. The children were learning to read like real readers; they were making selections the way real readers do based on interests, curiosity, and what their friends were reading.

Linda paid attention to the frustration expressed by her students, too. She started the year using the basal because there was much pressure to do so. As teachers, we were frequently told that the district had invested much time and money in the new basal and that we should use them. Linda quickly moved to allowing the children their own choice of books, too. We both had help from the Chapter I reading teacher.

We both met at least weekly with each student and also developed different forms for keeping track of student progress. Where possible, in the record keeping folder, the students were involved in keeping track of their learning and their progress. We won't share the forms that we used; we learned, after looking at many forms, that it is best to develop your own. Decide what you want to keep track of, work to include the children in that keeping track, and develop a form that you can revise easily, perhaps by keeping it on a computer. Also, just plain blank paper works quite well, encouraging kids to write about what they've read. You can study how they keep track and then develop a form that works based on what they are already doing.

Third graders seem to soak up a lot of vocabulary because the books they choose and the interests they pursue demand that. We encouraged the children to keep track of confusing or new or exciting words. This was serious language study and the children seemed to get into it.

We don't believe that children need to do a project on every book they read, but a project is a way for children to show what they have learned or to practice skills that are tentative. We had weekly discussions at which they might choose a book project to do; projects included posters, dioramas, book talks, book jacket design, book marks, plays, puppet shows, book commercials, or reading the book into a cassette for others to enjoy at the listening center.

We also changed our math program quite a bit. We moved into hands-on math activities to put greater emphasis on conceptual development, mathematical reasoning, and problem solving. We gave up the security of a textbook and spent our math money on manipulatives instead of workbooks. The children had access to the manipulative on open shelves and see-through containers. They used the materials at formal math times and other times, too. Everything was labeled so that students knew what the materials were called and where they belonged. The beginning of the year focused on allowing the children to explore the materials, and eventually we moved into problems, concepts, and more. We posed open-ended problems so that students could find many different answers and ways to justify those answers.

ASSESSMENT FOR MEANINGFUL TEACHING AND LEARNING

As we have discussed, our biggest area of growth has been in the facing of individual students. We knew that in whole-class teaching, many children were not getting what they needed. Letting go of teacher's guides and mandated curriculum and paying attention to what we knew about children and learning forced us to study assessment. Because we were not using a textbook, we no longer could rely on the unit tests to assess learning. We had to be accountable, with the students, for their learning.

In our weekly conferences, we faced individual students. Listening to our colleagues in the group as they discussed keeping track of children, we learned to take anecdotal notes as the children were working on their writing and reading and we also paid attention to the needs expressed in their writing. We watched for skills that they needed to learn to become more powerful writers. We filed the anecdotal notes in their individual student files and saved them for future reference by us and for parent conferences. We also grouped children when they had needs in common.

A new form of assessment for us was the use of student portfolios. The students chose any product that they wanted to include in the file folder. The folders were stored in plastic crates and kept in a spot where students always had access to them. Document captions were used to label the pieces to be put into the files. We also suggested products to include in the same folders. These portfolios were shared by the students and us at parent conference time.

AN INQUIRY PROJECT ON OUR CITY

A very important point during our first year with the study group was when the traditional (district-required) time to study our city arrived. We studied the city each year that we taught third grade, following the district's rather boring teacher's guide. In the study group, we discussed and brainstormed alternative ways to study the city in which we lived.

We then decided to do the same thing, brainstorm, with the children in our classrooms. We listed the things about the city that they knew, engaging them in a discussion of the city and its many parts. We eventually sent for the packet of information that the city's chamber of commerce sends to new residents, talked to architects, and took a walking and bus tour of the city. Our school is quite close to the state capital building and we went there for a formal tour and a search for more information about the city.

Our students made rubbings of different parts of the capital building by using crayons (on their sides) on newsprint paper. The students made maps of various parts of the city and got information from the city's welcoming committee. They made numerous phone calls to confirm or find certain pieces of information. Our students were quite engaged in their study of the capital as they sought to make sense of what it meant to be a member of our community. They discussed the roles of restaurants, shopping malls, and the university.

They decided that the welcoming committee's information was lacking and subsequently developed their own welcome packet for future or present residents of our city. They felt that the information in the old welcome packet needed to be updated and made more interesting. The packet that the children developed involved an immense amount of research about our city and its services; their demand for information led them to phone calls, letter writing, the computer, the library, and more. The final packet was quite impressive.

Our purpose in this chapter is not so much to show the children's work as to demonstrate our own growth and how it supported the kids in their growth. The study of our city was a landmark for us; we were learning to follow the children's lead in learning. Our many discussions with each other and the group helped us learn to rely on the children more. Our work with the group was an important part of our journey in learning to be better teachers; it also deepened our relationship with each other.

The children in our classes know that we are good friends. They see us laughing, joking, complaining, whispering, celebrating, and more with each other. We think this is a good thing for them to see. It is a wonderful thing for us to live.

Although the first year of our group was a lot of work, it was a most rewarding year for us because our students were reading and writing until the very last day of the school year. Some wanted to finish projects as others were putting things away so that the janitors could give the rooms their summer cleaning.

We still have many questions. We want to become more child-centered and want to explore what that means. We want to give the children even more control of the curriculum, as we did with their study of our city. We know that we will have each other to do this and hope that our group will also stay intact because it helped us move to where we knew we wanted to be heading. We know that we are on a journey and we want to continue because it keeps our teaching fresh and new.

Chapter 6

A Montessori Teacher, Learner, and Writer

Mona McKenzie
Lincoln Public Schools, Lincoln, NE

¤ ¤ ¤

During the first year that our study group met, I learned how much Montessori's views of children, teaching, and learning are like those of constructivist teachers. In this chapter, I present my growing understanding of Montessori as that growth took place during our study group. The group was a collaboration that helped me build classroom activities based on what I believe.

THE SPIRIT, TEACHING, AND LEARNING

The Montessori philosophy comes from Maria Montessori (1967, 1976), a woman who lived in the early 1900s and who became the first woman physician in Italy. She began working with infants and institutionalized children in Rome by observing them. She researched the idea that children needed stimuli that involved the senses, and she designed materials for those children. She believed good teachers need to learn to observe children, closely watching what the children select to work on in the class. Then, each child should be honored for her or his own uniqueness. She referred to this special part of children as their *spirit* and said that teachers should guide the children in lessons that free each one to reach their own potential so that they, in turn, will free all people.

Teaching children is a process of learning to know yourself and learning to observe and guide others. Teaching is a combination of the scientific processes of observing and deducing. It focuses on being open to where the person is developmentally and emotionally, and open to seeing their spirit. As a teacher, one of my goals is to find the methods or materials that lead children to further discovery of their spirit and the world in which they live while they are members of the classroom community.

Our study group was another community where I felt that spirit. Our group did for me what I was working on doing with the children in my class. Group members brought data to the group; we analyzed and shared things that worked for us. We were doing what Montessori (1964) described; we were "fusing the spiritual life of the student with the virtues of science to create a school for the service of living humanity" (p. 36).

The process we went through in our group was similar to what Montessori did when she began. We watched children and developed lessons that led them to independence. Group members worked as collaborators, helped each other, and discussed what worked and what did not work. I developed my observation skill, something I had not previously had the opportunity to do. In my classroom, children learned lifelong skills that enabled them to communicate with others; they learned to read from books that interested them, as well as to do research in books and through other resources. One of my children summed it up best as we went on a walk through our school when he said, "All classes are learning just like we do."

I saw my colleagues as learners, myself as a learner, my colleagues' students as learners, and my students as learners. All learners expressed themselves as individuals and as group members. I feel that Ridgeway is a spiritual place in this respect. Our group members worked for and with their own spirit and the spirit of the children.

The Classroom Environment

One of the main aspects of a Montessori classroom, like the constructivist classroom, is the time invested in preparing the environment as the best learning situation. My room is arranged simply, keeping clutter and extraneous stimulus to a minimum because I want it to be beautiful and useful. Montessori developed materials for the children to use with that in mind; the materials came from her observations of children at play and at work.

The Montessori environment is interrelated with other subjects. For example, plant and animal cards, which name the parts of or describe living things, are available to the children. The children also have access to many maps that they use for tracing and copying, labeling countries, and finding capitols, rivers, and other land forms. An important part of the environment is the language that is going on all day throughout the variety of subjects. Montessori materials are developmental and cover a wide range of ages and abilities; they encourage and support a language-rich environment. I felt fortunate to have these materials available to me, but I also found that collaboration with others, even though I had Montessori training, helped me further my sense of how to use the materials in even more appropriate ways. The classroom environment took on greater meaning for me and my students because of the questions and discussions that we dealt with in our group.

Literacy Activity

Montessori was concerned about language development and I was trained to use her ideas about handwriting, phonics, grammar, sentence writing, and story writing. In my classroom of 6-through 9-year-olds, language shelves were set up with phonetic work that begins with the initial letter sounds. Maria believed that the best time to work on beginning sounds was when the child was between the ages of 3 and 6 because that is when the child is most receptive to learning the letter sounds, not just the letter names. Once the child is beyond this, a different approach is used. The work is sequential and includes vowels and variations to phonetic spellings. The children use word cards that have patterns on them and other cards that have lists of words. They are also busy with word study that includes teaching of contractions, compound words, prefixes, suffixes, and work with root words. Homophones, homographs, synonyms, and antonyms are also taught.

All materials are introduced with lessons that I learned in my Montessori training; the children work with the cards to master and incorporate their understanding. Writing is done in a variety of ways. Story starters and ideas for writing are also on the language shelf. Children do much information gathering and writing. Skills such as note taking, outlining, reference work, rough drafts, editing, and final publications are taught as needed. Creative writing was another option during the day.

Grammar is taught to the children at a very young age, beginning in the preschool with a miniature farm environment. The lessons are continued at the elementary age for the children to learn the parts of speech in interesting, inviting, introductory sessions. Montessori found that children were interested in knowing the function of words at an early age and if you waited to introduce this, the interest was not as great nor were the concepts internalized as easily. That is what Montessori termed *sensitive periods*. These are periods when:

> ... a child's different inner sensibilities enable her/him to choose from her/his complex environment what is suitable and necessary for her/his growth. They make the child sensitive to some things, but leave her/him indifferent to others. When a particular sensitiveness is aroused in a child, it is like a light that shines on some objects but not on others, making them her/his whole world. (Montessori, 1966, p. 128)

Montessori learned of these sensitive periods through observation and they have been supported in further research by Piaget and other researchers. These sensitive periods are now the age groupings of Montessori classrooms: birth to 3, 3 to 6, 6 to 12, and 12 to 18.

For my own reading in our study group (my personal/professional literacy activity), I began with Graves (1991) and then read Calkins (1986). These two had a profound affect upon my own writing and the writing that was completed in my classroom. My students began to carry notebooks and we wrote quite a bit. I was amazed at what my students wrote as they got into story writing. The group supported me and challenged me as I read Graves and Calkins and thought of ways that these two contemporary researchers complemented my Montessori philosophy and classroom. The books and our group discussions offered strategies that were consistent with my beliefs and stretched what Montessori children usually do for writing.

The children kept track of their writing because it was bound in their notebooks, and some of this was eventually published as stories. I did not study their writing systematically the way Kim R., Kim L., and Kim Z. did. The notebooks documented their growth and at our study group meetings I addressed questions I had. I made a gentle transition, both for myself and with the children, into a more "writers workshop" approach.

Reading was another area that was changed, but not as dramatically. The children got more and more into researching to find information. Our group helped me examine the place of project groups in a Montessori classroom. Some Montessorians believe that children should be reading and comprehending before they enter the elementary class. In my situation, this is not always the case. Some of my Montessori students knew how to read and some did not. I still used a strong phonics approach in my language lessons, where it worked. But I also used strategies of what good readers do. For the beginning readers, I used sight words, pattern books, and predictable books that they were successful in. Then I moved to author studies that had a variety of books from easy to difficult. The children selected a book to be an expert on. Those who chose similar books became a small group that met while I had minilessons with some children individually. As the children become better readers, I did studies of different kinds of books so they could deduce literary elements and genre. The children learned reading skills and strategies through individual conferences and in small groups that had similar needs.

Practical Life in a Community

Practical life activities are another important aspect of the Montessori classroom. These help the children learn about becoming independent members of a community. In my classroom, this is done by providing activities that the children need for every day living. Learning cleanliness of the room and responsibility for self are included. It also means learning to use the community as a resource and going out into the neighborhood to find information or to help others or the environment. Working as a classroom community created bonds between myself and the children as we learned about each other together.

Our study group supported me as I moved the class into a study of our neighborhood. The children learned phone skills, letter writing, and interviewing techniques in an authentic way because they were involved in finding out about things they wanted to know more about. The children called stores, doctors, and other specialists in the community for information and they made appointments for people to come to the classroom or for the class to visit them to gain more information. We were becoming a community of learners.

One of the main differences between Montessori classrooms and some traditional classrooms is the view of curriculum. In a Montessori classroom, the curriculum always focuses on teaching the whole picture so the children will have a better understanding of how things are connected. We focused on the whole neighborhood and then saw how its parts were connected. From this, the children pursued individual interests, but with a broader understanding. Montessori stated, "Here then is an essential principle of education: to teach details is to bring confusion; to establish the relationship between things is to bring knowledge" (Montessori, 1976, p. 94). An example of this was the way I taught the history of the development of the earth before other sciences were studied. In language and math, the history of each discipline was presented to the children. I believe this to be essential, even when I am teaching reading and writing. Children need the whole presented from history in order to do different kinds of books, writings, and forms of poetry. They need lessons on phonetics and comprehension, not just one or the other. A master teacher does both at a time when it is appropriate developmentally, but this is not easy to learn. Knowing when to teach different things is what I think whole language is all about; it is knowing what to teach and when to teach it. The projects undertaken by the students of the other teachers in our group were consistent with this idea. In our discussions, we pushed each other to see the big pictures, the broad goals of what we were teaching and why, and of what the children were learning and why.

I had the benefit of Montessori training to facilitate that. I also had a powerful group of teachers to collaborate with me to carry that through in a practical sense, on a day-to-day basis. Our meetings kept me grounded and left me feeling that I knew what I was doing and that particular parts of my curriculum were either appropriate for the children in my class or something I wanted to consider changing.

COLLABORATION

Collaborating with our group gave me the impetus and support I needed to observe children in my class and really listen to them. That in itself is not an easy task and took practice and input from others. Observing was one of the main areas I improved in my teaching. This occurred because our discussions left me with questions about children and I had to return to my class and look hard in order to understand what was going on and to address my questions.

Another area that improved was my own personal writing and the writing that I did with the children in my classroom. One of the main things I learned was to have children journal every day. This was a thorn in my side. I didn't like to journal daily; why should I expect the kids to do it? When I began forcing myself to journal daily, I journaled about my classroom, what I did for lessons, and the children's reactions and responses to the lessons. This helped me plan for the next lesson. Eventually, I found this to be a peaceful time to gather my thoughts on what we did that day.

The children loved writing in journals and looked forward to it everyday. They saw themselves as writers and readers. It was a joy because I learned that children can be intense writers and that I really could write, myself. People in our group wanted to hear what I had to say in my writing. In our group, I was and felt valued. My colleagues told me what they liked about my writing, asked me questions to clarify what I meant, and gave suggestions on ways I might try to make myself better understood. The end result is that I was able to model this in my classroom—from a personal perspective as a writer, not from a textbook's point of view. The students also responded to one another in a positive way, asked meaningful questions, and supported one another in their writing. What had happened for me in the group was happening for the children in my class.

Another collaboration was when the four third-grade teachers (including Liz and Linda) and I decided to study spelling. We read articles and books that Rick Meyer helped us find, and then we discussed the articles and our practices. I changed the way we did spelling in my classroom. Previously, I followed a list or did some work with patterning that I had been trained to do. This involved a prescribed step-by-step activity that, I realized, was pretty meaningless. I changed by having the children look at words they were having trouble learning to spell conventionally. We also had some words on a common list, words that most of the children were having trouble spelling. Hearing Rick say it so often, I learned the phrase, "What do you notice about these words?" They thought hard about finding patterns or rules on their own and they discussed these. Some words just had to be memorized, but they were discussed as problem words that we all could talk and laugh about. I asked them the best way to learn words. Some could tell me and some could not. We discussed strategies. When they couldn't suggest anything, we went back to studying the words together. For some it was as simple as practice, while others made learning the words into a game. If they had difficulty spelling, they knew they needed to learn strategies that would help them with that; I was learning many strategies from my reading and our group's discussions and, in turn, the students also learned those strategies. Those who were good spellers became the experts we called on as needed. The discussions in our study group were similar to the ones I had with the children in my class. We talked about language and the way words are spelled in both places, in the study group and in my classroom. The collaboration about spelling in one place was affecting the teaching and learning of spelling in the other.

I also audited Rick's university class on assessment that focused on miscue analysis. It is not an easy process to learn but was helpful to me because I learned about the reading process and strategies that readers use. I listened to readers in my classroom and made decisions on strategies that they might need to learn. Rick's class was another community that helped me learn. Kim R. and Kim L. were in the class, too, so there was good overlap between the communities that I was relying on for professional growth.

The coming together of professionals to engage in learning, sharing, and helping one another was one of the times in my career that change came about through a process that we, as teachers, created together. The study group was a supportive environment of colleagues, and it stretched me, was sometimes stressful, and was especially important when I began to share my writing. I continue to grow from that experience. It made me examine my practices and learn to define them and be able to explain them on a practical level. I still feel close to the other educators in the group and often go to them when I have a question. I miss the group and look forward to resuming of our activities once the book is finished and we can, again, focus on the year at hand and the issues before us.

Our study group was a place of growth and struggle, but from my point of view, it was a tremendous leap in my education. Teachers were examining what they did and either finding ways to support their practice or exploring new ways and finding evidence of growth to support what they did. No longer were teachers just doing what they did because that was the way they learned how to teach. It was exciting to be part of this.

I believe we must each learn to know ourselves and to honor the gifts we bring to our classrooms just as we learn to honor the spirit of each child in our class. As we do that, we no longer fear our lack, but begin humbly to move on and learn what is next for us to learn. Montessori (1966) stated, "It is the spirit of the child that can determine the course of human progress and lead it perhaps even to a higher form of civilization" (p. 7). Honoring that spirit and guiding it with a group of dedicated teachers is an empowering experience.

Chapter 7

Learning From a Researcher, a Researcher Learning

Richard J. Meyer
University of Nebraska–Lincoln

¤ ¤ ¤

The mutuality of learning that occurred in the study group saturates this book. In this chapter, I focus on my role as a group member who was a resource for the group and also systematically studied the group.

The frame for my work in the study group was described in Chapter 1, in which I presented the idea of servicing-in. My commitment rested in the belief that the teachers living in the context of Ridgeway School would develop relationships and gain insights into the school culture and the way they were situated within that culture if they were provided a forum for conversations. My role at Ridgeway was confusing. Was I an outsider or an insider? Does there exist some place in between? It is easy to theoretically lay out the role of someone who wants to be involved in servicing-in, but living that was not easy. The tension of living inside and outside is discussed further in chapter 11 because it became an issue for all members of the study group in relation to nonmembers at Ridgeway. I wasn't an objective outside observer because I was a member of the group who was listened to, challenged, and engaged in active discussions of ideas, problems, thoughts, dreams, curiosities, and possibilities. And, I wasn't an insider because I was not a staff member at Ridgeway. At one meeting of our group, Mona turned to me and said:

> Because of what you bring out.… You gently guide us and teach us but you question and ask. You don't set one way. We learn what we want to learn because we want to and I see all of us doing that here. You know, and you don't say it has to be just a certain way and ideally, Montessori said that the true test is when human beings stop taking tests and start learning for the reasons that we are learning here today … (Transcription, 3/28/95)

Ahh, such flattery. And I believe that Mona meant what she said because she is direct and honest. Yet was I ever completely "in" while servicing-in? Probably not. I was not there every day; I was not living the life of a teacher there. But, I certainly gained an intimate knowledge of how the school worked and the teachers' views of the school, the community, and each other. In this chapter, I discuss my roles briefly. Although these roles are not dichotomous, there were two roles that I enacted at Ridgeway. One role focused on supporting and cultivating the study group's activity. The other role involved making sense of that activity, understanding subsequent teacher change and student learning, and understanding the place of the study group in the broader school culture.

A RESOURCE AND A RESEARCHER

My role in our study group was twofold: I was a researcher and a resource. I facilitated our sessions until folks began to take over with their own agendas. At that point, I found myself talking less and less and listening a lot more. In analyzing the tapes of our sessions, I seemed a bit uncomfortable with silences in the first few sessions and probably talked to fill the quiet. As our comfort with each other grew, silences were not such a problem.

The researcher role carried with it the responsibility of engaging us with the broader group of people who were involved in similar work. I wanted the group to know that we were not alone, as Hollingsworth (1994) so poignantly explains:

> I continued my search for other stories and theories that would help me better understand ours, and moreover, help us link our experiences in the group with others in the larger world. I searched for similar patterns in others' experiences to weave into the tapestry of our stories. I discovered many educators who suggested … that teachers require a dynamic understanding of self in relationship to both self and others across multiple contexts! Our group was surely providing a context for self/other relationship development … (p. 68)

So, I encouraged reading and writing and provided access to articles and books that might be new to group members.

I tried to be honest about the tension I felt between Mona's comment and Hollingsworth's remark. I worked hard to not be *the* expert, but to be one of the many experts in our group. I would not play the role of the outside expert who visits the school for one or two staff development sessions in order to *fix* that staff and then disappears. The deficit focus of the "fix it" approach to staff development frustrates teachers because it perpetuates the myth that teachers are "broken" and in need of quick repair by a distanced specialist. I wanted to disrupt that myth and I was working at composing myself as a servicing-in colleague, not an outsider "inservicer." I think it is important to include this distinction because other inquiry groups may want to establish relationships with someone outside of the school setting. When doing so, it is important to consider what role you want that person to play in your group. As you will see, I was learning to be a resource and a researcher. I hope the following sections portray the difficulty of cultivating these roles.

Becoming a Resource

I dealt with the pragmatics of reminding us to get started and, as the group became tired, to end so that we could all go home. "I always have such a headache after this class ... but it's a good headache," Kim L. said. I think that some of her headache had to do with the intensity of focus that we experienced. I tried to make sure that we honored our agenda. This became increasingly important when individuals agreed to bring their writing or their students' work to a meeting. We didn't want anyone's efforts over-looked. Before the teachers brought evidence or data from their classrooms, I helped us stay focused on what we were reading or discussing. I made this role public and all were agreeable to it; I said things like, "I'm not sure if we want to move away from this paragraph, yet; it seems that it puts tension on, ummm, some of the things that you're doing in your classrooms."

One of the most difficult roles I played was having us all, including me, slow down and be tentative and elaborate at the same time. I wasn't quick to leave an issue; I felt that quickness was typical in schools because of the rush to find a solution to a problem or get an issue addressed during a 10-minute lunch rush. I wanted to encourage a slower process to see what happened as we became more reflective practitioners (Schon, 1986).

I spent many hours thinking about what articles or books might best fit what we were doing and planning. For example, the Rief (1991) chapter was important in showing how to have children collect data by interviewing as well as demonstrating (DeStefano, 1981) how a teacher can write about his or her own classroom. Readings taught us all a lot; we discussed the content of the selections and we talked about what strategies the writer used in order to develop our own writing. We were reading for multiple reasons, as teachers, learners, readers, writers, and inquirers. This excerpt from one of our meetings shows the impact of our reading on our writing and thinking:

> Kim Z: I [read an article in Reimer, Stephens, & Smith, 1993] ... I liked that one a lot. I liked how it was written. So I was trying to model [my piece] similarly, thinking okay, how did she [the teacher in the article] go through her day; how did she tell me?

Rick: And then an important thing that she does in that work also is she analyzes. She gives you the 10 steps or whatever it is that she developed and that's kind of an analytical ...

Kim Z: Well, I thought about that during parts of this [Kim's own written description of a classroom event] ... there needs to be more of my reflection on this.... There needs to be my thought in there somewhere.... Sort of like after each section or after the very end or you know ...

Kim R: Or after spending weeks of researching [one topic], this is how I felt about this or that or the other thing [She's rehearsing (Murray, 1982) her writing aloud in the group.] (Transcript from study group session)

Another part of assuming responsibility for some of the organizational stuff of our group involved the pragmatics of our next meeting. As a meeting ended, I suggested that we set the agenda for the next meeting so that we would be clear on what to read, who might be presenting writing, and what questions the teachers wanted to address in their classroom and when we next met. This took a long time when I refused to make decisions; I was open to being asked to locate an article or book, but would not decide who would share, what we would read, and other learner responsibilities.

I did not want to be the center of attention although I knew that, especially in the beginning, many group members wanted to report things to me, have me confirm their activity, or ask what to do in specific classroom situations. There is tension in this type of activity. I do not deny my agency in the study group, but I did not want the teachers to become dependent on me as the expert. I wanted to facilitate teacher development and my own development, but not in the traditional ways that professors do that with students. I learned to listen, live with some silences, and, increasingly, respect the multiple conversations that took place at once in the group. As individuals' curiosities were piqued by something, many conversations often emerged. I wrote in my field notes one evening, while listening to the tape of that day's session:

While Kim R. and I have started a conversation about her piece of writing, on the tape you can hear the voices of other smaller subgroups that start to talk. They are impossible to transcribe because there are so many voices going at once; the important thing is that as needs came up in the group, we naturally subgrouped and talked to whomever it was we wanted to address. Clearly, individuals had to choose who to listen to or it sounded like the tape: lots of noise. I've come to really enjoy this flow of our group. (Field notes, 3/8/95)

I was trying to compose myself *with* a whole group of co-researchers. Listening to the tapes of our sessions inspired me to be more quiet as a researcher and a resource. A poignant example of my learning was when Kim Z. was struggling with how to analyze data. She asked, almost rhetorically, how she could organize all she had collected. I responded with great zeal, suggesting that she develop a list of categories:

> That's how you start, and then, what I do, is I'll make another copy of that whole document so I have it in two places. One, the way I wrote it, when I first sat down and write it so that's preserved. The other one's what I call a working document, and I work on it. I might go through it and use bold or different font and start to categorize it, so I'll take a chunk of that text on to ... okay, this is about moments that they leave the room to get information some place else. This is about an intense conversation between two people. Here's another moment where they leave the room. Here's another intense conversation. Here's when a new project idea evolved. Here's ... and so I go through and I have categories for every chunk that seems to be a self-contained or that I could arbitrarily say this is definitely a ... whatever category I establish. It comes from my notes. Those categories I put all together, so in a new file and in my computer I can cut and paste, so I cut that thing that says ... let's say it's ... let's say one thing I want to do is look at conversations between kids rather than who is going through the teacher and teaching. So every chunk that I have that's between kids I'll start a new file called "between kids" December 3rd, paste it in. December 6th, paste it in, December 9th, paste it in, so everything that's between kids ... here's what's starting to happen, the categories that Linda used on her chapter, they're starting to emerge for me because, well, somebody knows my kids talk a lot to each other, and when you read your notes and your thinking, okay, I have to think of like a theme for this chunk, that's when you're starting to develop major headings, possible major headings for your ... now a lot of times I'll go through and I'll go this category's not working because I'm not finding any other times where they leave the classroom to go to a resource, they're always going to the same place, they're always going to the media center, so that whole file becomes one sentence my kids leave a lot to go to the media center and that's it, done deal. But, conversations between each other, if that's a category ... [Then to write it, you'd find] anything that you want to put in for a kid. You put a post-it on it and you write Figure 1, just arbitrarily number them, Figure 1, Figure 2, Figure 3, and so on. And then you'd have text, text, text, that you've written those notes, notes, and then you skip ... double space, you write see Figure 1, leave another double space, and then you keep going so that I would know or a reader would know that that's where Figure 1 goes. When we get to the final piece, we'll have the Design Center shrink stuff, move the text up, and they'll do it, you won't have to do that. (Transcript from study group session)

If you read the entire excerpt, you can imagine how embarrassed I felt as I listened to the tape of that session and realized how little this lecture helped Kim Z. in the analysis of her data. I wrote in my journal:

> Eeeeek! I don't want to beat myself up too much for this, but this role of "the great problem solver" clearly did not help Kim Z. She was quiet and her eyes looked at me and I remember thinking that I had fixed her problem. Ugh. She was dazed, all right;

I had poured a bunch of jargon and anthropological stratagem over her head and almost drowned her! Be careful!

Subsequently, I encouraged individuals to bring data and have us all look at it, talk about it, and suggest ways of organizing, sorting, and analyzing. Part of my role, then, was to learn along with everyone on many levels: as a group facilitator, as a coresearcher, and as a resource.

As with any group, there are feelings that seem to run below the surface. I wanted to support myself and group members in articulating these feelings because they seemed to hang in the air and slow things down. The affect of the group might, I thought, need a more public place so that we could grow. I risked naming things:

Rick: [Linda has just read a draft about her growth as a teacher] I'm curious about how you felt reading it because you seemed kind of nervous.
Linda: Oh I was a wreck, it was really hard for me to share it cause it's just so much part of me.

I also demonstrated my concerns about taking risks in classrooms and the importance of having data to show that children were learning:

What if someone asks you, well I'm going to ask you … "What did the kids learn and how do you assess what they learned?" Isn't that part of what you're supposed to do? (Transcript from study group session)

For all the members of the group, this was the first time that they all sat down together with members of different grade levels, meeting for an extended period of time over many months. I certainly had never done this as a teacher. As the group discussed, imagined, and composed what we needed, our forum became a powerful thought and curriculum collective as ideas were presented and cultivated.

One example of such a cultivation of curriculum was when Liz and Linda explained that their children would be studying our city. The group began to make suggestions: take them on a bus ride, have them talk to that old man who knows about the capitol building, let them do rubbings in a cemetery, get the aerial photo of the city, and more and more and more. Then I asked, "What if you did this with the kids? What if the kids could generate questions and resources from their knowledge of the city?" I was suggesting that they rely upon the community (classroom's) funds of knowledge (Moll & Diaz, 1987). Moll and Diaz suggests that a community can get much done when the members of the community rely on the collective skills and knowledge of its members. We were doing that about the city; the kids might do the same thing. They could undergo this same process of brainstorming, and Liz and Linda might learn what the kids knew about their city (and didn't know, too), just as we had done in our group. Indeed, members of our class asked: What aerial photo? Who is that old man? Why rubbings in a cemetery? I wondered aloud about having the children engage in a similar process as a pedagogical strategy. They tried this strategy and it was quite successful, as they mentioned in their chapter.

By participating in the discussion of how to study our city, and then having the group reconsider what transpired in that discussion, I was learning to engage in metateaching or metapedagogy, thinking about teaching before and after actually doing it. Or, perhaps this was praxis as Freire (1970a) intended, where the teacher was involved in teaching and learning and also outside of it, analyzing and making decisions of what to offer or suggest next. I worked at being in the group and thinking about the group at the same time, making the boundaries between my two roles less distinct.

There are a few other things I did in my capacity as resource. I visited the group's classrooms as much as possible during the full days I spent in the school each week. This afforded the group a second point of view on a classroom. I asked questions of the teachers whose classrooms I'd seen, and this led us into discussions of facets of the classroom that may have not come up previously.

I wrote a grant to obtain an 8-millimeter camcorder, some tapes, some small tape recorders, and a laptop computer. We shared these items as they were needed in order to collect data, analyze it, and write. We didn't use these enough at our meetings, though. Looking back, I think we would have learned from and stimulated conversation by viewing and discussing tapes of the teachers' classrooms as a way of visiting those classrooms. Perhaps we'll do this in the future.

Another way of being a resource was suggesting events to attend. Many of our group members had not been to a large professional conference, larger than a state level International Reading Association conference, so I encouraged them to attend and even present at the Whole Language Umbrella and National Council of Teachers of English annual conventions. We have presented (Meyer & Ridder, 1996; Meyer et al., 1996) and were well received at these. Such experiences certainly excite and revitalize a group.

Becoming a Researcher

As a researcher, I took field notes (Spradley, 1980) at each session. Following each day at the school, I elaborated field notes, looked for emerging themes, and read and reread the notes looking for theories to explain why sessions unfolded as they did (Glaser & Strauss, 1967). As themes emerged (such as the ideas of composing and disrupting), I used constant comparison as described by Glaser and Strauss to confirm or disconfirm them. I discussed the emerging themes with the group and they agreed with, challenged, and stretched my thinking.

My field notes were not limited to our sessions. I took notes when I visited each classroom and compared what teachers said with what I saw. I did this to be a resource, but also to be a researcher. When I asked questions at a meeting about what I had seen in a classroom, our discussions focused on making sense of what another pair of eyes saw in a classroom. The teachers clarified the activities in which children engaged within the classroom, and they also thought and rethought those activities and opened them up to close scrutiny. The teachers and the children (through their work and the data we were collecting) were informants (Harste, Woodward, & Burke, 1984) about their classrooms, and our discussions were a forum for supporting, challenging, questioning, and studying tentative ideas.

I audiotaped all of the sessions beginning at the third one because I did not want to rush into taping. I wanted folks to feel comfortable and then suggested that if I taped our sessions I might better understand more of what we were doing and how I might be of some help. My goal was to balance my role as a researcher (my own learning) with my role as a resource to teachers. I remain committed to *not* using the school in an opportunistic fashion (i.e., a place to research *on* a school). I wanted to have a mutually beneficial relationship that would sustain itself beyond the year of district funding. My relationship with the group at Ridgeway, as it continues to evolve, would suggest that the group is accomplishing this.

In my discussions about research strategies, I think I helped the teachers in the systematic collection and interpretation of their data. They saw me play with data and tentatively invent themes that I thought were justifiable in the data. Then they initiated a similar process in interpreting the parts of their classroom and school that they were studying.

REFLECTIONS ON MY ROLE

My role in the group was, above all else, to share in the school experience with the group of teachers that I was coming to respect, know, love, and learn with in order to enhance the lives of learners in the classroom and to understand what such enhanced lives looked like. As I felt increasingly accepted as a friend, confidant, and resource, I learned about life at Ridgeway somewhat as a participant in the school culture (Agar, 1980).

I have tried to make clear my goal of composing anew what it meant to be a university researcher at a school site. We were colearners, and I worked at valuing the many faces and facets of inquiry and inquirers that I discussed in chapter 1. Sadly, I came to understand that facets of inquiry might not be valued at the university. I wrote the following journal entry in February of our first year together.

> I went to the Teaching and Learning Center's breakfast for nontenured faculty. [The Teaching and Learning Center supports faculty in improving their teaching, achieving tenure, and mentoring graduate students. I am not a tenured faculty member at the time of this writing.] I explained my work at Ridgeway and how important it was to me and the potential it had for graduate student research, including teachers as graduate students. One of the senior faculty who was on the panel looked surprised. "That's not work for someone like you," he said. "That's the work of tenured faculty who have that much time to invest at a research site. You're really walking down the wrong road with that project."
> This is such a hierarchical view of research. Only those who have achieved the status of tenure are entitled to engage in this kind of work? I don't think so. Only those who have waited seven years for that status finally get out into the schools? I just can't wait that long. Folks at Ridgeway are, as Vygotsky would say, "ripening." I want to be there now. Things are happening now. (February, 1995)

I was disrupting the view of inquiry at the university (for some) as I was composing myself as an inquirer. I felt vulnerable, much as members of our group did when we began to change some established regularities at Ridgeway. My view of inquiry is multifaceted, rather than hierarchical, and I stuck with it. This is not meant to self-aggrandize; I could see no other way to compose myself as a researcher.

Finally, I want readers to know that the many chapters in this book that I wrote alone show some of our learning from the years that our group has been together. Those chapters demonstrate our learning from the children and staff at Ridgeway as I worked as a resource and a researcher. As a researcher, resource, and colearner, I relied on group members to ensure that I accurately portrayed what happened.

Part II

Sustained Commitments:
Cultivating the Group, Voice,
*Politics, and Advocacy**

¤ ¤ ¤

Idealistically, schools are organized with children at the center, but there are many influences on children's and teachers' lives in school: the policies of the district, the district-mandated curriculum, the ethos of the school, and broader contexts such as the state and federal pressures that those in schools feel. Student and teacher inquiry are contextualized within a classroom, within a school building that consists of other teachers and children, within a school district, within a political and economic climate, and more. A school, then, does have layers to its context. These layers, unlike facets of inquiry, are hierarchical. The farther we move from the children in a school, the greater the power. Kids have less power than teachers who have less power than principals who have less power than district office administrators etc. These layers are shown in Fig. II.1.

The group of teachers, district office personnel, and university researcher (me) who have voices in this book wanted to engage children and ourselves in learning that was rooted in the learners' interests. Children's inquiry is at the heart of their learning and, therefore, it is at the heart of this book. And teachers' inquiry goes hand-in-hand with children's inquiry because teachers who demonstrate that they are learners inspire their students' curiosity and commitment to learning.

Our group found that engaging in inquiry precipitated responses within and across many contexts (layers). Indeed, it was the teachers' inquiry, supporting the children's inquiry, that opened the way for disruption of some of the regularities (Sarason, 1971) at Ridgeway Elementary School. Engaging in inquiry was like placing a wedge in existing school activity. I found that inquiry both was driven by and drove the processes that created the

---

*All chapters in Part II were written by Richard J. Meyer.

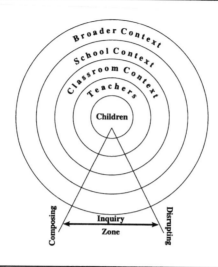

FIG. II.1. The zone in which inquiry takes place as a wedge created by composing and disrupting.

very wedge that supported inquiry. That's a complicated notion, but I show it with a diagram and then explain further (see Fig. II.1).

Within the contexts of their individual classrooms, teachers supported children's engagement in inquiry. Teachers and children composing themselves as learners turned out be quite disruptive to some aspects of life at Ridgeway. The tension between composing and disrupting was the zone in which inquiry was created and enacted; that zone was a wedge that was felt across the contexts shown in Fig. II.1. I use the metaphor of a wedge because a wedge unsettles things, puts tension on an existing system, and makes room for things to happen. Indeed, even within the group, the teachers' views of research were disrupted and composed, as Hogan and Clandinin (1993) suggest:

> It was not easy to unlearn the lessons we had learned so well in our own school experiences, in undergraduate and graduate experiences, and in the places where we worked as teachers. We learned to take notes in lectures and libraries and to give back the contents of those notes in examinations and in papers. We learned to take our selves out of our writing and our speaking when we wanted to be heard by our teachers and those in power. We learned how to quote authorities and reference them properly. We learned to complete long-range plans for our administrators that had no place for our voices and the children's voices. (p. 193)

In this part of the book, I continue the process of irising out as described in the Preface. I open the lens to include more of the contexts shown in Fig.

II.1. Having looked at the teachers' and students' inquiries in Part I, in Part II I broaden the discussion, presenting common themes and issues in their inquiries, ways in which the group initiated and sustained itself, political issues for work such as ours, and implications of our work for others interested in similar activity.

Chapter 8

Thoughts Across Chapters 2 Through 7

with Kimberly Ridder
Lincoln Public Schools, Lincoln, NE

¤ ¤ ¤

Inquiry was not a new set of procedures or lesson plans that we could pass on to each other, but a way of thinking about curriculum with our students in a way that enabled them to find and examine questions significant in their lives.

—Short et al. (1996, p. 22)

I have two goals for this chapter. The first is to discuss some of the themes that run through the teachers' writings in the preceding chapters and to suggest ways in which their writing demonstrates composing and disrupting. The themes of inquiry that the group had in common, their differences, and decisions made within the group "enabled [group members] to find and examine questions significant in their lives."

The second goal is to discuss why some members of our group did not write and to somewhat problematize that issue because other teachers may be involved in composing, disrupting, and inquiry and may not be writing. I want the chapter to acknowledge the tension that existed around writing. Writing was not easy for all who did write, nor was it even an option that some group participants wished to pursue. Recall that I was studying our group's work as a thought collective. The two goals for the chapter reflect my inquiry in that they are analyses across the preceding chapters and the group dynamics that led to those chapters.

The final section of the chapter is written by Kim R. and demonstrates the emotional roller coaster that this kind of work puts a teacher on.

THEMES ACROSS THE CHAPTERS

The discussion in this section begins with curriculum because it is the most salient common thread that runs through the teachers' writings. There are, in the teachers' writings, differing notions of where curriculum originates, how it is perpetuated, and the roles of teachers and children in composing curriculum. Next I address the role of relationships as those relationships supported development of the teachers and their students. At the end of this section of the chapter, I briefly consider some other themes that are rooted in chapters 2 through 7: being a member of a team, changes in family/school understandings, an inquiry-inspired view of literacy, and assessment.

Curriculum and Expressions of Ownership

Atwell's (1987) discussion of what children need to engage in written language activity applies to inquiry activity as well. In addition to the stuff of writing (paper, pencils, etc.), Atwell suggests that writers need time to write, ownership in making decisions about their writing, and response from another writer. The teachers in our group reorganized schedules to allow inquirers time to think, question, learn, search, re-search, write, and create in a variety of ways. Virtually all of the children's projects demonstrate the children's assumption of ownership of their learning and, to some degree, the curriculum. Ownership showed itself in many ways. For example, Kim R.'s students did not exclusively demythify their fears through their inquiry; they also changed what it meant to learn in school. In this sense, they were composing themselves as learners and disrupting prior beliefs about what happens in school. Liz and Linda's children saw that they could take ownership of a city-created document and change it. Kim Z.'s students took over the curriculum to pursue their interests in polar regions. Liz, Linda, and Mona's students became language scientists as they studied the ways words are spelled. In all of these cases, the students' own learning agendas became foremost in their teachers' minds as students and teachers composed themselves as inquirers. The teachers and their students disrupted curriculum and faced themselves as thinkers, writers, artists, mathematicians, biologists, architects, pet store visitors, ethnologists, and members of ongoing thought collectives. There were many facets of inquiry occurring at the same time: the students' inquiry into areas of interests and into themselves as learners, the teachers' inquiry into themselves as inquirers, the teachers' inquiry into the students' inquiry, and the inquiry involved in our group as we discussed the many facets of inquiry.

The students received ongoing responses from each other as they met daily in their inquiry groups. They received responses from the teacher and other adults in the classroom. Inquirers could adjust their projects based on daily feedback. Their final projects and presentations received spontaneous responses as well as formal responses requested by them and their teachers in feedback forms. As the students made plans for their subsequent endeavors, they used the feedback they received from those many sources.

Not all of the inquiry engagements occurred in the same way. Kim Z.'s class was focused on one theme that emerged from a whole class study that emanated from the district curriculum. Liz and Linda were also involved with something that originated at the district office, a regular unit of study on the city. Kim R. and Kim L.'s themes emerged from the children as they listened to the children's daily discussions and responded to their expressed interests. Both avenues were ways for children to compose themselves as learners and inquirers. Both avenues supported the children in addressing their own questions, building communities of learners, and focusing on lifelong learning. Mona pushed her Montessori-based understandings of language and literacy so that reading and writing within her classroom were enhanced by the thinking and research of Graves and Calkins.

The points of origin and the purposes of areas of study are issues that the teachers had to face. For Liz, Linda, and Kim Z., the point of origin was the district office. For Mona, there was a strong link to her Montessori training. But, as the students assumed increased ownership of the areas of study, the purposes for their study changed. There was a move from covering what was required to the creation of knowledge at the local (classroom, group, or individual) level. This is learning that disrupts the common notion that preplanned themes are an enjoyable way to cover curriculum. Themes need to be more than a disguised way to transfer knowledge. Short and Burke (1996) discuss this:

> Our movement away from believing that we needed to "cover" topics began when we examined the ways in which we go about learning and inquiry in our own lives outside of school ... our beliefs were challenged once we asked ourselves how we live as inquirers in the world. (p. 100)

There are, then, a variety of ways to "live as inquirers in the world." In the worlds of our group's classrooms, themes emerged from the children or began by teachers introducing a theme, such as the polar region; there ensued a journey into new and unexplored areas of thinking and creation of curriculum, not replication of something contrived for preordained outcomes. The learner-created curriculum emanates from interests, joys, fears, sadness, intrigue, and other aspects of living in the world.

The teachers in the group also took time to invest in ownership of their own learning. They engaged each other in responses to what they were attempting, and systematically keeping track of, in their classrooms.

Children and teachers composed themselves as learners when they were actively involved in learning about their worlds, they developed under-standings of the roots of myths that affected thinking and feeling, and they made decisions about how to face their world once they were enlightened by their inquiry. Short and Harste, with Burke (1996) used the inquiry cycle to engage in this process, reminding us that we don't reach the end of a learning journey, rather we reach our next question or curiosity. The teachers and children looked forward to what they might compose next and how they might go about it. When the district's prescribed curriculum was used, it was referred to as a minimum—the least that might be done. It was a point of origin, but not an end unto itself that could exist without consideration of the interests of local (classroom or group) consumers. The district curriculum was thinking that was completed for the teacher and the children; the inquiry-based curriculum in the preceding chapters is thinking with, among, and between the children and the teachers. Curriculum, then, becomes a state of being and becoming, rather than a quantity of prefash-ioned information.

Relationships That Support Learning

Some relationships formed within the group and some were brought to the group and enhanced there. As the initial year of the group progressed, two aspects of relationships enhanced the members' interactions and relation-ships. First, close relationships that existed before the group began were made public and were opened to others. Kim R. and Kim L. were good friends before we began our work together. They worked out together in aerobics classes, took graduate courses together, and supported each other through difficult times such as Kim L.'s divorce. Liz and Linda, as demon-strated in their chapter, were also close friends; when Linda's husband died, Liz's friendship, and the way it was extended into the group, helped Linda's return to school make more sense. The group was not intimidated by anger, grief, and difficult times.

The second aspect of relationships that supported the group as a thought-ful learning collective was the willingness of members to take risks and challenge themselves and each other in our forum. Thus, members risked caring for each other as well as taking the risk to challenge ideas. This proved to be a powerful combination. As this challenging and questioning began, the group seemed to thrive on it. The process led to enhanced relationships between members. For example, Kim R., Kim L., and Kim Z.'s relationship

developed (and Kim Z.'s relationship with her second-grade team deterio-
rated) over our time together to the point that Kim Z. requested a transfer
to the first-grade team in order to be continually challenged and to challenge
right back. Group members helped each other disrupt their notions of
possibilities for relationships; they supported proaction such as seeking to
be on the same team.

These relationships supported all the members of the group by demonstrating encouragement, commitment, conversation, and bravery as members engaged in composing and disrupting. This safe feeling was not always
present for the teachers in the group when they worked in their grade-level
teams. It became evident that grade-level teams are quite arbitrary in their
formation because teachers at Ridgeway are not involved in hiring. Our
group put tension on the notion of *team* as it existed at Ridgeway.

Disrupting Teams' Regularities

Members of the study group learned that inquiry in one classroom, when
supported by a study group within the school, disrupted other staff in the
school. Kim Z.'s example may be one of the most profound that our group
encountered. Her colleagues in second grade were excited for her success
and, also, somewhat resentful as Kim and her students received accolades
and attention from me, the district office, and teachers outside of the school
while the rest of the second graders continued their work as usual. Moving
ahead in composing herself and supporting her students as inquirers thus
contributed to disruption of relationships on the team. Rather than following the team's regular way of operating, which excluded the expression of
individuality and required that all four second-grade rooms use identical
materials and plans, Kim Z. supported her students and asserted herself as
invested in composing, which was, by its very nature, disruptive to the team's
former (and well-established) ways of being together personally and professionally. Teams are sometimes vehicles that tug individuals towards mediocrity because members think that membership in a team demands
homogeneity of curriculum across classrooms. The teachers in the study
group found such homogeneity impossible because of the relationship
between the students, the teachers, the emerging curriculum as it was
enacted, and the inquiring minds within their classrooms.

Families and Schools are Affected

Inquiry activity supported families in composing new relationships with
Ridgeway, disrupting the view that many held that the school was not
accessible. The large crowds at project presentations and learning fairs are

evidence of changing home–school relationships. The family feedback was glowingly positive and families began walking their children into the school in the morning and meeting them at classroom doors in the afternoon. The children were encouraged to show their families around "their" classroom. "It's your classroom," Kim R. said to the children when they asked if they could show their families some work in progress. "You may invite any of your family or friends in to visit."

I did not study parents, but they reported at conferences and via letters that their children were enjoying school. Parents wanted to see the rats that their children discussed, the spider webs that their children built, the bubble that had Arctic animals in it, and so forth. Their curiosity and their children's enthusiasm drew them to a school that sounded different from what they had attended.

An Inquiry-Inspired View of Literacy

The teachers supported their students in using literacy as a tool for learning. Goodman (1996) suggests that one of the goals of reading instruction is to make individual words transparent so the reader learns to construct meaning, not focus on individual words. He means that the *word*, as a surface structure, is a window into meaning and not an object of intense and belabored study. The children and teachers you met in the preceding chapters lived Goodman's understanding of the reading process. The student in Kim Z.'s classroom that read using marks that she added to the text is one such example. She added symbols to her writing so that she could remain focused on meaning. Students who learned to read through writing their own reports while making references to their notes and books are further examples. And, the teachers who wrote to learn, to express, and to understand what they had lived are also examples of individuals writing and reading to construct meaning. All of these learners composed themselves as meaning makers.

It is noteworthy that the students and their teachers were composing themselves as writers within the nonfiction genre, for the most part. There were times during most school days when the children could write stories, poems, songs, and so on; their inquiry, however, (both the teachers' and the students') usually involved nonfiction written language activity. Historically, beginning readers read and write fiction; these beginning readers and writers engaged in nonfiction. This may be an important area of further study, enhancing reading and writing programs with a focus on nonfiction (or at least more of a focus than presently exists).

But the children were not bound by written language as the only way to make meaning. They also used other sign systems such as clay, paint, string art (spider's web), costume design, and architecture. They dreamed, planned, played, and enacted their interests and expressions of what they had learned. The many ways that the children found to demonstrate their learning are noteworthy because their demonstrations were often surprises that far exceeded expectations. The teachers and students began to expect the unexpected, delight when it showed itself, and sense connections between other sign systems and written language development. These connections are an area for further study of inquiry-inspired views of literacy.

Assessment Via Systematic Collection

Although the systematic collection of what was happening for the teachers and for the children (and parents) varied from teacher to teacher and from classroom to classroom, collection and subsequent analyses were a common theme of our group's process. Teachers gathered data to discuss, studied it for the questions that rested within it, used it to document growth, and designed the classroom setting to cultivate it. For some, it led to writing for this book. For all, it led to rich classroom learning environments. Ongoing systematic collection was not easy, and the commitment to engage in it involved the disruption of established ways of using time in the classroom and the school. It meant composing of the self as a record keeper like the ones Power (1996) describes as dedicated to "taking note" of what occurs in their classrooms; it also involved helping children compose themselves as record keepers and decision makers, consistent with the ultimate use of record keeping.

Kim Z. and her students kept track as a whole class effort in which the children and the teacher were partners in the collection. Although Kim R. had many project groups going at one time in her classroom, she chose to take notes systematically and intensively on the group studying rats. This was not an easy decision because she wanted to study every child's growth, interests, and changes over time. But it was not feasible to take notes, analyze writing samples, and try to write the words the children spoke in many groups at one time. Her focus on one group allowed her to understand that group, in depth, as a window into understanding the inquiry of the many groups in the classroom.

Kim L. kept track of five groups, but she had different amounts of data from each group. The *Kids Group* spent a lot of time talking, and Kim L. did not record (with tape or by writing) most of their interactions. She relied on breadth rather than depth to obtain (for herself) and to present (to families and in writing in this book) what unfolded in her classroom.

Liz and Linda retraced their lived experiences. They read articles and books and also found papers they had written. They recalled conferences they attended, important teachers they experienced, and the lessons they learned with their students. They were building a sort of portfolio, a collection in a transactional relationship (Rosenblatt, 1978) with their lived experiences.

Parents, the students, and the teachers were involved in the assessment of all of the classroom inquiry projects. They reflected upon efforts and products and projected goals for the future. The teachers developed new goals with the children based on the many sources of data that they generated and collected. Some of this activity led some members of the group to writing, but not others.

NOT WRITING DOES NOT MEAN
NOT LEARNING

I would be remiss if I did not report that writing about inquiry was an issue in our group. The excitement about writing a book generated thoughtful discussions that may not have occurred had we decided not to write. Clearly, teachers and students can be inquirers without writing books, but thinking about making our work public in some form (in our case, a book) changed the group dynamics. We became sharply focused on very specific facets of classroom activity. The intense reflection required for writing was positive because members' learning was articulated; we also knew that our conversations could not focus on future endeavors and that felt limiting, at times.

Teachers are not accustomed to writing, indeed they are not expected to write about inquiry in which they might engage when they are involved in composing curriculum with children in schools. It's not part of their job descriptions and they are not typically afforded the time needed to engage in writing. For members of this study group, becoming writers involved discovering their literacy (Graves, 1990), disrupting their understanding of their jobs, and composing themselves in a new light. Participation in writing seemed to confirm the changes that individuals were making and supported them in becoming descriptive and analytical about what they and their students had accomplished. I began to wonder if perhaps schools are organized to keep teachers from writing, not as some insidious plot as much as the historically rooted design of the role of teachers as enactors of curriculum, not as substantive thinkers and writers of it (Shannon, 1990).

Three group members did not write. But who should tell their stories? I have included sound bytes of some of their voices (as quotes from our sessions together) in some chapters of this book and have tried to acknowledge their influence on the group, but I can not write pieces for them. It is important to discuss why they didn't write, to think about why it matters if teachers do or don't write, and to consider whether or not someone else should write for them.

Pam did not write because she was busy writing a grant to support the initiation of study groups at other schools as well as teaching early childhood special education at Ridgeway; she was doing two full time jobs. There was no time in her day to write for our book; she attended few sessions as her other obligations became very demanding. Pam's learning from the group became an important part of how she carries out her present job facilitating study groups in other schools. She has become articulate about study groups because she organized them with other teachers; thus, she published her learning from our group, if we view publishing as her involvement in making her learning public. The two other members who did not write are discussed later.

Disassociation From the Group

The anonymous member of our group was involved in her first year as a classroom teacher. I wonder if our group of teachers seemed to her to be what Power (1996) refers to as "superteachers" who "make [non-super-] teachers feel very insecure and inadequate" (Power, 1996, p. 47). The teacher read the first drafts of this book, which did not include anything she wrote but did include her voice in transcriptions of our group meetings; her responses to herself included dissatisfaction with how she sounded. She wanted neither her name on the cover nor her identifiable voice within the pages.

As a first-year classroom teacher, she dealt with all the complex issues of being a first-year teacher: the parents and students didn't know her (no reputation or relationships); she was very concerned about classroom management; and she worried about the site of her next year of teaching because first year teachers were most vulnerable to transfers since they lacked seniority. Ultimately, she was transferred because Mr. Z. felt her special education training would be put to better use if she was a specialist outside of the classroom.

The oral discourse of our group helped this new teacher think about the activities in her classroom. She thought aloud so that group members could respond, question, and support her work, and, in turn, her thinking influenced group members. Yet, I can not write a chapter about her and her students' learning because such action on my part would be akin to usurping her voice and her understanding of her classroom. I also can not include her children's voices (or hers) because I did not spend sufficient time in her classroom to paint an accurate picture. Perhaps the feelings she had of having her classroom taken away from her also enter into the decision not to write. She was focusing on the future and possibly moving away from Ridgeway.

As I reflected on the teacher's withdrawal from the group and the book, I wrote in my journal:

> Teacher and student inquiry may, for many reasons, remain quite local. I am learning to honor this choice, but it's not easy because I think that when teachers make their learning more public it may affect change more broadly within and across schools. [The teacher] was a teacher who did interesting things and supported her students' learning and growth, but the activities remain with her, her students and some classroom guests who saw the process and results. And, her and her students' learning remain inaccessible to others.
>
> I do find myself resentful, feeling guilt for feeling resentful, and, mostly, increasingly aware of my vulnerability. When my work at Ridgeway is viewed as research, a teacher's withdrawal makes me vulnerable to being a researcher with no data and no evidence. This just is not resolving itself ...

One of my concerns is that teachers who do not make their learning available to wider audiences perpetuate the isolation that so many teachers feel. The importance of thought collectives, and thought collectives connected to other thought collectives, seems almost urgent in that they are grassroots movements intent on changing teaching and learning as it occurs in school. Teacher study groups need to consider ways of coming into and expressing their voices in their groups, how and if they wish to make their learning public, and the political nature of such activity.

There is tension here because this first-year teacher learned a lot from being in the group; she developed as a teacher and her students gained from her participation. As I said above, teachers do not have to write when they engage in inquiry. Still I wonder how schools will change if teachers keep their learning to themselves. This is an important issue for us to face as teachers, teacher-researchers, and university-researchers. Publication is an issue not for self-aggrandizement but for systemic and systematic change in schools. Later, I discuss different options for publishing, but, again, the important idea here is making learning public, because such publication will contribute to the disruption of schools as they are and, hopefully, the composing of schools that are more invested in authentic learning. Ultimately some form of connectedness is the deeper issue. A teacher need not write to learn or to feel connected to other reflective colleagues. It is connectedness that may undo the cellular nature of schools that Lortie (1975) describes; and that connectedness will support teachers as they compose classrooms for inquiry.

Do Administrators Have Time to Write?

Jane did not finish her piece because she is an administrator with an extremely heavy load and she must run from school to school and meeting to meeting at a pace that is extremely demanding. And, she did not finish because she is a dancer. Literally, she attends at least two dance classes a week, is extremely active, and does not like to sit still to write. She has a good job for her personality: She gets to move between the district office and the many early childhood classrooms in more than 30 schools in the district. Basically, her life as an administrator prohibits investment of large periods of time for writing (see Wolcott, 1973). Jane's unfinished piece is poetic and demonstrates the many directions in which she felt pulled:

> Isadora Duncan (Cheney & Duncan, 1969) wrote, "If I could tell you what I mean, there would be no point in dancing." I am a dancer. Although my business cards say Public School Early Childhood Consultant and my address reads a school system district office, I am a dancer. I am a dancer who is trying to listen to my own song and the songs of the 31,000 children and their families in my community. Education has always been the backdrop for my singing and dancing.
>
> What was the year like? It was like swimming in mud, letting go and taking it back a million times, trying to catch a greased pig, and juggling too many balls at the same time. I was going through some major personal changes while adding 40% to my already full-time job (two days a week were committed to this project). I said [Ridgeway] was the priority, but every time I wasn't in the district office, I felt like I was still letting someone down. Then when I did go in for a meeting at the district office or another school, I felt guilty because I was letting the project down. Taking on a change of this magnitude needs to be given more space and support than I allowed ... yet I learned so much.
>
> What happened? We all grew. I had some informal hypotheses I was testing. They revolve around my understanding of leadership and change and resistance and district office support and what teachers really want and most importantly what children can really do when we remove some of the walls. We met some resistance from teachers, children, and families. Webster defined resistance as "A force that retards, hinders, or opposes motion" ... I naively believed, because the 'motion' we were proposing was so pure and good for children and because the entire staff from Ridgeway had asked for this movement or motion to occur, that resistance would not be an issue. I wanted my leadership to facilitate process and clarify conflicts. I know now the price of pushing to make things happen, and choose to allow the process to unfold.

Jane dealt with issues that shed light on what other administrators in her positions might expect if they become involved in similar processes. She revealed in interviews that she met resistance at the district office from colleagues who thought that the work at Ridgeway was undermining pre-viously purchased curriculum materials. Others at the district office felt and expressed the tension between developmentally appropriate practice and other district policies. She was confronted with questions about how to evaluate what was happening at Ridgeway. Jane did not write about these, but she faced them daily on her job.

She also experienced resistance from teachers who told her that they had perfunctorily signed the proposal to engage in the funded year of study. They wanted money to hire substitutes so that their teams could plan together, but they did not want to question the developmental appropriateness of their practices. This tension between insiders (those willing to engage in systematic questioning of their practices) and outsiders (those invested in maintaining Ridgeway as it has been or making superficial changes) is presented in greater depth in chapter 11.

The school system may be set up for teachers to not write, but the administrative track is even more rigid about this. Many administrators find themselves involved as business managers rather than educational innovators and leaders. How many books are there by principals who wrote while still in their job? We may know of some (super?) teachers who do this (Atwell, 1987; Rief, 1991), but it's difficult to find super-principals who have the time or inclination (Harwayne, 1992; Meier, 1995; Wortman, 1996, are exceptions). It's just not part of their job, yet. I'm left curious about how administrators compose themselves and what they disrupt (or perpetuate) as they do so.

Writing and Thinking

Choosing not to write did not exclude anyone from discussions about another's writing. Nor did not writing prevent anyone from stretching their own thinking by participating in what other group members wrote. I submit that writing, as others have shown (Langer & Applebee, 1987), shaped the thinking of group members, particularly the members who engaged in it. Writing slows things down, demands reflection, and asks teachers to experience what their student inquirers experience: learning by being curious, finding information, trying things out, and reflecting. Each writer's work enhanced the individual writer and the nature of our thought collective; and each nonwriter's participation also shaped the nature of the collective.

I look forward to the many ways, in addition to writing, that teachers and their students might demonstrate their learning. We might see a classroom portfolio, a web site, a video, a learning bubble, an audiotape, a painting, a photo montage, a sculpture, or welcome packet as evidence of teachers' and students' engagements in inquiry. Books like *The Rat Pack* (chapter 3), that include a meshing together of children's and teacher's voices, may become more popular in classrooms, schools, and districts as a way of assessing. Perhaps, in the larger market of published trade books, they will be enjoyed by teachers and families, thereby supporting the composing and disrupting

of views of school. These are all evidence of students and teachers composing curriculum, composing relationships, and composing 'self' as thoughtful
citizens. Further, they are evidence of those same folks disrupting myths and
long-held beliefs about teaching, learning, relationships, and curriculum.
What remains to be seen are the ways in which teachers and students make
decisions about making their learning public and, if they choose to have it
made public, the impact such publication has upon lives in schools.

A TIME CAPSULE

The last part of this chapter was written by Kim R. during the summer after
the first year that our group formed. It is a condensed and intense summary
of her first year as a member of our group. The power of this piece is that it
demonstrates a teacher composing herself, and the tension that she felt with
the concurrent disrupting that had to occur. It shows dreams and nightmares, building and tearing down, hopes and fears. It offers insights into
what Kim was feeling as she planned, organized, challenged, and reflected
upon classroom activity. Her piece serves as a segue into the broader view
of issues of teachers studying together that is presented in the following
chapters.

¤ ¤ ¤

Setbacks and Accomplishments, Tears and Joy
By Kimberly Ridder

The days prior to our research and development year were flooded
with ideas, dreams, hopes and more ideas. Kim L. and I spent hours
hovering over the computer, meticulously designing important forms
to be utilized in our emerging, developmentally appropriate classrooms. Feverishly, we labeled file after file to hold our precious crea-
tions: writers workshop, readers workshop, project groups, assessment,
math workshop ... you name it, we had a file to represent it.

The walls of our classrooms seemed extremely bare as we prepared
for the arrival of our students. No "cutesy" Susie's zoo posters this year;
our walls would soon be completely covered by the work of our budding
scientists, doctors, and artists. Bulletin boards that were usually covered with teacher-designed "Welcome to School!" signs were left nude
except for computer-typed signs that read, "Reserved for student
projects." Display windows were also empty except for thin layers of

summer dust nuzzled inside them. No longer would we spend countless days agonizing over what to exhibit in our windows. This year the windows belonged to the students!

As we excitedly described all of our plans to the principal, he shook his head in disbelief. He knew what we were like, every year jumping head first into something new. But this time he looked at us as if we had really gone off the deep end. "It all sounds wonderful," he offered, "I just hope that you are not disappointed, you have some pretty high expectations." Us, disappointed? Never! We just knew that this year would be different from all the others. We were certain that this year our students would come to school ready and able to participate in all of the fabulous opportunities we had to offer them. So what if there wasn't enough time in our busy schedule for a recess; the students wouldn't need it. They would be so immersed in our academic offerings that they would forget all about having a silly recess.

Everything was ready! The tables were sparkling from the thorough scrubbing they had received the day before, clutter- free except for the plastic coated name tags taped there to give each child a personal space, their home in the neighborhood we were trying to create.

As we anxiously awaited their arrival, we envisioned their small smiling faces and big bright eyes sparkling with excitement of the new year. We could almost feel the energy we knew would radiate from them as they walked through our classroom doors. When the bell rang, we jumped from our serene thoughts to greet our new friends. As the children walked through the door, we began to notice that they weren't quite as we had envisioned them only minutes before. Niomi's eyes were far from sparkling as she entered the room. The description of her parent's party the night before more than explained the reason why. Christina worked exhaustively to find her seat, carefully scrutinizing each of the perfectly written name tags. Finally she succumbed to the assistance of a peer, knowing she was unable to read even her own name. Casey's sunny personality shone through, when he informed us that he didn't have to listen to "No teachers," and that he hated reading and writing. And K— radiated energy all right, but the energy was directly aimed at the person with whom he had a conflict at breakfast. Interestingly enough, K— spent his first day of school in the office with Mr. Z., writing an apology note to the breakfast paraprofessional whose face he had spit in.

The rest of the day wasn't much better. We learned that Brandon enjoyed playing the game of hide and seek. The only problem was that the game wasn't played on the playground where it belonged, but where ever and whenever Brandon felt the urge. Hide and seek went on during bathroom breaks, in the library, during story time, and even in the middle of Mr. Z.'s "Ridgeway's Student Expectations" speech. It even turned into a game for the rest of the class, as they began to offer clues to Brandon's many creative hide-a-ways. "He's behind one of the coats outside Mrs. MacKenzie's room." "He's in the lost and found bin" or, "Mrs. Ridder, Brandon's on top of the stall in the boys' bathroom." Sure, we wanted our students to be creative, but this wasn't quite what we had in mind!

A student named T— also proved to be a unique challenge. Only months before, he had been adopted by an American family from an orphanage in a different country. The absence of any formal schooling and lack of exposure to language was immediately apparent because of his lacking social skills and inability to articulate even his own name. But because he was already 8 years old, it was decided that T— should skip kindergarten to be with kids more his own age. He was functioning at a developmental age of three. His eyes widened with excitement as he looked around the room: paint, animals, blocks, and a water table. Because he had never seen any of these things, it wasn't long before he was distracted by the stimulation of the environment. The rabbit, the blocks, and the art center were far more interesting than a teacher. T— did sit down once to join the rest of the group; it was only to get his lunch ticket. He was starving! Who wouldn't be after an activity-filled morning like his!

When the final school bell rang, Kim L. and I found ourselves collapsing into two of the miniature chairs in our completely dismantled classrooms. Our once sparkling clean tables were soiled with markers and crayons. Books were left laying carelessly throughout the rooms and crumpled pieces of paper lay littered on the floor. As we reviewed our day's plans, we noticed that nothing we had written down had gone as planned. All of our hard work and preparation seemed a travesty now.

When I looked at Kim L., I noticed a tear quietly rolling down her cheek. Words weren't necessary. I knew exactly what she was feeling and before long, I, too, was crying over all that seemed lost. Together, we began putting our newly designed files back in to the filing cabinet, to be pulled again at a more appropriate time.

To our despair, Mr. Z. was right. We were disappointed. He did not gloat, but instead was there to listen, comfort, and encourage us to continue on. He offered suggestions from many years of experience and sent us on our way, knowing that what we had experienced would be a lesson of a lifetime, a lesson we would not soon forget.

We experienced many setbacks during our research and development year, but we never completely let go of our dreams. Instead, we slowly and deliberately introduced our ideas to the children, but only when we felt that they were ready. Many of our ideas went exactly as planned, but far more were modified over and over again to meet the diverse needs of our students. Together with our kids, we experienced the pleasure of success and the difficulty of dealing with failure. Simultaneously, we learned how to celebrate our learning accomplishments; but more importantly, we learned how to laugh together at our mistakes and concede and adapt when things didn't go as planned.

Looking back at that first day, Kim L. and I are now able to laugh, remembering our detailed plans to apply at McDonald's or at Younker's to sell shoes. I remember thinking it impossible to even get through each day, nonetheless implement our extravagant R & D ideas! But now we are appreciative of everything (well, almost everything!) we had to endure in our pursuit of a more developmentally appropriate program. All the past year's memories, still freshly engraved in our minds, will remain with us as we again begin to plan for new students and a new school year, a school year that is fast approaching.

Chapter 9

Becoming Inquirers

¤ ¤ ¤

To reconceive writing and reading means bumping up against a personal definition of literacy, and against a school's definition of curriculum and evaluation. To reconceive teaching means crashing against a personal autobiography, often one that holds old stories of literacy failure. To reconceive learning means wandering around in time and space, colliding with personal stories of learning that happen in places outside of school. Those stories need to be told and heard.

—Sunstein (1994, p. 230)

Members of the study group dealt with the many aspects of "bumping up against" self, curriculum, and life in school as we met and they worked at composing and disrupting themselves, their relationships with others, curriculum, and the ethos of Ridgeway. The telling of their individual stories, and the viewing of events as stories, occurred within the study group. Having looked at individual teachers' inquiry in chapters 2 through 7, in this chapter I broaden the discussion, focusing on the group. Readers interested in a more detailed description of the pragmatics of our group should read Appendix B, in which I discuss how we began, organized, and ended our sessions. The focus in this chapter is on how the group initiated its inquiry activity.

INQUIRY IS RELATIONAL

Inquiry is relational because it involves being in relationships with others in many different ways. At Ridgeway Elementary School, teachers, who are friends, supported and challenged each other; they asked each other questions. They supported their students in inquiry. The students had relationships with each other. The children's inquiry groups had collective relationships with each other, intragroup relationships, and relationships with the adults that helped them engage in inquiry. There are also vicarious relationships through inquiry, such as the relationships that children in one class had with teachers other than their own when those children's inquiry was the subject of discussion in our group of teachers.

There were old friendships and new ones. There were moments of feeling included, excluded, excited, confused, confident, and doubtful. The very fabric of inquiry is woven with relationships. Relationships, the social setting of learning, constitute the context. We may be studying a child's reading, our own response to an article or book we've read, or trying to figure out how to make our city something a child will be curious about, and we are always studying, intuitively or explicitly, our relationships. It is within relationships that we can be curious, improvise, discover, and create. Bateson (1989) says, "Each of us has worked by improvisation, discovering the shape of our creation along the way, rather than pursuing a vision already defined" (p. xv). Members of the group composed themselves, relationally to and with others, as we initiated inquiry.

INITIATING INQUIRY

The quote from Bateson's *Composing a Life* is consistent with the processes the teachers lived as they composed themselves (and I composed myself) as inquirers and supported the children at Ridgeway in becoming inquiring students. But we began by reading, not thinking about systematic studies of classrooms. We read pieces by Crowell (1993), Perrone (1991), complete issues of Primary Voices (Reimer, Stephens, & Smith, 1993), Wells et al. (1993), Dewey (1938), Rief (1991), McLaren (1989), Katz (1994), parts of the ASCD yearbook (Beane, 1995), and a group of articles that focused on inclusion. In addition, individuals read Avery (1993), Graves (1991), Short and Harste with Burke (1996), Harwayne (1992), and Calkins (1994) and shared their learning through book talks and discussions of ways in which the works influenced classroom activity.

An individual's sharing might emanate from points at which she disagreed with the author, agreed with the author, discovered something that she didn't know or hadn't thought of, or because she resonated with something the author said. For example, as Kim R. read more and more of Avery (1993), her excitement increased. She had found another first-grade teacher who was learning that children need to construct their learning and their learning environment. She said:

> Well this is one example; they are talking about room arrangement and how when you have your room totally ready and, you know, the kids haven't had any say in what you do. You have the desks here and you have all the things up on the walls. And everything's ready and beautiful and she [Avery, 1993] said "When tempted to do too much, I remember Lisa, a first-grader from years ago who one day in late March pointed to a word taped to a window and asked 'Mrs. Avery, why is that word on the window?'

> The word 'window', I taped it there and obviously Lisa had no idea what it said or why it was there. The children must understand the purpose of everything in the classroom and so now what goes up are items connected to classroom learning." (Transcript from study group session)

This is reminiscent of the piece Kim R. wrote as part of chapter 8 in which she describes planning the first day of school without the children and winding up the day dissatisfied, confused, and overwhelmed.

The readings were more than informative. They provided support for the teachers as they found *both* other teachers who are learners *and* researchers' work that encouraged them as they changed their practices. As our reading and conversations progressed, it became apparent that some members were already engaged in inquiry. They were approaching their classrooms as sources of questions and curiosities, so I suggested that we engage in some type of formal study of the classrooms. An increasing number of teachers are engaging in such work:

> ... veteran teachers are conducting school-based inquiry, evaluating programs, and studying their own practices—with one another and with university-based colleagues. (Darling-Hammond, 1995, p. 7)

There were feelings of excitement and terror at the thought of engaging in inquiry. After all, wasn't *research* something that was often put before teachers by someone else as evidence of what they needed to do; they hadn't thought of contributing to existing knowledge. Having met for a few months, the reading and conversations inspired group members to give it a try. We each had interests and we had a group that was committed to discuss things, curious minds that wanted to wander and wonder.

During our first few meetings as a formal group of inquiring minds, many ideas were explored as ways of addressing our interests. Kim L. reported that her work as a teacher had changed:

> This is more work and it's harder. We don't spend our time cutting stuff out for the kids to put together. They [the children] are doing a lot more thinking about what it is they are doing and where they are going. (Transcript from study group session)

Even though each teacher was just beginning her research focus, classroom activity was changing. The teachers' roles were changing because they initiated the systematic collection of data, brought it to sessions to discuss, and left sessions with ideas and more questions. Liz said that since she and Linda began the self-study of their literacy teaching lives, she saw children in a different light. "No more cutsey stuff," she explained; her children were studying important (to kids) topics. "Two years ago, I wouldn't have said all kids can learn," Liz said at one of our sessions. Now that her children were identifying areas to study, they were investing time, owning their work (Atwell, 1987), and experiencing authentic learning, and Liz was seeing them all learn.

Looking back, I found that our early sessions were characterized by frequent changes of focus across individuals and topics. I wrote in my journal:

> I have felt this way before. I think it's because teachers just don't get enough time together to talk to each other. Our group reminds me of a bullet being fired in a cave; it ricochets all over. Our conversations seem like that. It's hard to focus on one person because so many have something to say, something to question, something to wonder about. Can this be helpful? Does this support teacher's inquiry. I'm not sure. I have to wait and see. (Journal entry)

The teachers began bringing questions and data to our meetings; data came in all forms. Kim Z. said that she wasn't sure how to keep track of the classroom activities. Mona brought work that her students had done. Kim R. and Kim L. brought a letter they received from Judy Graves, a speaker they heard at a workshop (see Appendix A), and the response they drafted. There were writing samples, readers on audio tapes, and anecdotal records. We had begun. And things became more complex.

Inquiry and the Roots of Disruption

Kim Z.'s focus on a specific area of study that her students identified (life in the Arctic) led to our first discussion of this work as something that affects others in the school (like the wedge discussed in the introduction to this section). Typically, the second-grade team all studied the same thing at the same time, using the exact same materials. When the team's preplanned Arctic unit was supposed to have been completed, Kim Z.'s students were curious and wanted to continue. Kim Z. told our group that the district "garbology" unit had arrived from the science consultant at the district office and that she had told her team that she would not be doing it in her classroom. She was anxious because a departure from team activity, such as this, had not been done before. At this point, she was wondering if the rest of her team would decide that it was acceptable to study different things at the same time (across classrooms). This was the first report to our group that some of our work may have disrupted the context, in this case the second-grade team. The rest of the second grade team was concerned about this departure from the team norm; they would not depart from the team's plans.

Kim Z. looked beyond her team and began wondering about how some big ideas all fit together:

... from my mind and my readings: whole language, constructivism, and other words. Are these the same thing, all over and over again, or are they different? (Transcript from study group session)

Later in the same session, as Kim Z. described some activity within her classroom, she did not resolve her question but she realized that the children had truly engaged. They were "taking ownership [and] responsibility for their own learning" (Cambourne, 1995, p. 185). Kim Z. smiled and said, "Ahhhhh, I've created learners." She meant that she and her students found new energy and enthusiasm for learning and that calling what she was doing by a certain label ("constructivism" or "whole language") was not the same as naming a process to signify the understanding of the complexity and affect of such work. This means that Kim Z. understood that she was composing herself as a teacher-inquirer, the children were composing themselves as learners, and that these acts disrupted the way things were at Ridgeway.

Composing a Place to Think

Enthusiasm spread throughout the group as individuals reported on learning by themselves and their students. This seemed new and different because of the focus on teacher and students as learners, rather than seeing classrooms as a place that enacted curricular guidelines imposed from outside.

As the year progressed, our group meetings felt like data analysis sessions. Individuals' data became sophisticated as they brought photos, elaborate anecdotal notes, videotapes, and quotes of child language. For example, the group heard of Kim L.'s first-grade children locating a life-sized skeleton; they had labeled all of the bones with sticky notes and were tracing each others' bodies and drawing organs inside themselves. They were making plans to get a calf heart from a supermarket. I worked to locate articles and books for us to read and learn about other teachers who were engaging in inquiry. Mona moved the group into some philosophy when she presented some of the foundational ideas of Montessori (1966). The group read, wrote, thought, philosophized, and reported to and with each other.

Our beginning sessions tended to move along from person to person as each had some "air time" to explore and think out loud. I wondered if we were glossing over important issues and, at the same time, felt the urgency for each group member to have time to speak. I wasn't sure how to resolve this tension between each person talking a little bit and the need for individuals to have extended air time to think aloud. Smaller groups seemed to be one possible answer, but the group did not want to separate; they liked being together and pretty much demanded that we stay as one whole group in spite of frequent multiple discussions.

The tension between many individual speakers having a brief turn and focusing on one person in depth was tough to resolve. Kim R. helped resolve this as we began one session in early March:

> You guys, I asked this before, but I never really got any help, and I really need help [we had, apparently, moved too quickly to the next person at our last meeting] ... I have all this stuff and I have to organize this into a meaningful way for me and for others to look and understand what I've done, and I don't know how to do it, and this helps me maybe think ... I have it ... you know, I have the whole thing day by day of what we did ... I want to sit down and do this [put it all together in writing], but I don't know what to do. This is kind of like what I can go back to, to look and to say, "Oh, this is what we did this day, and this is what I said to them, and this is what some of them responded with." ... I also want it to be so I can go back and say, "Okay, on this day, and I can use that quote that a child used" ... I've got another one of these [notebooks full of kids' work and quotes she collected], and I'm starting my third, and I'm starting to get overwhelmed and I need to do something with it.... Today, I wrote ... "They said let's go to the library and find some books." "What kind of books are we going to look for," I asked. "Books on caves and volcanoes," said Teresa. I mean, it's coming out more, you know, but I wanted to write it, I was tired of waiting. I couldn't wait until after school to write so I wrote. I thought I'm not getting into this, I need to write this down before I forget ... (Transcript from study group session)

Then, we focused on Kim R. for a full hour. That evening I wrote in my journal:

> Kim Ridder apologized for taking so much time and said that her questions from last time were not answered. We spent an hour listening to and helping her with how to write all this up. She has a "mountain" [her word] of material: kids' work, her notes, her journal, her scripting of kids' working together, kids' portfolios. We discussed who the audience was; who was she writing this for? What did she want? What did she want others to know? She did wonder if others thought this a waste of time, but it was so powerful—about writing and the self and how to put those together. She wants every journal entry in there.... She was going to start to write something and that she wasn't going to read anything besides her own writing for next time.

Kim R. had changed the group. At our next session, she read what she had written. We spent considerable time listening, commenting, asking questions—living the lives of a writer's support group.

The following week, Kim Z. took the floor and read what she had written, perhaps inspired by Kim R.'s commitment to write and take a bigger piece of time to be the focus of the group. Subsequent sessions tended to focus on one or two people's writing and thinking. We listened, supported, questioned, cheered on, and pushed each other to write because we were finding that our writing was indeed "shaping our thinking" (Langer & Applebee, 1987). We were not just beginning any more, but were deep into what it means to be inquirers.

The teachers were composing themselves as inquirers; they made the shift to more concentrated focus on individuals' work as they expressed the need for that time. We didn't discuss readings as much, though folks continued to read. They composed themselves as a forum in which to present ongoing inquiry and the writing that originated from it. They disrupted what teacher-learning looks like; they would not be empty vessels waiting to be filled. They were composers of knowledge, a role that involved a fundamental disruption of how teachers are supposed to learn.

COMPOSING OUR RESEARCH

The teachers were growing in ways that were similar to a maturing relationship. They were learning about intensity, passion, and depth of a sustained commitment. Each member of the group decided how to collect, organize, and re-present what was occurring daily in their classrooms and, as well, some of what had already gone by, unrecorded. Kim Z. reflected this feeling:

> Well, I'm still writing on that … [the children studying the Arctic]. But, see, now this time I'm trying to journal more [the children studying the zoo], where, you know, day by day…. the observations,… totally a journal, with my photos inserted,… Because I don't know if I can go back and remember everything that we did [in the Arctic study]. (Transcript from study group session)

This kind of thinking aloud encouraged others to take risks in their thinking and in their practice. The group supported members in their feelings of having been granted permission to try new things, as Mona said:

> [the group has given] me permission to do all the things that I kept wanting to do but was sort of looked at aside like you shouldn't do it. Even though it very much is part of her [Montessori's] philosophy. (Transcript from study group session)

As they became more systematic about data and writing, they felt the full range of emotions that writers feel: angry, scared, annoyed, frustrated, threatened, embarrassed, amazed, empowered, strong, serious, foolish, and more (Dillard, 1989; Goldberg, 1986). Mona expressed some of these feelings, helping all feel a bit more at ease in sharing their work:

> … when I first began writing this it … was like I was out to prove something to someone. And then I started reading The Art of Teaching Writing [Calkins, 1994]. And I thought, "Why am I writing that way? I don't like to write that way." So the second Saturday morning, I got up and I wrote the next thing which is what I'm going to share with you and I don't know what I'm going to do with this part yet. And this part isn't as long as that part so we're all okay. [Laughter] But I think this is going to

lead into what I will write at the end of the session. (Transcript from study group session)

Mona's words were significant to us because they demonstrated the anxiety, the tentativeness, and the desire to keep going. Our group was making a shift; as the teachers found patterns, composed new ideas, and were surprised at the nature of inquiry activity in their classrooms and in their own lives, they were writing more. As writers, they wanted a support group for that activity. Their writing was an important part of the inquiry process; it was one vehicle that supported the composing and presentation of their learning.

A Writers' Support Group

I suggested that we could write up our inquiry so that it would be available in some form that other teachers could read. Jane thought this would be useful in presenting the year's work to the board of education as a way of being accountable. I wondered about other teacher groups that might be interested in the work and nature of this group. The relationships and connections that the teachers in this group were making were worth sharing; they relied on each other, looked forward to seeing each other; and they wanted to partake in each other's thinking. Their relationships may be demonstrated by Kim Z.'s thought, one sleepless night: "And you know what? I laid awake thinking [about writing about kids] the other night at 3:00 in the morning. I should have just called you [to Kim R]."

The teachers were sharing pieces, in progress, during the weekdays between our meetings. As Mona was leaving class one evening, Kim Z. turned to her with a comment about her writing:

Kim Z: You're just so insightful and reflective.
Mona: Oh that's nice of you to say. I feel comfortable in sharing with this group, you know, that's really nice and I love what I'm learning this year. I'm learning a lot.... Because I have help and I have people say this is good, try this. That's really neat for me. This is a wonderful experience. (Transcript from study group session)

The group had, by April of our first year together, reached a point of honesty and sincerity that allowed members to question, name, and respond to each other and issues of life and teaching at Ridgeway with honesty, caring, and the intensity of emotion that often accompanies "interwoven conversations" (Newman, 1991). Still, with each successive meeting, we worked to check up on each others' feelings as it became evident that we were taking more and more risks. Linda's feelings about reading her piece express the growing willingness to take risks and the vulnerability attached to it:

> Oh I was a wreck. It was really hard for me to share it because it's just so much a part of me. It's a part of my heart and if you wouldn't have liked it, I would have really been hurt. You know, it's really a part of me and I don't know, I just … (Transcript from study group session)

Mona explained the way we began to resonate with each other in terms of her understanding of Montessori:

> And I really believe when you go into Montessori, each person, like we do in this group,… you get out of it what you're going to get out of it and that's what you end up doing is sharing of yourself with others. And so that's what we're all doing. (Transcript from study group session)

The group helped each other face the difficulties of teaching and changing, even supporting each other when it was decided not to face an issue, such as Kim Z.'s unresolved feelings toward her team:

> **Kim Z:** And how do I feel about it? I mean I still have very mixed feelings about the feelings I get from my team right now, you know? I don't know if I'm ready to evaluate that. You know what I mean?
>
> **Rick:** Yeah, well it just might not be time to write about that.
>
> **Linda:** It would be hard to write it if you're not sure yourself. (Transcript from study group session)

As the first year of researching and thinking together progressed, the group's seriousness was reflected in its intensity, thinking, researching, and analyzing. We evolved from a researcher-inquiry support group to a researcher-inquiry-writer support group. Our added function, writing, made our time together much more complex as we dealt with issues within our lives, within our classrooms, within the school and district, within the group, and the writing that seemed to add another dimension to the nature of inquiry. We discussed the idea of portfolios as systematic collections and demonstrations of classroom activities (Graves & Sunstein, 1993) but decided to write a book because we became intrigued with what such a book might contain and how it would portray the group. The thought of being published re-energized the group. Readers need to know that the first and second proposals for this book were rejected. Our third draft was accepted provisionally, and we made major changes to reach this book.

With the increased focus on writing, group members who chose not to write were facing difficult decisions. Any member, whether writing or not, could and did present and discuss classroom data. The study group still functioned as a thought collective, and we engaged each other in conversations rooted in writing and thinking. Of course, not all groups need to write; our group needed to write to learn. Most important for any group, though, is safety.

Safety for Writers.   Once Kim R. and Kim Z. shared their writing and took an extended period of time to get responses to it, others in the group also took risks and began to share. As the group evolved into a safe setting, members could deal with the difficult issues each faced in writing. They faced how hard it is to be a writer:

> **Kim Z:**   Really hard. It's so hard that I say, forget it for the night, I'll do it tomorrow.
>
> **Mona:**   It is scary.
>
> **Kim Z:**   I mean I worked from 6 until 10 o'clock last night, reading, going back and reading things, trying to figure out looking back at pictures and I didn't spend a lot of time writing. I don't feel like ... since I only have 3 pages ... but I kept changing things, I thought, "No, that doesn't go there," and I don't know, it's hard. And I didn't expect it to be so ... you know, I didn't expect, you know, I don't know. (Transcript from study group session)

And the teachers persevered through the difficulties of becoming writers because of the need to express what they were doing and because they supported each other in taking risks as writers, sharing that writing, and listening to feedback from each other. Kim Z. said:

> No, because I thought about that because I thought about putting this stuff in about working with Kevin [her student teacher]—having the support of another colleague right in my room ... Because really, I seriously don't know if I would have done it by myself, you know, without him right there saying, you know.... (Transcript from study group session)

And there was plenty of encouragement:

> **Kim L.:**   Seriously, do you want me to read this cause it's not too good?
>
> **Mona:**   Yes, yes, yes, read it.
>
> **Kim R.:**   It's not very good.
>
> **Kim Z.:**   Yes, it is.
>
> **Kim R.:**   It's not very good and it's really rough. I told you it was kind of embarrassing.
>
> **Liz:**   Oh we know it will be terrible but share it with us anyway. [joking voice]

Kim Z.:	It's good. She's such a perfectionist.
Kim R.:	Yeah, talk about it … [to Kim Z., another perfectionist]
Kim Z.:	Read it, read it. [Kim R. reads her piece] (Transcript from study group session)

Kim L. wanted to be encouraged, but didn't want to hear encouragement that was not rooted in her piece, as is shown in her response to someone saying she should read her piece because it was good:

Kim L.:	Mine's real rough. It is, I mean, it's just a quick thing.
Unidentified:	It's good, read.
Kim L.:	You haven't even looked at it. (Transcript from study group session)

She wanted the piece accepted as tentative, rough, and not viewed as good solely because she was reading it. It truly had to be heard and, she expected, in some way valued and evaluated by the group. She wanted and feared criticism. She wanted it because she wanted her writing to be clear, crisp, and interesting. She feared it because: the piece might not be good; it may be boring; and the host of other reasons each of us harbor as we fear rejection of our thinking, our writing, and our selves.

And slowly, over time, each teacher in her own way began sharing her thinking, her data or evidence, and sometimes her writing. They took risks, asked for what they needed from the group, and realized that we had created a safe forum for this work. As Kim R. said:

> I'm not scared anymore. I used to feel scared about bringing my writing to you guys, but I don't feel scared any more…. It doesn't hurt my feelings or anything. At first you kind of think, "Oh God, they hate it," but it's not that way. (Transcript from study group session)

One nagging question was whether or not they wanted anyone beyond the group to read their writing. The original passion about touching other teachers with their words became too real as folks began completing pieces. Kim R. said, "I don't know them and I don't know if I feel comfortable sharing…." They overcame that; here they are, their voices in print. But it was not easy. Even as we readied things to make copies just within our group, the one teacher who does not want to be in print expressed hesitancy about sharing anything in writing. She never shared any writing with our group during the year she was a group member, although she had a crate full of data that she discussed with the group. At one meeting, trying to encourage her to write, I said:

> You can tell people how hard this was. You can write: "I want you to know how hard this was, I did this, and then I did this, and then we did this in the group and then I

did this on my own, and then I had this anxiety attack for 3 weeks" … and retell that story to share your journey. That way is probably one of the most honest things we can do, because [as a reader, a teacher would] read through and it's like, "everything's so wonderful in her class and how'd she write such a great book?" [Thinking of themselves, they would wonder], "where's the anxiety here?" I don't see any problem with putting that in…. (Transcript from study group session)

Our support for one another didn't always work, as in the case of this teacher.

Publishing.   As we wrote, the idea of being published thrilled and threatened. Liz wondered if her piece would be rejected while all the others got in. "It's all or none," Kim Z. told her. We were in this together. Writing the proposal for our book was a burst of energy. We were busy writing abstracts and a table of contents, and planning what it might look like.

When the first book proposal was rejected, it hurt. It sent us spiraling down, as we read the reviews as though they were razor blades cutting to the core of our inquiring lives. But we worked to convince each other that it was worth it to keep writing and that the reviewers had invested time and energy to help us frame our work so that it was more useful. We also considered other ways to publish our work such as district presentations, local and national conventions, and more.

The teachers were getting a lot out of the writing, whether it was their own or another group member's: it taught them about themselves, it was affecting their relationship with each other and their understanding of children, and it was shaping curriculum decisions and enactment. It helped them compose themselves and helped make sense of the disruption that they felt within, among, and beyond the group, and it did the same things for me.

We met after the summer, following our first year together as a study group, and an interesting phenomenon had developed, one that I should have anticipated. The teachers had lost energy in their inquiry projects. Those projects focused on the last school year and they were focusing on the next school year and didn't want to relive the previous one by trying to write a chapter. We met and discussed. Later, I wrote in my journal:

I realized that the group worked when we had a structure imposed from the outside. The school year was one type of structure. It seemed that we needed a commitment that was more contractual in nature, but this is power over. I need to rethink this. Kim Z says that earning course credit makes it all worth while. This may be quite accurate. Credit towards a degree is a payoff (even if it's a course that they pay for). I don't find this unreasonable at all.
Or, perhaps teachers want to focus on the current year, regardless of credit. After all, I know the urgency I feel for the courses I am presently teaching; it would be hard to write about a course that I taught last year.
Teachers' writing may need to be a lot quicker than I ever thought. Perhaps it needs to be done during the school year or immediately in the summer afterwards, otherwise

it will fall to me to be the major voice. Perhaps this means that books are not that feasible. Perhaps teachers would rather write for professional journals; it sure psyched up our group when I published their work in the Nebraska Language Arts Bulletin (Meyer, 1996b). [The Bulletin is a state-level journey that I edit; I included shortened versions of some of the teachers' pieces in one issue.]   Maybe presentations at conventions is the way to go, though travel money for teachers is nil. This just is not easy work.... (Journal entry)

By the beginning of January 1996, we were back on the writing path because our book proposal was accepted, the new school year was off and running, so that anxiety was reduced, and we found we missed the thought collective as a place to share thinking and writing. Individuals were making important decisions about their written work. Liz and Linda were questioning the way their piece sounded "so dry and boring; it's just a timeline," Linda said. They were excited to move on in their writing, and curious about what it might look like. We helped each other with revisions. Kim R. was almost finished with her piece from the previous year and felt motivated to finish it quickly; her inertia encouraged others. Kim L. found Year 1 to be a good "warm up" and wanted to systematically study one facet of her classroom during the 1995–1996 school year and contribute that to the book as her students' next steps in inquiry. Mona said, "I'm writing again; it feels good." Even though the teachers in the group were in very different places in their writing, one thing became quite clear: When we consider all the constraints and pressures in teachers' lives, it becomes more apparent why it is not easy for them to write.

Other Ways of Being Heard

The group became quite popular in the summers between school years. Members of the group presented at district-level workshops. We (Meyer et al., 1996) had a proposal accepted and presented at the annual Whole Language Umbrella conference in St. Paul, Minnesota. Kim Z. did not attend because she had a baby. Kim R. and I presented at the 1996 convention of the National Council of Teachers of English (Meyer & Ridder, 1996). I also presented part of our work at the National Reading Conference (Meyer, 1996c). The teachers' work was being made public, and in that sense it was being published.

Life in a school, a personal life, the thrill and interest of a new school year and the waning interest in the previous school year, and many other issues contributed to the viability of our group. In some ways, a new school year called for new beginnings, for "re-becoming" inquirers. As the second year began, the group's dynamics for staying together began to interest me. My understanding of what held us together is presented in the next chapter.

Chapter 10

The Dynamics of Sustaining a Study Group

◻ ◻ ◻

To free curiosity; to permit individuals to go charging off in new directions dictated by their own interests; to unleash the sense of inquiry; to open everything to questioning and exploration; to recognize that everything is in the process of change—here is an experience I can never forget.

—Rogers (1969, p. 105)

Our group worked much as the unforgettable experience that Rogers describes. We met every Wednesday, regardless of the multitude of obligations that the teachers had. We were excited by "new directions," supportive of each other as we searched for and learned about those directions, and "unleashed" inquiry as we composed ourselves as learners with the students of Ridgeway and each other. Eventually, members felt safe to question each other about anything; and they did that.

You may notice that I sometimes refer to the group as "we"; I do this in instances where I am aware of being an insider, a co-learner, a cotraveler with my colleagues in the group. Other times, as a resource and a researcher, I sense myself studying the group, including my role in it. This is the tension between being an insider and an outsider. I return to this issue later in the book, but do want readers to know that it is something I want to problematize in teacher study groups. There are other "insider/outsider" issues, intimated throughout the book, that I also discuss later.

PARTS KEEPING THE WHOLE TOGETHER

On the same page that Rogers describes the exhilarating nature of such an experience with a group, he also notes that he does not always achieve this with a group. In this chapter, I present some of the ways of our group, to

161

shed light on how the group became a sustaining thought collective that we "can never forget."

Our conversations were at the heart of our group, making it a forum for reflection and passionate discussions; they were a place to experience the freedom to learn and to question and to challenge. Group members focused on issues, difficult situations, and new ideas. They expressed and grew from their sorrows and joys, both personal and professional.

This was not the first group of teachers to find that change takes place in a context; others have found the specificity of context (Clandinin, Davies, Hogan, & Kennard, 1993; Cochran-Smith & Lytle, 1993; Goswami & Stillman, 1987). There were, at Ridgeway, three broad areas related to the context of our work: individual or personal issues, issues within our group, and issues that related to the whole school or district. We devoted some of each group session to these parts of life at Ridgeway because: (a) individuals were feeling and expressing the intensity of change; (b) the presence of the group was felt by individuals and by the group, and members wanted to discuss this; and (c) we were disrupting some of the regularities of the school and needed to discuss that, too. Had this been a typical staff development or university course, the time devoted to these issues might have been considerably less because teachers from different schools tend to summarize, gloss over, or choose not to disclose "troubles at home" (meaning their home school). The teachers needed to face these issues as part of the context in which they undertook inquiry. Naming the issues that helped members (Fine, 1987) led to a deeper understanding of the context. With that enhanced understanding, we could make better sense of just what we were composing and disrupting, its influence on our colleagues, and the changing school climate.

In the first three sections of this chapter, I discuss individual, group, and school issues that our group faced; dealing with those issues helped the group bond over time, as safety increased, and supported the groups continuance over time. Then, following a discussion of the principal's role, the rest of the chapter focuses on the group's desire to learn and the ways in which that desire sustained the group.

Individuals' Issues Related to Life at Ridgeway

Kim Z. was upset that she was disrupting the usual activity within her team. She didn't want to follow the curricular schedule that the team built; she wanted curriculum composed with her children (Short & Burke, 1991) and wanted it to have an inquiry base (Short & Harste with Burke, 1996). Her decision to move to first grade affected her professional and personal relationships with the second-grade team members. Recall that Kim Z. was not the only one facing individual issues. Liz, on the third-grade team, also experienced frustration, but not to the point of the team physically splitting apart:

> I was getting real frustrated.... And I can remember one team member going, "This is just too much for me, I can't do everything [you're asking of me].... " She just ranted and raved and then it was over, you know? But she felt comfortable enough with us to just rant and rave and cuss a little bit.... And then we ... kind of processed that. (Transcript from study group session)

The group members used meetings as a forum in which to make sense of what happened to them in relation to other faculty at the school as things changed. Perhaps what happened is best explained by Lester and Onore (1990) because our collective action was influencing the school:

> The possibility for change in this school [in their study] was intricately tied to both empowerment of teachers to initiate changes though a commitment to new ways of seeing teaching and learning as well as the involvement of an administrator in an intellectual understanding and commitment to the implications of those changes.... when experimentation begins to occur in many isolated classrooms and when experimentation begins to reveal the impossibility of reconciling institutional demands with individual goals and to exaggerate the inadequacies and contradictions of an eclectic approach to learning, the individual teacher's decisions or choices simultaneously begin conditioning the larger school community. Collective action and change on the level of teacher's worldviews can come to influence the institution. Rather than having a teacher's choices controlled by the institutional practice, the institutional practice can come to reflect the collective beliefs and practices of teachers. (pp. 190–191)

Mr. Z., discussed later in this chapter, was allowing the group to meet; Jane, a district level administrator, was supportive of it and vocal about her support. And the group was just large enough to "begin conditioning the larger school community" by disrupting individuals and teams. It was essential that the teachers talked to make sense of what transpired; they could feel the weight, at times, and needed a place to process what was occurring.

Kim R. ventilated about the member of her team who "has put up a real wall. She's been against us from the beginning and she's just bound and determined that what she's doing is not projects [inquiry]." Kim R. and Kim L. struggled with the tension they felt. At a team meeting, Kim L. asked the teacher to talk about something that she was doing with her students, and after school, at a study group meeting, Kim R. said (to Kim L.), "And it was good that you got her to share today about some things that she does." In spite of this, there was a growing sense of insider-ness (those teachers in the study group) and outsider-ness (those not); although we did maintain an open door policy, we received no visitors or newcomers except for a one-time visit from the computer teacher. We spent time at each meeting listening to individuals as they made sense of the changes they were feeling. As individuals changed, they found that their view of their teams changed as well. The composing of self was, in turn, sometimes disrupting to the teams to the point, in Kim Z.'s situation, of asking to be transferred. And that disruption underscored how composing of self is disrupting to self because of the discomfort that can accompany growth.

Our group came to care about individual members on very personal levels, too, as evidenced by our regard for Linda as her husband got sicker:

> **Rick:** Are other folks coming?
> **Liz:** Where is everybody?
> **Rick:** How's Linda's husband?
> **Kim Z.:** She brought him to the hospital today.
> **Kim L.:** I saw her leaving this morning.
> **Kim Z.:** And that she's going to be gone the rest of this week. He … basically, he wasn't eating, so they brought him … she brought him into the hospital, and now she has to basically be there to give him food, to regulate his intake so she's going to stay home and do that with him … and if he doesn't start …
> **Kim L.:** Is it because of that chemo and stuff they got in him, or …
> **Kim Z.:** He just doesn't want to …
> **Kim L.:** Just doesn't want to.
> **Kim Z.:** Yea, I think he's just so exhausted, he just … (Transcript from study group session)

We came to know about each others' spouses, our families' school lives, their health, problem students, and worries about placements for the next school year. We empathized with Kim L. as she struggled to complete her divorce proceedings, continue to teach, raise two children, and be present for our group.

We spent time making sense of the new leadership at Ridgeway because it was a safer environment than it had been previously. Our first year together as a study group was Mr. Z.'s second year as principal of Ridgeway. I place reactions to him and understandings of him in this section on individual issues because the previous principal affected individuals in our group quite differently. Some felt neutral about the former principal, others celebrated the arrival of Mr. Z. because of the pain they felt during the prior administration. Kim Z. had a difficult time with the principal that was at Ridgeway before Mr. Z. That principal made Kim Z. feel vulnerable and led to her being hospitalized with an ulcer during one spring break. The teachers in our group reminded each other of the change as a way of stressing that they didn't feel as vulnerable as they had previously:

Kim Z.: I mean there's differences in the building and yet … I think most of us get along fairly well.

Rick: I … you can correct me if I'm wrong because you all live here, but I *used* to think that leadership had nothing to do with that and that the principal … it's like teachers did what they wanted and we're all such independent souls and just knowing you … I wasn't here when the former principal was here … but just knowing you and seeing your difference as far as the way you view yourself and what you do and other experiences that I've had with leadership, I'm just starting to feel that leadership is so important. I hate to admit how important it is because I want to think of the independent teacher being …

Liz: … but you've got to have that support behind you because that person controls your job.

Rick: Yeah.

Kim Z.: Well, and I got called on something today that ended up being somewhat of a misunderstanding but I didn't feel like I was getting in trouble, you know what I mean? I felt like he [Mr. Z.] needed to bring this to my attention as a professional, here's what I need to say to you, what do you need to say to me? Okay, I respect you for that, we're okay, smile and I'll say hi to you still in the hallway later on and you know it has no bearing on your job …

Liz: And no tears.

Kim Z.: Right and not tears, my stomach doesn't hurt, you know.

Rick: You used to come to class [as a graduate student 2 years ago in an on-campus course that I taught] and I thought you'd been punished and sent to your room.

Kim Z.: I was in the hospital over a spring break with an ulcer one spring because of it. I mean it's a lot different. It makes a ton of difference.

Rick: … a principal changes a school … the tone of the whole building. I hate to admit that! But it's being really borne out.

Kim Z.: Right. (Transcript from study group session)

I do not want to paint too rosy of a picture because every principal makes decisions that hurt people. The point here is that our group helped individuals live their lives, and make sense of their lived experiences, at Ridgeway. I may be stating the obvious, but this group function, addressing each as an individual, helped sustain the group.

And, within that context, we could never forget that "we are who we teach and we teach who we are" (Meyer, 1996a). The teachers' personal lives, saturating their teaching, reading, writing, inquiring, and learning, were part of the group. Kim Z. summarized it quite well:

> I think that's true though. Now that you say that, I never really thought about that but maybe that's why this year is better for me too in a sense. I mean there for a while, my life was just a wreck, I mean, relationship-wise and stuff and now I've been married a year and kind of calmed down, you know. Things are okay that way. You know, you kind of wonder if that [personal life] makes a difference. (Transcript from study group session)

And we didn't neglect to celebrate our successes. As Linda said:

> You know it's the way to do it when you have kids come to school everyday and they're disappointed when Friday they can't come. Monday we made that announcement. "Friday we have another day off?"
> "Can't we come?" [the kids asked]. You know, and I had quite a few. I know I'm doing something right. I never had that before this year. I knew I'm doing something right when I had those kinds of comments [from kids]. (Transcript from study group session)

Mona was the most convinced that things at Ridgeway were always happening for the best, for the children and the teachers. She believed that the children sensed this as much as she did.

> It is [a great place to teach], and I know if it [a day at school] was just horrible I could come to any of you and it would be okay. And … the kids are so antsy this time of year, it was a rainy day, was it Monday? We walked the long way around back to our classroom, by our new classroom in back [Mona's multiage classroom would be in a different room next year], and I said, "We're going on a detective walk, and I just want you to think about what you're seeing and then be able to write it down when you get back to class." And this is what Ben wrote [reading Ben's piece]:
> "We went on a detective walk around the school. I saw ladders outside. When we returned I realized that some things are the same."
> I said, "Ben, clarify that. What exactly do you mean by that?"
> He means our classroom and the other classrooms in the school building. And he wrote, "All of the classrooms do studies, all teachers try to keep their children warm." (Transcript from study group session)

Individuals within our group sensed that the group tried to keep them warm.

Our group also relied on each other for some of the nitty gritty of teaching. For example, one member wanted to know if it was possible to have an inquiry group of one, because only one child wanted to research a particular area (see Kim L.'s discussion, chapter 4); another wanted support in changing the furniture arrangement in her room. As the arena for thinking became safer and safer, individuals brought an increasingly wider range of individual questions to the group.

The teachers helped each other learn to listen to the students to learn about how they might use time to meet the students' needs. When an issue was brought up, individuals offered subtle and not-so-subtle different points of view. We had the contrast that Mona could offer from a Montessori perspective, Jane's views on attachment (the subject of her masters thesis some years ago), Kim R. and Kim L. on moving literal and figurative walls, and more. Kim Z. expressed the support she felt:

> Well, and I know that I wouldn't have been as successful as I have been with what's going on in my classroom if I didn't have these guys [Kim R. and Kim L.], because they've been doing it for a whole semester, and I feel brave enough finally to say, "I can do what they're doing," you know, but they've tried out, they've tried some of the management things, the procedure ... I mean, I can go to them and ask, "Did you do this, will it work?," you know, and that's helpful. (Transcript from study group session)

Our group was the thought collective in which we discussed, agonized over, mourned, and celebrated what individuals were composing and disrupting. Individuals' issues overflowed into issues that related to our group and its place at Ridgeway. Although I separate the individuals' issues from group issues in the sections within this chapter, all of these were operating at once. The teasing out or separating of the pieces helps explain what happened within and around our group to sustain the group as a place to think.

Group Issues Related to Life at Ridgeway

Our group felt vulnerable because we were, to some extent, polarizing the school. We were instrumental in bringing some tension to the school. We also composed a different view of what a team might be. The tension and the different view of teaming contributed to sustaining the group.

Tension in the School. In February, at an intermediate grade-level meeting (Grades 4 through 6), one of the intermediate grade teachers complained to Mr. Z. that the younger children at Ridgeway (below Grade 4) were doing "a lot of fluff," rather than the important curricular activities that would get them "ready" for the upper grades. Word of this meeting spread, and when our group met the following afternoon we spent time venting some of the anger felt toward the upper grades as well as justifying practices that group members were enacting. The teachers in the group felt that inquiry was being attacked as a useless or "fluffy" way to teach and that other teachers were suggesting that it lacked substantive content.

Mr. Z. informed the faculty that there would be a meeting of all individuals involved (essentially the entire school staff) in what he called a "circle meeting"; the staff would sit in a large circle and listen to each other. Mr. Z. was good at this sort of thing. The following week I learned that, although the feelings were made public and no one seemed swayed, the facing of each other defused some of the tension because Mr. Z. validated the entire staff.

The upsetting feeling of the upper grades was reflective of the disruption that emanated from our group. Study group members were getting attention from teachers in other schools as they wanted to visit group members' classrooms. My presence was seen as favoring the primary grades, although I was willing to visit and work with any grade level teachers at their request. The teachers in our group were changing curriculum and this was threatening. Perhaps, as they looked at group members' classrooms and saw the increased excitement, the variety of displays, the flow of parents that increased over the course of the year, and, most importantly, sensed that teaching was changing, they began to feel uneasy. The study group talked about creating curriculum (Short & Burke, 1991), not merely covering it. The group wanted themselves and their children to be substantive thinkers, not technicians (Shannon, 1989).

The tension was real and it was building. It didn't move beyond the stage of small groups complaining to each other once Mr. Z. held the circle meeting. He was articulate in letting teachers know that a variety of approaches was acceptable and that the teachers in the building needed to respect each other. This pushed most of the tension underground; it arose occasionally at group meetings when a rumor would circulate the building about what "someone" said. Our group meetings were a place to process these rumors so that group members could continue the work that exited them most: their classroom inquiry.

Teams ... for What?   Teams of teachers organized by grade level remained a sensitive topic as the group began to analyze the beliefs on which we thought teaming rested:

> **Kim R.:** But I'm really saying that I think the biggest change has come since we sectioned our building off into teams.... fifth grade team has their meetings and first grade team [has theirs, separately], and it's like you all have to be doing the same thing and you all have to be exactly alike and that's a lot ...
> **Rick:** Is that true of teams in this building?
> **Kim L.:** Not any more, but I think. . .
> **Kim Z.:** Initially, I think that's what [the former principal] wanted.
> **Kim R.:** That's what we were.
> **Kim Z.:** She loved our [second grade] team. She loved how we all planned together.

Kim R.:   She liked us [first-grade team] because that's how we did it, too. We all planned everything together. We had the same thing. [Curriculum was] divided up into the same exact things [for each class]. We ran off [copies of work for kids] for everybody in the team. We ran off all the centers. Math was the same. I mean now what this [our group] has done is we're all going our own ways so we're not that little team that does every thing together. You see what I'm saying?

Rick: Yeah. The team is very different now.

Kim R.:   I think it's divided our school.

Rick: Well, your team's also divided [within each team as individuals wanted to go in different directions].

Kim L.:   That's what I mean.

Liz: It hasn't for us [third grade] in that we've talked ...

Linda: For a long time. You and I [to Liz] talked together for a long time.

Kim R.:   The word "team" ... team to [some people] means we're our own little group that we all have to be doing the same exact thing. And that's not what a team is. A team is for sharing and doing this kind of stuff, support, and ideas. A team is not to be, "Well, here's my idea that I'll copy for all of you." (Transcript from study group session)

Teaming appears, in the eyes of some of our group members, to be a vehicle to control teachers and to guarantee that curriculum is homogeneous across classrooms. The group was coming to terms with this as we began to view teaming as a push toward mediocrity and single-mindedness. They found that teams tended to limit individual growth and team growth because the team tended to enact the simplest, most easily duplicated, and least adventurous suggestions.

The presence of this group, its collective thinking, the work of the students, the various exhibitions of that work, and the groups' increasing prestige within the district are some of the many facets that began to bind the group, strengthen it, and enrich its working context. When members felt threatened from outside, the group drew together. When the outside pressures were less intense, the group stretched each other. We came to know each others' habits, comforts, and snack choices; indeed, we came to know each others' lives. And, within that context, the group was disrupting old notions of teaming and composing a new understanding of a team as a thought collective that served as a forum for support, defense, enactment, thinking, being tentative, taking a risk, sharing writing, asking questions, and challenging self and others.

Whole School Issues Related to Life at Ridgeway

Schoolwide issues affected all teachers at the school, including our group's members. One such issue had to do with a proposal Mr. Z. made just prior to our first year together. Knowing that there were enough children identified as "special education" students at Ridgeway to support one full-time special education teacher per grade level (each grade level is a team), Mr. Z. suggested that the special education teacher become a classroom teacher, disperse her caseload of special education students among all the classrooms of each grade level, and have smaller numbers of children in each class. The plan was for primary grades only. For example, the first-grade team originally thought they would have 60 students distributed among their three classrooms with a fourth classroom for the special education teacher. That teacher would have pulled kids out for special instruction, or she might include the children in the regular classroom and work with those students in their own classrooms during the day.

Instead, all of the children (including the special education students) were distributed evenly among the four teachers, giving each teacher 15 students. The classroom teacher, with the help of the special education teacher, would write the required Individual Education Plan (IEP) for the special education students in her classroom. The teachers liked having smaller classes, but felt uncomfortable including certain special education students in their classrooms because they did not know enough about how these children learn and didn't feel they were getting the support they needed in finding out. They weren't sure they wanted to continue the plan into the 1995–1996 school year. Mr. Z. decided that the plan would be continued. According to our group, he did not consult with any of the teachers when he made this plan. I quickly located articles on the success and failure of inclusion. Although the group did not agree to take any action on Mr. Z.'s decisions, our reading and discussing helped to ventilate and plan for the special education students in classrooms.

As the 1994–1995 school year was drawing to a close, Mr. Z. made other staffing decisions. Kim Z. would teach first grade, as she had requested, and one first-grade teacher would move to the second-grade team. The discussions of such school-related issues were foundational to sustaining the group.

We discussed staffing because staffing decisions that Mr. Z. made were carefully chosen and complex. In addition to moving Kim Z. to support her growth as a teacher, he wanted to move a kindergarten teacher out of her classroom; he also wanted one member of our group (anonymous) to use more of her special education training so he moved her into a more specialized position as a pullout teacher for the intermediate grades. We talked considerably about these decisions at our group meeting. Mr. Z. was moving people whom group members suspected he might want out of the school. The kindergarten teacher moved to a different school when the opportunity to do so arose over the summer. The member of our group remained at Ridgeway half time and worked half time at another school.

When the group member was told that she would be moved out of her third-grade classroom, she was upset. We listened, supported, and tried to see a bright side. I was angered by the move because I viewed it as oppressive and intimidating. Teachers could be held in tow by a decision that sent fear through the entire teaching community of the school. But was it? That remained the nagging question, for me. Was this a move to better the school by placing staff in positions where they could do the most good? Was it a way to gently usher out of the school those teachers that Mr. Z. regarded as less than competent? Did he intentionally want to create a state of panic among the teachers to remind them that he had this power so they should not push too much for greater control in their own classrooms or teams? Were the teachers' fears based in the former administration? Mr. Z.'s rationale, always publicly stated, was that he wanted people in positions where they could do the most good for the kids at Ridgeway. He was willing to "eat it" (his term) when there was anger about a move that he made; by "eat it," he meant that he was willing to take some people's anger, tears, or expressed disagreement. He knew some people didn't agree with the decisions he made, but he assumed full responsibility.

Our group served as a forum in which we made sense of such school-wide issues. As things came up, we worked collectively to understand decisions that affected the entire school staff. This often meant discussing things to help relieve the tension. Mostly, group members pushed each other to understand the context, their work within that context, and the learning of children there. We were meaning-makers (Wells, 1986) and our collective acts of making meaning, whether for an individual, the group, or the entire school, served to bond us, seemed to "free our curiosity," and supported us in "charging off in new directions" (Rogers, 1969).

THE PRINCIPAL

Mr. Z., the principal of the school, affected the school across the various contexts discussed up to this point. As I suggested earlier, many teachers claim to teach as they please in spite of their principal. Through the decisions he made, Mr. Z. knew how to make himself felt within the school and within our group. I do not undertake a complete study of leadership in this book, but in acknowledgment of Mr. Z.'s influence on individuals, on our group, and within the school in general, I include this discussion to complement some of the information already presented about him.

Mr. Z. has been a principal for almost twenty years. His warmth and sensitivity helped our group, not because he participated (he didn't), but because his support allowed our group to flourish amid all that was going on at that time at Ridgeway. Mr. Z. took an active role in helping all the teachers adjust to a new principal. He described the former principal as "a traditional, suspicious kind of a principal." When he arrived, "the staff was pretty aggressive, pretty union-ish, pretty angry ..." because the former principal had upset some staff members.

Mr. Z. is not afraid to confront tough issues, such as the way things used to be at Ridgeway:

> [Things were] really good from the very beginning [of my tenure as principal]. My very first faculty meeting I had everybody take their right hand and I said hold it up like this, so everybody held it like this. I said, "Now, put it like over ... put it over here." [He was moving his hands as though he was turning the pages of a book.] So they all put it over here. And I said, "Okay, in front of you, you have the history of Ridgeway Elementary School. Let's all turn the page together." So we all turned the page. I said, "Now we're on a new page, no one's allowed to turn back." And no old stuff [about the former principal] has ever come up, ever. (Mr. Z.'s quotes in this section are from transcripts of a taped interview.)

He believes that a principal has got to show much appreciation and support for teachers and staff because there may come a time when the principal wants to do something that the staff may not agree with. He said:

> ... when you're dealing with people, you have to make a lot of deposits in their accounts so that the day you need to make a withdrawal ... I mean, sometimes I have to say, "Am I usually pretty reasonable?" And they usually say, "Yes," and I say, "Well, please allow me to be unreasonable in this issue." So I try to do as much depositing as I can so if I need to do a withdrawal it doesn't hurt quite as much.

This is consistent with his idea of "eating it." He supports the teachers, makes decisions, and will take the flak that accompanies unpopular or discomforting decisions. His leadership style is one that supports risk-taking and he, quite willingly, listened to teachers' ideas:

> But I do think that a teaching staff is a much bolder and more confident teaching staff if they think the principal is going to be kind of calm about anything that hits him.

And he was calm. He ran circle meetings, told folks that he had decided to move them to different positions, let the staff know that the study group had his blessing (as did everyone else's work in the building), and worked towards a sense of mutual respect. Mr. Z. explains his role this way:

> I manage the building. That's what the teachers want, and I'll do as good a job as I can managing the building and I'll empower them to be the instructional leaders, you know, along with me. There are a lot of times when I feel more like a hospital administrator working with the doctors ... than I am like the master teacher.

His role, then, is not the curriculum leader, instructional leader, or agent for the district curriculum. He trusts teachers to make sound pedagogical decisions and content decisions.

> ... teaching is so much more complicated [than when I began]. It used to be, I'd get a new teacher, I'd give them a social studies, math, reading, and science book, and I'd have a manual slapped in between each one of those. I'd say, "Don't forget you're going to need to buy plastic bags for unit three in science," and then I guess maybe I was the instructional leader, because I at least understood it.

According to Mr. Z., the district's adopted curricula are open to local interpretation in the school. Although I found that teachers tended to think that the curriculum was not open to much interpretation because they felt pressure from the district office to enact mandated curriculum, Mr. Z. felt that each school could adjust to their local population and needs: "I do know one of the things the district did right was to let individual buildings kind of self-actualize as opposed to having a model."

Mr. Z. referred to himself as a "recovering control freak" who had faith that his teachers would plan together for what would be best for the students. He knew what was going on in the building; he knew if a team was functioning well or if there was tension, and he knew about disagreements among staff members. He seemed to have eyes and ears all over the building. And he wanted to make sure teachers had arenas for professional growth.

The Ridgeway Institute was Mr. Z.'s idea; he wanted a place where teachers could learn from each other by "sharing their expertise." The Institute was in place the year before our study group started. Teachers presented areas in which they became experts on a monthly basis. The teachers learned from each other about portfolios, math ideas, literacy strategies, and more. The Institute led to writing the proposal that secured money for the first year of our study group. Mr. Z. decided that the Institute idea might work better at each grade level, so the idea of grade-level study teams was born. Teachers viewed this as increased time to meet, study, and plan for their students. Mr. Z. met with the teams for part of their study time, and he also encouraged adjoining teams to meet (first grade met with second grade; second and third met, etc.). He worked a lot at getting people to talk to each other because he believed that if you put folks together, they tend to communicate and get along better.

Mr. Z. also knows that "parents still aren't coming to school, they're still not participating in their child's education." He was encouraged by the number of parents that attended the various presentations given by the students of teachers in our group.

The study group was lucky. It grew out of the desire to meet across grade levels and was supported by Mr. Z. The participants in the group were involved over and above their obligations to their grade-level teams; Mr. Z. helped keep the possibility of meeting acceptable. His view of teachers assuming responsibility for their own professionalization, and his assumption that teachers will want to do so, helped sustain our group.

ABIDING STUDENTS OF EDUCATION

The individual, group, and school issues with which we lived served, in some ways, as boundaries for our discussions. And, as those discussions pushed at our composing and disrupting processes, we worked to cross or expand our boundaries. The changes that the group facilitated within and beyond the classroom reflected growth towards inquiry and movement away from prescribed curriculum and away from traditional relationships between group members. We were discovering what it means to be an "abiding student of education," as described by Dewey (1904):

> The tendency of educational development to proceed by reaction from one thing to another, to adopt for one year, or for a term of seven years, this or that new study or method of teaching, and then as abruptly to swing over to some new education gospel, is a result which would be impossible if teachers were adequately moved by their own independent intelligence. The willingness of teachers, especially of those occupying administrative positions, to become submerged in the routine detail of their callings, to expend the bulk of their energy upon forms and rules and regulations, and reports and percentages, is another evidence of the absence of intellectual vitality. If teachers were possessed by the spirit of an abiding student of education, this spirit would find some way of breaking through the mesh and coil of circumstance and would find expression for itself. (p. 26)

In this section, I dig deeper into how this group worked together to create an "unforgettable experience" in which teachers could compose and disrupt. It is my hope that readers will see the group as a thought collective that sought to support teachers as learners, which is what I believe Dewey meant by "abiding students." We sustained our group beyond the year of funding by remaining committed to each other. That commitment rested on the creation of curriculum (composing it), support, and sharing of self and ideas from things as basic as record-keeping strategies to things as complex as philosophy.

Mutually Composed Curriculum

Our group explored ways of disrupting and composing curriculum; the time spent on such an endeavor was a shift in thinking about curriculum. Children became integral partners in the planning process. Group members changed their classroom schedules, allowing larger blocks of time for children to pursue interests and co-compose curriculum. Members began to listen to kids differently, as Kim Z. notes, reflecting on her changing ways of paying attention to potential curricular avenues:

> Maybe in the past I would have had this unit planned, and I would have had in my mindset this is what we're going to do, this is what I have planned. By golly, we're sticking to this lesson plan, I don't know ... I don't know that I would have done this [pursued student-expressed interests], but one might just, you know, brush those off with just an answer there and never go into it or explore it any. (Transcript from study group session.)

Kim Z.'s thinking resonates with Dewey (1938):

> The plan, in other words, is a cooperative enterprise, not a dictation. The teacher's suggestion is not a mold for a cast-iron result but is a starting point to be developed into a plan through contributions for the experience of all engaged in the learning process.... The essential point is that the purpose grow and take shape through the process of social intelligence. (p. 72)

Kim L., Kim R., and Kim Z. focused on child-developed projects. Kim Z. tended to have the project focus around one theme; Kim R. and Kim L. focused on a broader spectrum of individual children's expressed interests. At one time, Kim L. and Kim R. had groups, within and across their two first-grade classrooms, studying machines, sharks, the basement of the school, snakes, and the human body. Kim L. and Kim R. welcomed all the areas of study that interested the children. The first year, they helped the students form groups to focus on four or five of these areas, explaining that the children needed to join a group because pursuing too many individual interests was not possible due to lack of adult help. During the second year, students' individual interests were addressed. Kim R. explains how the curriculum was developed with the children:

> Kim R.: We [Kim L. and Kim R.] observed them and wrote down what they were saying to hear what they were interested in, and then we went to brainstorming after ... "this is what we heard when you guys were talking." And then we went to [the large group and had] them choose something they were really interested in and then went into the groups. Then brainstormed again and ... first we webbed; yesterday we webbed. I said, " Earth, tell me

about it," and we just webbed and they told me about it, volcanoes and caves and mountains and all the stuff came up, and then after we looked at it ... "I see more spider legs [parts of the web with children's words]," [a child] said, "spider legs around caves."

I said, "You're right, I wonder why?"

Teresa goes, "And that's what I want to learn about." You know, it was: bingo!

Rick: She knows [what she wants to learn about].(Transcript from study group session.)

Our group's reading and making sense of language and literacy led to composing and disrupting curriculum. For example, Liz was worried that her kids were not reading enough books, so she studied the problem as an inquirer: "But I feel frustrated that they're not reading enough because when it comes to book club it's just 'Let's just do our play.' But today there were three or four around a tape recorder reading, you know, it's reading." Thinking aloud in the context of our group, she realized that reading is more than just books; it is reading when children read their own writing, too.

Linda changed her understanding of what it means to immerse children in language:

> ... we study Jack Prelutsky as an author and I found even my quote "nonreader" can read the poems that they have read over and over again and I never thought about that ... And I don't know why I never picked up on this.... And I can't wait to do it because my ESL [English as a second language] kids can even read the lines of poetry. (Transcript from study group session)

The teachers' work in curriculum development did pay attention to the district mandated curriculum. Yet, by allowing the children to focus on areas of interest, the teachers in the group found curricular goals being covered while excitement and areas of interest were being uncovered. The group meetings were forums for reporting and supporting the composing of curriculum as a mutual effort between and among teachers and students, thus sustaining interest and excitement within the group.

Supporting the Composing of Curriculum.   The teachers supported each other in the composing of curriculum by challenging each other. They reminded each other to look at the district curriculum not as something that confines but as a sort of minimalist document of expectations. As Kim Z. stated:

You need to know those objectives, and you need to go … sometimes, I mean, you need to go to that curriculum just to say, oh, I get it, this is what they mean by that objective. It doesn't necessarily mean you're going to use all that material to teach it, but I mean when I first started teaching I [referred to the district curriculum]. (Transcript from study group session)

In the following interchanges, individuals moved from a question, to sharing an event, to seeking clarification, to gaining information, to having an idea realized before us. This is composing at its finest. The anonymous teacher was having her students write letters to have guest speakers discuss an area of study. She wasn't sure if those being invited could read the children's invented spellings. Kim R. offered a suggestion based on her use of letters with first graders:

Kim R.:	They [the students] didn't see that, but they wrote the letter and I put a cover letter on it and sent it [because some resources can't read invented spellings].
Unidentified:	Okay, okay. Because I wasn't sure.
Rick:	Yeah, I think you might need a cover letter on school stationery so they know that it's not frivolous.
Kim R.:	And I also … they were going to call the restaurant, and I called prior and said this person's going to be calling in 15 minutes and this is what they're talking about, so …
Rick:	For the ground work.
Kim Z.:	One thing you need to do, I meant to bring mine … I'll bring them next time, I sent home a parent letter after we got done with the Arctic stuff and kind of explained to parents that this is a different way of teaching and that some refer to it as the project approach, and this is why I chose to do it this way, and I would like your input, and I asked them … if their child talked to them more about this, seemed more excited about this learning as previous teacher directed things, and I asked them, "Have you visited the learning bubble, what did you think?" and other comments, and I've got to bring them, because I've got the nicest comments, I mean,… just some incredible comments from parents. And one mother, who I'd never expected … and previously didn't know that much about her, really talked to me about … obviously she's going to school [to be a teacher], and talked about, "This reminds me of cooperative group work," and … she's read this person, and I … I mean, what a dialogue to get going between me and a parent, you know, so you need to write some kind of follow-up to send home after you've had parents in, I mean, it's great feedback. (Transcript from study group session)

The first-year teacher in our group decided to write a letter to parents explaining some of the inquiry that the students were doing. She told parents that they would be invited to the final project; she was composing a relationship with parents through the children's work.

Aspy (personal communication) suggests that when we listen to another person we should lean towards her, cup our hands firmly within our laps, and show the other that we are ready to receive what they have to offer. He had me, in counselor training, hold eggs while listening to other trainees. That's how our group worked. We held each others' thoughts the way one holds an egg, not too tight but not too loose. Within that context, we could make discoveries, ask questions, show what we were doing within our classrooms, deal further with curriculum, discuss classroom organization, and face the emotional issues that confronted us. And ask more questions!

Asking Questions

The teachers made discoveries, crystallized their understandings and planned for the future as they immersed themselves in their questions, students' questions, and the questions of colleagues in the group. The questions reported in this section are from transcriptions of our taped sessions. There were questions about children's transitions. Kim L. asked:

> Do you think kids have trouble if they're in a Montessori classroom after a certain grade making the transition to more traditional type of classroom where there maybe learning isn't as child-centered?

Questions about curriculum, such as Kim Z.'s question, "What are they doing? What are you guys studying now?"

Questions about children's role in the curriculum, such as that asked by Mona:

> I've got a question … can I ask you my question before I forget it? … Where she was saying that children, when you're doing a project approach, that they tend to pick areas in which they will excel and do well, you know, and that's how the group leads and takes off like that, do you think … [that] if you started at the beginning of the year, and you continually saw people always in certain roles in their project group, and not … you know what I mean, if they were always picking the area, like some one's really, really good at art, so they always picked that way to … is that okay, is that not okay, do you need to encourage, you know, what do you do? Do you see what I mean?

And questions, such as the one that follows asked by Mona, about the roles that children might assume in an inquiry-based classroom:

> And what if it's always … somebody … who's always just going off on this tons of writing and everything. I mean, that's great and wonderful and you never want to stop

that, but what if it never allows anybody else in the group to take on that role, you know, what if they always see T— as the writer, whatever group she happens to be in?

There were questions, such as Rick's about finding tentative solutions: "Have you resolved that?"

Questions about how time is spent (from Linda): "I read this [Kim R's draft] and I kept wondering how much of the day did you spend doing the writing and the projects?"

Questions about accountability (again from Linda): "That's one thing I wanted to know too was how were you able to [keep track of progress] ... I know just by teacher observation but did you do any formal types of things?"

Questions, like the ones that follow from Kim Z. that demonstrate teachers assuming leadership in the group: "Why don't you read what you wrote?" and "Do you have something?" and from Linda: " So everybody read and write [for next class], and bring data to share, right?"

There were questions that seek support and encouragement, especially about writing, such as this one from Kim R.: " Seriously, do you want me to read this cause it's ... not very good and it's really rough?"

Finally, there were those questions that challenge each others' writing, such as those asked by Kim Z.:

Where does that go, though?

The part where you were saying about how it's connected to real life, ... and that's really good. I'm wondering is there a part in there, or is there someplace in your paper where you're going to say how they end up choosing things that are the curriculum?

Questions became an important part of our group because they signified safety, tolerance, and curiosity. The teachers' questions—their abiding curiosity—helped to sustain the group. They also knew that they had to become good record keepers in order to justify, with evidence, that questions were being addressed and that the children were learning.

Record Keeping

The teachers in the group became systematic at record keeping. Some began with portfolios for themselves, their classrooms, and the children. The children's portfolios were, in most cases, owned by the children. The children made decisions about what to place in their portfolios and wrote captions of some sort for the contents. If a teacher wanted things included in a portfolio, but the child did not wish to include those items, the teacher might choose to maintain a classroom portfolio. As time passed, the teachers took extensive anecdotal records on their children, others audiotaped children reading and talking, others videotaped classroom activities on a regular basis, took photographs, and most developed record-keeping sheets to keep track of specific areas that they were interested in studying.

Kim Z. began extensive record keeping when her students decided to study the zoo in our city. Here, she makes public her commitment to collect data more systematically. You can see her making decisions about what to collect and how to go about it, even though she may not yet know what will emerge from all the data:

> I don't know what it's for [all her notes, organized in a notebook]. I thought it would be for maybe if we ever went and talked with [other teachers at their schools]. Because what I started doing was I kept a journal and I had thoughts and reflections for each month and I tried to write at the end of each month about each area. But I quit, I mean I haven't. Some areas I still do, I still keep track of and some areas I kind of haven't, you know? But then I started this other thing. I remember where it's at; it's in my other bag, I have three bags, see, look. And it's the journal of the zoo stuff and I've been keeping that day by day ... I've been making copies of everybody's stuff, practically, so I have lots of authentic kids' stuff. (Transcript from study group session)

The district requires that teachers list the units or themed areas that they studied during the year. Linda and Liz reported exciting changes from years gone by. First, from Linda:

> ... when we went to fill out the reading cards, we talked about this yesterday, we said, "Okay, what units have we covered?" We didn't have enough room to cover all our units. We had to pick and choose. What I thought was cool, too, during that ... when you were pulling that out, we asked the kids, "Well, what did you study? What did you read about?" And the cards were all different. It wasn't just something you could have run off and put [the same thing] for the class. [Kids said,] "Well, I studied ... " (Transcript from study group session)

Then from Liz:

> And personal goals. Everybody met a personal goal this time, and they all knew what they were and, [said] "Yeah, I did it," and they could prove it [because they had a product to show that they were proud of ...] (Transcript from study group session)

Sessions during which the teachers presented their record keeping were actually data analysis sessions as we worked to understand what was unfolding in their classrooms. The growing pool of data intrigued and excited group members; the pool, and discussions about it, served to bind and sustain the group.

Philosophical Discussions

Discussions of the philosophy on which our practices rested reflected the professional integrity of the group and helped us to bond, as individuals spoke from the heart. The group was made up of substantive thinkers who planned instructional strategies and activities that were rooted in ways of thinking about learning. Sometimes they brought up issues of philosophy for clarification. For example, recall that Kim Z. wanted to know the difference between whole language, language experience, literature based, and constructivism. The conversation that followed from her question led the group to look at the theory and language of our profession and how it affected our understanding of practice. On another day(2/28/95), we discussed the difference between cognitive and metacognitive processes and whether or not planning inquiry with children was metacognitive activity.

The teachers were aware of their thinking as being atypical, as reflected in a conversation during one meeting. Kim Z. had been visited by teachers from another school who heard about her children doing inquiry:

Kim Z.:	… that's the thing that always just gets me about how people just want to change and then they just jump into this and they …
Liz:	They don't have the philosophy, they …
Kim Z.:	… haven't read anything, they haven't studied anything. They don't have the philosophy and the background knowledge, I guess, and they don't understand why they're doing it. And I think you understand why you've made this change and it's because of … what you've read and people need to know that … you see how you've changed because you've read.
Liz:	People will not change unless they want to. That's why this just stuck out at me, you know? We have to provide the opportunity for that change to come from within rather than trying to impose it from without.
Kim R.:	But you can look at those classrooms that do it because they think it's the way to do it …
Kim Z.:	Or because somebody else is doing it, so they're just kind of copying.
Liz:	Right, they copy what they're doing …
Kim R.:	… but they don't have any reason for why they're doing it.
Kim Z.:	No philosophies.
Kim R.:	They don't understand what's happening and what they're looking for. (Transcript from study group session)

Mona provided constant demonstrations of the relationship between theory and practice, rooted in her Montessori background. Her references to "Maria" inspired other members of the group to look at their referential frames for the activity that was enacted in their classrooms. And Mona changed over time; she still felt very committed to the passion and use of metaphor that she learned from Montessori, but Calkins' work (1994) influenced her view of how children use, learn, and invent language. Mona encouraged our group to challenge her, she read books that stretched her, and she brought questions to us when she felt disruption between what she was doing and her emerging beliefs, indeed she used our group as a forum for such thinking:

> [In] my teacher training we were taught how to use the materials, how to teach. We were taught what to look for at the age of the child, you know, how they exactly develop. But we were also taught to watch to see what they show us and where they're at. And we're taught to observe and that's why I love being with you [our group] because I can develop those skills more because you're going through the same pains that I go through ... trying other things and it's good to have that and I've never had that before. (Transcript from study group session)

The group supported Linda as she faced the differences between what she believed and what she enacted. Linda admitted that she "fell back to what was more comfortable." Classroom activity was not an enactment of her philosophy, but our discussions supported her as she got back in touch with what she believed and her expectations for classroom life. Linda was making sense of how she could live out her philosophy. She reminded the teachers (and me) that we have philosophical roots to our thinking and that our actions may reflect cohesion or tension with those roots.

And our philosophical discussions reflected our reading—reading which influenced our thinking and classroom strategies.

> Mona: Well, this is the second time around [her second attempt to write about her classroom], but that's okay. I learned in this book [Graves, 1991], that's okay.
> Rick: That's *real* okay.
> Kim L.: That book turned you around?
> Mona: Yes, it did. It really did. And I took notes so that I can share.

The group was composing a bond based in classroom activity, presentation of self, relationships, individuality, philosophy and, in some deep way, joy.

JOY

There is politics attached to joy that makes it something that is truly double-edged. Where there is joy, in a school, there may also be anger and tension. There was joy in our group. Tired, at the end of a day, we would meet, eat, talk, share, think, wonder, wander, stress, pressure, challenge, query, and much more. There was joy in finding each other. It is not easy to find each other at Ridgeway. Kim R. believes that teaming undermines a sense of the school as whole. Ridgeway teachers eat lunch in their individual teams' planning centers, and the teachers rarely gather as a staff in the lounge except for formal faculty meetings or staff development sessions scheduled there by the district or principal. Our class gave the teachers time to talk across grade levels. They discovered each other.

Joy was expressed in our discussions: Kim L. and Kim R.'s children involved in projects, Kim Z.'s study of the zoo, Linda and Liz learning about self and their kids' study of the city, Mona's children experiencing her spirituality and joy of learning, and me discussing issues of the group and the school.

There was the joy of knowing that a caring group would assemble each week and that there would be folks present interested in our joys and sorrows from home and from school. And there was the joy of engaging in sustained discussions of what folks were collecting from their classrooms. As members discussed what they had done, they began planning for what might be next, opening themselves up to the possibilities that the children would present. Our meetings became a forum for the celebrations of learning—children's and teachers' learning.

The group tended to focus increasingly on sustained activities as the stories of children, learning, language, teaching, life in the classroom, or curriculum continued over time. Members looked forward to hearing weekly progress reports on these. There was joy in knowing that these stories had an audience.

"How is T—?"

"Did Theresa do any more on that book?"

"Where is K—? Has he moved?"

And there were the joyous reports, such as the following from Kim R., of children coming to understand the power of being in a community of inquirers—how the community can help, support, hurt, and amend itself to stop hurting others.

> That's Eva. She's the one that sits through group and says "You know we wrote a book and we had people's names in the class and we used those peoples names because we knew how to spell them," but she goes, "We hurt people's feelings because they thought we were writing about them and the other people didn't think we should, so we're not going to use people's names in books. We're going to make people's names up so we don't hurt anybody's feelings anymore."

And there were aesthetic connections, too:

Kim L.:	Zach, who was a member of the machine group, said, "Hey, that looks like an inclined plane." [Pointing to the sign they use for 'greater than' during calendar time.]
Rick:	Talking about the great events … that's a sophisticated connection.
Kim Z.:	Yeah.
Kim R.:	Boy today when we put the music on, Eric said "That must be Venus." I said "Why? Why do you say that?" He said, "It just sounds like Venus." He goes, "That's Venus right there and this music sounds like Venus."
Rick:	And that's the classical piece?
Kim L.:	Uh huh, The Planets.
Rick:	The Planets is a classical piece somebody wrote and he recognizes Venus!
Kim L.:	Yes.

We did not merely listen and applaud each others' efforts; we asked questions that pushed each other and we thought aloud about the implications of one teacher's work on others in the group. This was the joy of intensity; it gave headaches and it stimulated our minds.

The teachers' joys and sorrows and those of their students permeated the many facets of inquiry as self, curriculum, and relationships changed for individuals, the group, and the school. Increasingly, the teachers and I learned to express ourselves regarding our inquiry; we found that the cultivation of voices was personal, professional, and political. This cultivation is examined in the next chapter as I continue irising out to the broader meanings of the group's work.

Chapter 11

Teachers' Voices and the Political Nature of Their Work

◻ ◻ ◻

*A teacher must grow from the spacious hope of being much more than a talking textbook,
more than a mere functionary who implements tests and mandated curriculum.*
—Shor (1987, p. 26)

In this chapter I continue the process of irising out in order to broaden the view of the work of the study group by showing the political aspects of teachers composing their voices so that they are "more than talking textbooks." I suggest that composing voices was political work because it disrupted what others expected from the teachers and even what they expected from themselves. Supporting students in composing their inquiring voices (Watson, Burke, & Harste, 1989) was also political because the group disrupted traditional expectations of child-learners.

TEACHERS' VOICES

Inquiry led the teachers to speak, write, read, listen, think, search, and push themselves to understand the contexts in which the members of the group taught, learned, and worked daily. It led to understanding what it means to speak, to write, to put the "self" forward in some way. It led to the composing and understanding of voices. I use the plural form, *voices*, because group members became quite aware of the differences across individuals' voices in expression, classroom practice, and the ways in which each made sense of inquiry. Hargreaves (1996) submits that "much of the literature on teacher's voice has made it into a romantic singularity claiming recognition and celebration … in a decontextualized way" (p. 16). The plural is meant to contextualize and represent many voices, not one, and include not only teachers, but the variety of the students' expressions of questions and their ways of learning to face, pursue, and present their inquiry. The teachers included the students' voices by incorporating student inquiry into their chapters, addressing Corbett and Wilson's (1995) concern that "Despite … repeated calls for reform aimed at students, young people themselves occupy, at best, a minuscule part of the literature on the process of change and reform in education" (p. 12).

The teachers' inquiry (and our ongoing group meetings) were a forum for discussion of students' voices. The students' inquiry projects were rooted in their voices; for example, recall how Kim R. and Kim L. circulated their room and listened to their students to facilitate the bringing of students' voices to whole class meetings where curricular decisions were made. The teachers' chapters re-present their students' voices. The students followed their interests, presented their projects, returned to their thought collectives to initiate new areas of study, and were heard by families, other teachers, and administrators as the projects were presented. Their expression of their voices, of their passionate interests, disrupted some parents', teachers' and administrators' (and university researchers') thinking about the possibilities of children's learning. Since the children's thinking was presented in their work via their teachers' writing, the main focus of this section is on the voices of the members of the study group. I stress here, however, that the students' enactment of inquiry remains at the heart of the politics of inquiry. The successes, passions, and intensities of the students' work was fundamental to the composing and disrupting that took place at Ridgeway. Of course, their teachers had to support and encourage them by composing an inquiry-setting, but the students' composition of "selves-as-inquirers" was instrumental to the politics that saturated the activity of the study group. It was the students' activity and their teachers' support of that activity that precipitated what happened at Ridgeway.

Goswami and Stillman (1987) discuss teachers as agents of change who can use their own research as a vehicle for that change. Cochran-Smith and Lytle (1990) add that such work involves teachers "collaborat[ing] with their students to answer questions important to both" (p. 8). Change is a process of teachers coming into their own, finding their voices, and choosing to express those voices as inquiry. And, teacher change is paralleled by the students as they (students) engage in inquiry. These are complex processes that penetrate to the moral essence of teachers as they make decisions to express self, follow their own professional paths, and, at times, know they may be alienating or even hurting others (colleagues) in their quest for their own voices. Gilligan (1993) expresses the intensity of this work:

In separating the voice of the self from the voices of others, the woman asks if it is possible to be responsible to herself as well as to others and thus to reconcile the disparity between hurt and care. The exercise of such responsibility requires a new kind of judgment, whose first demand is for honesty. To be responsible for oneself, it is first necessary to acknowledge what one is doing. The criterion for judgment thus shifts from goodness to truth when the morality of action is assessed not on the basis of its appearance in the eyes of others, but in terms of the realities of its intention and consequence. (pp. 82–83)

The teachers in our group expressed their separation from others as they moved away from mandated curriculum.

Teachers' Voices and Mandated Curriculum

Responsibility is an aspect of expression of voice when it involves the move away from mandated curriculum. The teachers in our group read, discussed, wrote, and found other ways of learning and responsibly expressing their learning. They were proactive in that they planned, asked questions of themselves, and challenged each other. Abandoning mandated curriculum was not a wild and carefree abandonment of regulations for the sake of some nebulous and vaguely uncertain activity that lacked goals. The moves that teachers made toward supporting their students in ownership of learning were enacted in responsible ways that included record keeping for account-ability for the ultimate goals of reading, writing, thinking, and inquiring. Plans may have been tentative because classroom activity is dynamic, social, and constantly changing, but the teachers' understanding of and insights into the students' learning were expressions of their professional responsibility. I do not want to appear to be suggesting that all teachers abandon mandated curriculum. Inquiring, learning teachers who are "abiding student[s] of education" (Dewey, 1938) are in a position to voice and enact change because they can justify their students' activities. They are responsible.

The teachers worked to separate their individual voices from the ex-pected (by the district office) single voice within the district. Although the district office was asking for change in some areas, such as early childhood, the teachers continually received conflicting messages that seemed to ask them not to question or think or speak (by wanting them to use adopted curriculum in reading, math, science, etc.). Thus, while being asked to change, they also faced the expectation, from other district administrators, to receive and pass on the district prescribed curriculum and not to question decisions made at the district office. They were expected to be silent and accept that the information-dispensed-as-knowledge at the district office was to be, in turn, dispensed to the children in a banking manner (Freire, 1970a). They were expected to be quiet and well-functioning conduits of the curriculum, passing it from the district office to the children in unspoken agreement with (rarely questioning or confronting) the ready-made decisions that preplanned curriculum carries with it. But our group acknowledged what they were doing in "terms of the realities of its intention and consequence" (Gilligan, 1993, p. 83). Each curricular decision took on new meaning as group members looked for honesty in their own and their students' teaching and learning activity. Honesty demanded that both teachers and students engage in inquiry as a way to learn, with the view that learning is self-expression (voice).

The movement toward inquiry meant that the curriculum could be locally created by those willing to undertake the endeavor. It meant that decisions about many things would be made by the teacher and the students reflective of the social nature of classroom activity and mutually expressed needs and interests. This meant that as the teachers and students composed themselves, they disrupted some of the regularities of the district.

Teachers who confront mandated curriculum also confront their views of themselves, their views of their students, and others' views of them and their students. The pressures of all these views, especially if some of that pressure is toward mandated curriculum, may level teachers' aspirations for themselves and their students. Teachers' aspirations are leveled, similar to the leveled aspirations of students (MacLeod, 1995), by a system that is so much in motion that it obfuscates the identity of its teachers and students. Teachers are often viewed en masse as "the teachers of this district" with a lack of specificity to their particular contexts; generic aspirations for an entire district are a form of racism, classism, and oppression that undermines or limits the possibilities of what might occur in school.

The instituting of mandated curriculum is similar to the discussion by Belenky, Clinchy, Goldberger, and Tarule (1986) of "received knowledge" (p. 36). Received knowledge is transmitted by some *other* and considered valuable and prestigious because the other is in a perceived position of power. In the carrying out of mandated curriculum, some teachers might consider themselves "learners," in the sense of received knowledge, because they could "hear, understand, and remember" (Belenky et al., 1986, p. 36) and, in turn, institute the curriculum. But teachers-as-conduits are not the same as teachers-as-learners; being a vessel for some one else's thinking is not the same as being an inquirer.

Some teachers might react negatively to what I have just explained. They would suggest that they close their doors and do what they please. Yet, at Ridgeway, this was not the case. Most teams planned together, and the planning was a collective move toward mediocrity as teachers agreed upon common content that would be covered. The ethos of the school (Lortie, 1975) was one that supported team work, but the activity of the team typically involved a curriculum that did not reflect teachers' voices or the interests and imaginations of their students.

Unsilencing Voices for School Change

Belenky et al.'s (1986) discussion of "self, voice, and mind" applies to the teachers' expressions of themselves (aloud, in writing, or through other sign systems, such as a learning bubble) and their lived classroom and school experiences. Belenky et al. suggest that silent voices are typically among the "most socially, economically, and educationally deprived" (Belenky et al., 1986, pp. 23–24). Teachers are somewhat socially deprived, they are economically devalued, and their education is typically treated as low prestige. They are often silent because of their interpretation of the power structure of schools that treats teachers in ways that perpetuate deprivation. They are deprived of decision making and input, and assumed to lack competence. Fine (1987) and Sirotnik (1983) suggest that many students are silenced in schools. I would add that teachers are also silenced. It is quite likely that some teachers' voices are silenced by their understanding of the power structure of schools and the functions of teachers within that structure. Dewey (1938) sensed this (quite long ago) as a series of contrasts:

> To impositions from above is opposed expression and cultivation of individuality; to external discipline is opposed free activity; to learning from texts and teachers, learning from experience; to acquisition of isolated skills and techniques by drill, is opposed acquisition of them as means of attaining ends which make direct vital appeal; to preparation for a more or less remote future is opposed making the most of the opportunities of present life; to static aims and materials is opposed acquaintance with a changing world. (pp. 19–20)

Teachers' growing awareness of their oppression places pressure on them to trust in each other as a support system for cultivating their voices. This means increased sensitivity to the present system and the realization that, "trust is obviously absent in the anti-dialogics of the banking method of education ... [leading to] [h]opelessness [as] a form of silence, of denying the world and fleeing from it" (Freire, 1970a, p. 80). The work of our group suggests that within the hierarchical nature of the school system, teachers can feel the absence of trust and the hopelessness that results in silence, or they can come together to try to create the critical mass that Lester and Onore (1990) describe as essential for sending ripples of change through the school. This is complicated because the nature of the ripples will vary, and the commitment by teachers to engage in rippling work within schools involves many decisions, such as the amount of time and energy teachers commit to work towards change; the nature of individuals' composing; how individuals deal with disruption; willingness to study context of classroom, school, district, and community; willingness to act upon emerging awareness; and many more.

For the members of our group and for their students, coming to know their own voices was liberatory work:

Authentic liberation—the process of humanization—is not another deposit to be made in the [people]. Liberation is a praxis: the action and reflection of [people] on their world. (Freire, 1970a, p. 66)

Our meetings served as a forum for the communication that Freire sees as foundational to understanding positions and world views, to make sense of the ethos of the school context, and to coalesce initiatives for acting upon that context.

Some teachers at Ridgeway did not trust or want this liberation. Some feared it would only be retracted later, and others felt that it was not their job to inquire. One teacher put it this way, in the year-end interviews I conducted:

[Don't ask me], "What do you want to be doing?" No, it's like I'm here to teach the children, these [district curricula] are my objectives that I have to reach and so [if] there's a new program.... You need to tell me, "This is what you have to do that needs to be accomplished...." I have no problems with someone telling me, "This is what you need to do." I mean he's [the principal] my boss and that's just where I come from. The boss is the one that makes the decisions, not I.

There were, then, traditional and valued beliefs about the role of a teacher that were disrupted by the group. The point here is that expressing voices is not easy; it is a conscious decision and can be confusing because of various and conflicting pressures on teachers.

Historically, teachers have been quiet. They were "trained" to be technicians rather than substantive thinkers (Shannon, 1989). Shannon suggests that:

To understand their work, their experience, and their school culture, teachers must look again at the everyday events of their lessons. Not through the rationalized subjectivity that suggests that basal reading materials, tests, and bureaucratic structure are necessary to keep pace with modern demands on literacy, but through discussion of these objects to determine what they mean for teachers' and students' thoughts, feelings, and actions. Since teachers can only create new knowledge based on their current understanding, they must be subjects in the educative process and the discussions must be based on teachers' lived experience. (p. 136)

Thus, as teachers become inquirers, their inquiry becomes a vehicle for discovering or creating, enhancing, and expressing their voices. This is true for students, too. It is through inquiry that teachers and students can "make connections between their experience and current social structure" (Shannon, 1989, p. 137) in the school, get a sense that school "doesn't have to be this way" (p. 139), and "act on their new knowledge" (p. 141).

The tension between composing and disrupting was difficult because it involved teachers facing the very moral fiber of their lives. They had been taught or intuited that expression was inappropriate for a teacher. As they composed and expressed their voices, they realized that voice is, in part, an agent of their morality; as all the members of the group initiated the search for their individual voices, group members began to sense:

> the centrality of the concepts of responsibility and care in women's constructions of the moral domain, the close tie in women's thinking between conceptions of the self and of morality, and ultimately the need for an expanded developmental theory that includes, rather than rules out from consideration, the differences in the feminine voice[s]. ["s" added] (Gilligan, 1993, p. 105)

An "expanded theory" (Dewey, 1938) of teacher development needs to include teacher responsibility and care in the construction of teaching activity that cultivates the teaching and learning voices that are composed via inquiry. That inquiry may reveal oppression, anger, hope, and the untapped uses of imagination that inquiry sustains.

Finding Voices as Writers

Some members of our group felt silenced because of previous "research" or writing experiences that were harsh and negative. I put *research* in quotes because Liz and Linda, for example, recall spending hours in a library trying to make other people's work fit into an assigned paper. But this was not research; it was merely reorganizing other people's words. The study group supported members in the cultivation of their written voices. Each member of our group faced him- or herself as a writer. Most believed that they had no place in writing and that they should, if they wrote at all, write in a style that would please a traditional high school English teacher or college professor (formal, with strict adherence to standards of paragraphing, grammar, and more). The group disrupted old beliefs about writing and writers as they composed their written voices.

But finding writers' voices disrupted more than previous beliefs about writers and writing. Their writing disrupted their day-to-day lives and the lives of others in the school. It changed the tone and tenor of lunches together, of after school talk, and of relationships with other teachers. It began to bind the group; they were energized and, at the same time, further excluded others in the school who were not involved in a similar writing endeavor. Others were not intentionally excluded by the group, but felt that way reflective of the writers' excitement and emerging commitment to express and share learning.

Writing changed group members' lives (Langer & Applebee, 1987). Those who originally asked, "What's really new about what I'm doing?" began to see the sharing of their learning as a contribution to the growing

number of voices of inquiring teachers. It helped to read Avery (1993) and
Rief (1991) because they are women teacher-inquirers who wrote about how
hard teaching is and how to craft a classroom, and who demonstrated
(through their writing) that teachers are writers and perceptive inquirers in
their own classrooms. Group members supported each other in the move to
find voices as writers:

> Kim R.: You're getting ... you've gotten much better at journaling.
> Kim Z.: Yeah, that's my problem. I *have* to *write* this down, I need to just
> do it, obviously. (Transcript from study group session)

Kim Z. knew it was time to write; her writer's voice became urgent. She
questioned issues as they emerged in her writing, such as wanting to know
what to do about using the word "one" instead of "I" as a teacher researcher.
Kim L. responded, "I'd much rather read something that says 'I,' because
you know it's coming from them instead of somebody [else]." Kim L. intuited
that "one" is objectified and impersonal, distanced from self and work, and
implied a disownership of thinking. Our dealings with writing were, then,
emotional, pragmatic, and practical.

We dealt with audience quite a bit, as members wondered who would
read their work:

> Mona: I've been, you know, I've been thinking I can't write this, and I'm
> going, gee, maybe I can because of what I said today, but then
> who's the audience?...
> Kim R.: ... what I envision it for is for you guys, for Mr. Z. [the principal],
> for anybody that comes to Ridgeway next year that wants to
> understand what we're doing in our classroom.
> Kim Z.: ... first think [you're] writing to me, like you're telling me more
> about it, because I'm always coming down to ask her, and ... write
> it for J— or D— [other teachers, not in the group], too, trying
> to convince them that this is the way to go.
> Kim L.: Yeah, make it ... "this is my philosophy, this is the way I believe,"
> and write from that perspective. (Transcript from study group
> session)

They were proclaiming self, voice, and expression.

Cultivating voices also involved taking extended periods of time to focus
on an individual's writing; the teachers weren't used to being in the
spotlight, especially with their own writing. When Kim R. presented her
piece to us and expressed the need for time to discuss the piece because of

her feelings of confusion, excitement, and curiosity about being a writer, she concluded, an hour after we began, this way:

> **Kim R.:** Sorry, I had to do that.
> **Rick:** Don't be sorry, that's what we're here for, I think.

And then she withdrew her apology, or perhaps offered a bit of a justification for taking the spotlight because of her attachment to and urgency about what was happening in her writing: "I mean, it's very important to me right now, so...."

And when Kim Z. suggests that Kim R. work to continue to revise her writing: "Now hurry up and get it done so we can see, okay?"

Kim R. responded in a way that demonstrated that she was finding something within herself that she sensed may be slow to develop: "It's not going to be a hurry-up thing" (transcript from study group session). And it wasn't. Kim R., in the process of discovering herself and finding her voice, was also teaching the group by demonstrating to all of us her own journey toward finding or claiming or reclaiming and expressing her voice. Group members saw these same things happening with their students. The children became slowed-down thinkers as they supported each other in the elaboration of their questions, questioned their elaborations, and helped compose ways to present what they were learning. Recall the resistance Kim Z.'s students (chapter 2) expressed when she tried to teach her unit on teeth; her students had tasted learner-centered inquiry and expressed dissatisfaction with a teacher-directed unit of study. Having expressed their inquiring voices in their study of polar regions, they resisted reversions by their teacher. When Kim mentions this in her chapter, she almost sounds as if she was betraying herself and her students by thinking classroom life would be smoother if they "rested" from the intensity of inquiry via a teacher-constructed area of study. The children found their voices and they resisted departures from that type of work.

Finding voices as teacher-inquirers meant that members believed they had something to say that others might want to hear. They wanted the impact of their work and their students' work to extend beyond their own classroom walls and discussions in the teachers' lounge. They cultivated a sense of worth that extended beyond their original notions of what it means to be a teacher. They let the thoughtful voices within their minds step outside, feel vulnerable, and gather support in order to compose and disrupt even more. Although most members eventually expressed their voices in writing, everyone in the group—whether they wrote or not—acknowledged the group as a place to rehearse, examine, and cultivate their voices. Expressing their voices to take action upon their worlds was political activity.

FACETS OF INQUIRY BECOME POLITICS
OF INQUIRY

Teacher research in the study group involved the "systematic, intentional inquiry" (Cochran-Smith & Lytle, 1990, p. 2) in which teachers engaged while their students were engaged in their own "systematic, intentional inquiry." Conversing, recording, thinking, and questioning led to further reading, conversations, and questions about language, literacy, curriculum, self, teaching, and learning (Perrone, 1991). The group's questions and processes for dealing with those questions developed into its ongoing agenda. The facets of inquiry are the points of view of the inquiry process; they include the students' inquiry, teachers studying their students, teachers studying an area of interest, a study group as a forum of inquiry, and a study group as something to study. These facets became political because of what they disrupted.

Teachers, Students, and Politics

Inquiry is reflection in action, reflection on action, reflection after action, and reflection for subsequent action. It supports group-generated (within the thought collective) awareness, understandings, and plans for action. Graves (1983, 1986) suggests that teachers interested in writing begin by writing what they know. When teachers write and talk as they are coming to know, they not only find their voices in their emerging understanding, they also plan actions based on that understanding and that leads to subsequent writing, talking, thinking, and action. Teachers expressing their learning publicly by enacting and supporting inquiry as classroom activity are involved in political acts.

Greene (1995) proposes that the purpose of education is to make sense of our lives. Teachers in study groups take that seriously; they work at making sense of their lives. For example, recall that the district office supported the teachers at Ridgeway in their R & D year by paying for substitute teachers so that the teachers had time for planning and thinking. Our group grew out of those planning days. The district office did, however, perpetuate the technical nature of school (the view that schools are not forums for sustained thought) by withdrawing support after 1 year, resulting in the teachers at Ridgeway feeling abandoned. Work of this nature—change—demands sustained financial commitment that might require reviewing how district dollars are spent because change takes more than one year (Fullan, 1991).

Teacher inquiry is vulnerable when district offices initiate districtwide adoptions in many areas (reading, math, social studies, etc.) This is based in economics; the district curriculum implementations are based on the purchase of certain items at regular intervals (different curriculum adoptions in different years). Yet, successive implementations, typically of ideologically conflicting programs, leave teachers confused. Sustained district level support for genuine inquiry may assume low status because of the pressure from various interest groups (corporations) in selling to the district. Teacher inquiry may send messages that terrify corporations responsible for the manufacture and sale of curricular materials because teacher individuality and curricular specificity imply that negotiations with an entire system might disintegrate into having to face individual teachers and respond to their and their students' demands for materials, texts, and other curricular support. Reexamining school financing may be beyond a study group's function at this point in time, but it may be something that groups consider in the future as they face the politics and economics of inquiry.

Student assessment is another political arena. Testing companies have a vested interest (profit) in perpetuating standardized tests that may not demonstrate students' learning. At Ridgeway, we have not reached a conclusion about this, although during our second year together, Mr. Z. became quite intent on showing improvements in grade-level scores on standardized reading tests. This calls for advocacy for other types of assessment.

Time is political because if teachers are not given time to engage in serious reflective activity, the group's work can not be realized. The political, social, and economic contexts of school work to perpetuate and reproduce the existing school, putting tension on individuals who want to move in new directions. Schools perpetuate the cellular (Lortie, 1975) nature of teaching in which teachers feel isolated. But schools need not be this way. Inquiry groups may support teachers in stepping out of separate cells and into a common forum that serves to disrupt the cellular context and compose purposefully overlapping and interdependent relationships.

Inquiry-as-interdependence creates tension because "[a] change in the individual influences social dimensions, which in turn influence the individual" (LeFevre, 1987, p. 37). The group changes; then individuals change; so the group is different. It is time to face the specificity—of individuals and of contexts—that makes generic curriculum impossible, generic in-servicing unrealistic, and the search for kits or boxed sets that fix our schools, children, and teachers as insultingly deficit focused.

In light of inquiry-based curriculum that is context-specific and learner-centered, the findings of Moll and Diaz (1987) seem appropriate for the teachers in our study group:

> The key to understanding ... is in understanding the dynamics of material, local settings. To succeed in school one does not need a special culture ... success and failure is in the social organization of schooling, in the organization of the experience itself. (p. 311)

Moll and Diaz point to the structures of participation (Philips, 1971) of a particular school setting and how the complexities of those structures affect what teachers can do. Asking questions, engaging in sustained conversations, and taking action are political statements. Knowing this may help other groups understand or deal with the complex and various responses they encounter when they engage in inquiring, composing, and disrupting.

Inquiry was political in that the group disrupted the typical cultural capital of school (Lareau, 1989). Every child's and teacher's natural curiosity assumed higher value than performance on worksheets or involvement in the traditional ways with words in classrooms (Heath, 1983; Mehan, 1982). The teachers crossed cultural borders, disrupted expectations, composed themselves, and cocreated a context for authentic learning. They felt the joy, anger, and self-doubt that accompanies such activities: friendships changed; decisions were made to change grade levels; nongroup teachers viewed group members as not teaching, calling their work "fluff"; and other resentment from colleagues was tacitly and explicitly expressed. Our group's capital was the thoughtfulness of the teachers, looking for ways to cultivate children's capital into authentic learning with lifelong profits.

The view of teachers as "reflective practitioners" (Schon, 1983, 1986) is an increasingly common referent to teachers who are thoughtful about their students, teaching, and learning. In our group, as with others (e.g., Goswami & Stillman, 1987; Hubbard & Power, 1993; Patterson, Santa, Short, & Smith, 1993) the teachers sought to engage with each other and with their students in ways that took into account an awareness of each other, the context, and the specificity of Ridgeway. This is what Dewey (1938) meant when he discussed social intelligence.

Social intelligence at Ridgeway involved the formation of a group of inquiring teachers who were willing to stay together so that their composing and disrupting could be supported within a group. Inquiry was not merely the process of asking children what they knew and what they want to know, followed by the use of perfunctory research strategies in a library. Inquiry was a political act for teachers and for children as they researched interests utilizing primary sources for research, such as securing two rats to study how they communicate, reproduce, eat, and more. This was political work because it disrupted centralized curriculum as it supported learning and because it changed relationships among and between teachers and students. Changing relationships and curriculum was political because it involved change in the distribution of power and prestige in classrooms and, to some extent, in the school and the district.

Inquiry is a vehicle toward attaining the educative experiences that Dewey (1938) discussed. This was true for the children in inquiry groups, for the teachers in their classrooms, and for the members of our own group. The student-inquirers, the teacher-inquirers, the contexts of inquiry, and the fact that inquiry is life-changing are complex, political, and interwoven aspects of this work.

> Every thematic investigation which deepens historical awareness is thus really educational, while all authentic education investigates thinking. The more educators and the people investigate the people's thinking, and are thus jointly educated, the more they continue to investigate. Education and thematic investigation, in the problem-posing concept of education, are simply different moments of the same process. (Freire, 1970a, p. 101)

Inquiry, then, is not a strategy for classroom use that can be instituted because of a district mandate. It is a process of problem-posing for all learners and is political because it disrupts expectations of or demands for homogeneity of context, content, and activity.

Staff Development and Politics

My work as a university assistant (nontenured) professor was political because of my changing roles at the university and my activity at the school site. As I composed my relationships with the children and staff of Ridgeway, I also disrupted my relationships with some of my colleagues at the university. Although there is a move toward school-based research, I felt resentment for my lack of presence at the university. I was redefining scholarship (Boyer, 1990), and I was disrupting what it meant to be a good citizen of the college and a university teacher. Teaching and learning with my colleagues in the study group, away from the campus at a school site, were parts of my emerging pedagogical and scholarly agendas. Although such activity made some university colleagues uneasy, it reaffirmed what Short (1993) suggests: "Teacher educators who do research in their own classrooms offer the profession both a different perspective on the learning environments of preservice and inservice teachers and a way to transform those environments" (p. 155). I was composing my understanding of servicing-in and participatory professional development as I studied in and with the study group.

Recall that at the beginning of our work together, I thought that the group would focus on the literacy activity within the participating teachers' classrooms because literacy is my area of interest. The further we walked down the path of inquiry, the more I was confronted with the political realities of what it meant to be an inquirer and a member of this group. As the group engaged in inquiry, we underwent a process of conscientization, which Freire (1970b) defines as part of the process of:

> continual problematization of the learners' existential situations as represented in the codified images. The longer the problematization proceeds, and the more the subjects enter into the "essence" of the problematized object, the more they are able to unveil this "essence." The more they unveil it, the more their awakening consciousness deepens, thus leading to the "conscientization" of the situation.... (p. 221)

Site-based inquiry (composing of curriculum) supports "continual proble-matization." Indeed, continual problematization may be the essence of composing and disrupting because the tension between those two may become the arena, a political arena, for inquiring minds, as it did in our group.

Although Stuckey (1991) is discussing literacy, the same may be said about teacher inquiry; inquiry is:

> ... a social restriction and an individual accomplishment. Individuals read and write, or don't, and individuals do with their literacy what they can. The subjectivities of minds, and the ways in which people make their lives and thoughts, and the ways in which people are coerced, entrapped, colonized, or freed, must be addressed as processes. At the same time, the processes must not become the issue, since the conditions for any process, and especially for the literacy process, determine the possible outcomes. That is why, for example, teaching literacy depends on the circumstances rather than on the textbook. Our attention needs to be focused on the conditions in every instance.
>
> A theory of literacy is, thus a theory of society, of social relationships; and the validity of a theory of literacy derives from the actual lives of the people who make the society [the school]. (p. 64)

I was instrumental in helping the group study the conditions, processes, and outcomes at Ridgeway. Part of my servicing-in role involved helping the group (including me) understand what was happening to group members and their students. Stuckey continues her discussion by addressing how literacy programs can support change:

> To do this, we must remember who we really are. We are not just private individuals in whose private minds the printed word works powerful deeds. We are, to be sure, natural individuals, but we are social before we are born, and the commerce we do with our literacy is always, fundamentally, social. We are arranged by our relations to literacy, to how and why literacy is produced, and to the efforts of what literacy is about. The extension of these relations describes how close to the edge of survival we live. (p. 95)

The teachers in our group at Ridgeway founded a thinking and enacting collective that supported us in the social and political work of inquiry across the many facets of self, colleague, group, classroom, school, and district. They were composing the "commerce" that they would do with inquiry, and their students were also composing a classroom commerce rooted in inquiry. Inquiry became a sort of capital that afforded children prestige among their classmates (and teachers who valued it as well). Inquiry was also a form of capital in the group as we supported, cajoled, questioned, and presented our inquiring selves to one another and, eventually, in other forums. The conditions in which this work took place changed over time, in part because of the composing and disrupting that the group supported. My agency involved my commitment to participation, liberation, and democracy, which contributed to these changing conditions.

There were many feelings at the school that accompanied the study group's work. The feelings of exclusion of some staff who were nonmembers indicated that they perceived themselves as outsiders. And, some group members, quite aware of how much work it entailed, considered themselves insiders. Group members assumed status, and insider–outsider tensions were expressed in a variety of ways.

INSIDERS, OUTSIDERS, AND INQUIRY AS POLITICAL WORK

One of the most difficult aspects of my work with the teachers at Ridgeway emerged as I became increasingly thrilled and amazed at the inquiry that the children and their teachers were engaged in. As I worked with group members, it also became apparent that I was not spending time in other teachers' classrooms. There wasn't time, they weren't in the group, they didn't seem interested; the list of reasons (excuses?) seems virtually endless, a veritable litany of supporting evidence for me choosing not to engage with nongroup members. I was, then, complicitous in creating a group of insiders, and because there were insiders, there were outsiders. The insiders were group members; the outsiders were the other teachers in the school.

During the interviews that I conducted with staff members of Ridgeway at the end of the first year of our group, some teachers expressed feelings about being excluded and some did not. Those who didn't mind were content to plan with their own teams and not invest additional after-school time in a study group.

Outsiders Feel Less Prestigious

Some of the teachers who felt resentment wanted me to invent a means to include them in such a way that they would not have to attend after-school meetings. I tried meeting with some of them during their lunch periods and at other times during the day. They wanted to learn how to do "it," but I was not sure what "it" was. I think they wanted their students involved in projects because they thought that such activity was what the district office was now demanding. There was a thick feeling of anger at meetings I had with nongroup members; the teachers did not want this to be difficult. They wanted to be able to say they were doing "it" so that they would feel current and concordant with what they perceived to be district demands. There were issues of status at work here; these intensified as our group's prestige rose and nonmembers felt less valued.

Outsiders wanted prestige similar to that being granted to members of the study group. They thought they could gain it by having their students "do" projects; but they didn't see that students' inquiry is part of teachers taking control of curricular decisions, teachers expressing themselves, children assuming initiative in their own learning, and more. Outsiders' desires to maintain the image of doing what appears to be demanded by the district is the antithesis of what their (insider) colleagues were doing. Group members wanted to express their own voices and support their students as inquirers; this is a fundamental shift in what schools do, is political, and is confusing to those who want to be good teachers but have not engaged in experiences like the study group or some other consciousness-raising activity. There are other aspects of *insider* and *outsider* that need to be explored as part of the effort to help other groups affect change.

An Insider Moves Outside

I want to review the teacher who disassociated herself from this book. After I had invested well over 1 year in data analysis, I received a call from her one evening. She had read a draft of the book and decided that, "I just don't want to be associated with it." I truly felt faint. How could I systematically go through the entire book and remove any trace of her existence? I could not. I would make her as invisible as possible, but needed to acknowledge that she was a group member who made a decision. She was taking her voice (or wanted me to take her voice) completely out of this book. Did she not want to be part of "us" because of some fear that such an affiliation would hurt her career? She said that she didn't like the way she sounded in the book, "so much like a first-year teacher."

"That's what you were," I said to her.

"I know ... I just don't want to be associated with the book." She kept saying that over and over. I couldn't help her understand the important role that a first year teacher has in a book of this nature. I suggested that readers would see that the teachers were involved in many different ways of engaging in inquiry; they would want to see what she dealt with.

She was having none of it.

I returned to the tapes of our sessions and the hundreds of pages of transcripts. Were there clues as to why someone would not want to be heard? I saw that she resisted writing; she told the group of some difficult writing experiences as a child and in college. Perhaps she felt intimidated by the other teachers' writing. I wonder if I helped to make her feel like an outsider because of the prestige that writing took in our group once we committed to write a book.

One of the reviewers of this book wondered if the production of a product affected the group. I would say that it did. It forced teachers to focus on a point (chapter) in time; it may have contributed to making this teacher feel like an outsider. Hearing that she was being transferred out of the classroom and, at the same time, learning of our commitment to write this book, she may have felt overwhelmed. Her actions underscore that every group is different, fluid, organic, and affects members in a variety of ways. She also made me wonder about my role or position.

As a researcher, this was a terrifying place to be. What if the other teachers pulled out? What, I began to wonder, is my relationship with them? Is this another insider–outsider situation? How inside of Ridgeway was I? How outside?

Researcher, Resource, and Outsider?

A critical aspect of political activity is to keep turning things over, to continue problematization in order to gain insights into roles, issues of power and authority, relationships, and more. I wonder if a group like this needs an outsider. O'Laughlin (personal communication) asked me, "Do the teachers need external authorities to justify their work?" I am not sure; I have not been in a group that is all teachers because, in my present position within the university, the operational definition of my job prevents me from being a member of a group that is exclusively teachers. Members of the study group may have needed an outsider's permission, agency, and participation to initiate and sustain their activity.

I helped the teachers in our group publish, present, and gain prestige in the district by learning how to be visible. And, I am the White, only-male-in-the-group, university professor. The teachers' relationships with me supplement the privileged roles they are assuming in the school and district; and it also hurts them because of what privilege disrupts. In my capacity, with those descriptors (White, male, "higher" educator), I am different; and I am an outsider. This is the politics of insider–outsider positioning. I am not the only researcher to wonder about the presence of an outsider; some believe that even the changes that we "see" may not be there: "We know, for example, that adults are expert in pretending that reform is taking place without taking any real ownership in the process, particularly when there are sanctions for not changing" (Corbett & Wilson, 1995, p. 15). This resonates with the discussion, earlier, about nonmembers wanting to appear to be engaging in what the group was doing.

I was lucky, as an outsider, to have been part of the thought collective that developed; and I know, too, that I was instrumental in creating the collective. I am privileged also in that I have, as part of my job, the opportunity to write about what happened. And, as part of that, I struggle with how not to usurp or misrepresent the staff and children of Ridgeway. This leads to the politics of reward structures, which are different between the university and the public school.

Insiders and Systems of Rewards

Although a professor might gain rank or status by writing a book, teachers rarely receive anything for their participation. If they gain recognition and prestige, they may also be subject to resentment by some staff members. Our group decided that each author, except me, would get 10% of all royalties from the book. I would get 40%; nonwriters would not get any money. We didn't agonize over this decision because one nonwriter didn't want to be associated with the book and the two others were Pam, who left the group after the first year, and Jane, who was comfortable (almost insistent) that the writers get the royalties. We wanted to discern a way in which Ridgeway children could receive royalties, perhaps by purchasing trade books or other materials. After discussing the fact that such donations could lead to committees of teachers and administrators making decisions about how the funds are used, we decided to earmark the money to the writers in the study group and they could, in turn, donate it to their own or their colleagues' classrooms.

Members of the higher education community know that collaboration with public schools is, on one level, highly esteemed by many schools of education at the present time. Groups such as the Holmes group and Goodlad's (1994) National Network for Educational Renewal stress the importance of partnerships in improving teacher education and teaching. We gained much from our partnership as we developed a relationship that was based in "a community of discourse engaged in reflection, conversation, and action" (Fosnot, 1989, p. 139). Our partnership eventually resulted in me teaching blocks of undergraduate methods courses at Ridgeway and having the undergraduate students' practicum take place in Ridgeway classrooms. Since I knew many of the teachers and they knew me, the site-based practicum was more consistent and useful for all involved.

The relationship with the university, specifically with me, helped the teachers consider the tension between theory and practice. The group faced their practices and confronted the theories that they were reading about. Clandinin (1993) explains it this way:

> In our inquiry we tried to make sense of how theory and practice might be connected; we tried to engage in a dialogue between our practices and theory, a dialogue mutually informing to both theory and practice, to researcher and practitioner. In this view, theory was not seen as superior to practice but as in a kind of dialectical relationship

to practice. The dialogue or conversation between theory and practice resulted in new understandings of both. (p. 12)

Darling-Hammond and McLaughlin (1995) submit that when

... relationships emerge as true partnerships, they can create new, more powerful kinds of knowledge about teaching and schooling, as the 'rub between theory and practice' produces more practice, contextualized theory and more theoretically grounded, broadly informed practice. (p. 599)

It is the nature and definition of a partnership that I am wondering about at this time. If I left Ridgeway, there would be no partnership with the university, assuming that since I am the agent of the university involved with the school then there is, operationally, a partnership. Could someone take my place? Of course; and if they did, the nature of the partnership would change as the relationships changed.

Work between public schools and universities is relational and quite specific to the individuals involved. My relationship with Ridgeway Elementary School is just that: It is *my* relationship. It can not be generic. It is not as much about a school as it is about the individuals and the complexities that unfold therein. The "rub between theory and practice" is also a rub between individuals' ideologies. This is not meant to be construed as a hopeless view of partnership; rather it is an effort to contextualize and specify collaboration. Collaborative work is harder than previously construed because it takes more care than has been previously reported and the commitment is a complex one of time, effort, energy, specificity, genuineness, and more.

Yet, I wonder if this type of work is prestigious in higher education when it does not quickly produce sufficient numbers of articles in journals that would lead to promotion and tenure. Boyer (1990) addresses this issue as he tries to redefine scholarship, but its affect on nontenured faculty remains to be seen. The political nature of children's and teachers' inquiries may not reap extrinsic rewards until some existing structures (tenure, salary advancement) are disrupted and subsequently or simultaneously composed to allow for much specificity and individuality for both teachers and university faculty. As servicing-in work strives to make transparent some of the walls between the university and the public school, these issues need to be named, faced, and addressed.

The purpose of the discussion in this chapter was to make the politics of this work public so that others engaging in inquiry will understand some of the subtle and not-so-subtle responses they might receive when they are involved in inquiry with their students and each other. If the complexity and intensely political nature of this work is underestimated, it may be at the expense of inquiring minds.

Chapter 12

Implications: What's Next for Our Group and Yours?

¤ ¤ ¤

We can't be literate alone. Words change our thoughts. We go forth to do something in the world, to make our contribution. Others value us and help us to value ourselves. Our literate friends listen, talk, write, read, think, support, and challenge us. This community buzzes.

—Hansen (1987, p. 64)

Our journeys as inquirers are far from over for many reasons, the utmost of which is that the community "buzzes" because this thought collective is a powerful forum for meaning-making. In this final chapter, I iris out further to provide a broad view of issues that may inform our group, and yours, in the continued understanding and cultivation of inquiry.

SERVICING-IN

The work that our group undertook has implications for understanding and refining the process of servicing-in, particularly in light of what occurs as servicing-in is enacted as inquiry. Richardson (1994) suggests that "[w]e know little about how to work with teachers in helping them improve their practical inquiry" (p. 9). Complicating this further, Darling-Hammond (1995) writes, "Policymakers increasingly realize that regulations cannot transform schools; only teachers, in collaboration with parents and administrators, can do that" (p. 5). I would add that an outsider may be necessary, and that children, as the focus of transformation, are also voices that need to be included, especially if we are to reach the "deeper forms of student and teacher learning" (Darling-Hammond, 1995, p. 5) that are necessary for sustained transformation. Indeed, "breaking the mold" (Leiberman, 1995, p. 595) that restrains teacher development demands that we acknowledge that "The ways teachers learn may be more like the ways students learn than we have previously recognized" (p. 592).

The complexity, intensity, and the nature of the commitment of teacher inquiry contribute to our lack of knowledge of how teachers grow because there are generic (district, state, and national) expectations of teachers living and working in very different contexts. Specificity of context is acknowledged in the servicing-in relationship because inquiry and teacher knowledge are generated at the school or classroom site, sensitive and responsive to the differences that individuals are willing to express at those sites.

When teachers are supported emotionally, cognitively, and even spiritually by an outsider and by each other, an atmosphere of caring (Noddings, 1984) may be created. Caring, as moral and ethical activity, is foundational to the inquiry activity that emerges when individuals mutually construct an agenda for study of self, others, curriculum, learning, and lived experiences in their classrooms. All participants may benefit from the relationships that are created. The children at the school ultimately benefit because, as their teachers compose themselves as inquirers, the teachers work with the children to compose an ethos of inquiry within their classrooms. By ethos, I refer to Lortie's (1975) definition of ethos as "the pattern of orientations and sentiments which is peculiar to teachers and which distinguishes them from members of other occupations" (p. viii).

The relational nature of caring supports the dissolution of the objectification of teachers as they find voice, energy, and direction within self and between each other in a thought collective. By "dissolution of the objectification of teachers", I mean that servicing-in involves negotiation within a context in which all voices are heard, honored, challenged, and cultivated. It means working to end the coldness of a curriculum that is prescribed far from the school site and void of knowledge of the children and teachers expected to cover it. This is difficult and intense work that rests in conversations across school years. Clark (1990) writes, "[T]he term conversation suggests ... that any text must function within the larger context of a succession of texts that respond to each other in the process of defining knowledge that the community of people who read and write them can share" (p. 36). Successive conversations are not easy to sustain (Short et al., 1996) but are needed to build a history of a group, together, as the meaning-making of previous years helps members understand coming years. Servicing-in celebrates how exhilarating this work is and acknowledges how exhausting it can be.

The energy that is needed for teachers to grow is often overlooked in the literature on teacher-as-researcher, but there are descriptions of parents' anguishing attempts to change their relationships with schools. Lareau (1989) talks about "the dark side of parent involvement" (p. 148), suggesting that parent involvement increased stress, made parents feel that their children were increasingly vulnerable as those parents expressed themselves on behalf of their children, and could have negative effects on home life. The teachers in our group increased their involvement and felt many of the same feelings of the parents in Lareau's study.

Servicing-in means teachers take on a second job, one that I call metateaching or metapedagogy. They teach *and* they systematically study their teaching. The exhilaration and exhaustion may be demonstrated by an example.

One Wednesday afternoon, as we met in the common space between Kim R. and Kim L.'s classrooms, I looked around the room and thought I saw some very tired folks. "This is such hard work," I said. "I feel like we need a rest."

"Not me," said Liz. "I feel energized by all this. I'm ready to go go go."

I looked at her in amazement. Her response paralleled the responses of Kim Z.'s students when Kim suggested that the second graders needed a rest from inquiry and should engage in a prescribed unit of study. They resisted, the way Liz was resisting now; the activity that makes inquirers tired also invigorates them. In my journal that evening, I wrote:

> She's [Liz] the mother of children who participate in school activities, she supported Linda when Linda's husband was dying and after he died, and she taught a diverse and challenging class of third graders. As a professor, I can focus on research because it is part of my job. The members of our group stretched their job descriptions, truly a reflection of their dedication, thirst for knowledge, and commitment to self, each other, and children. The composing of self as an inquirer is not easy. It demands the confrontation of so much ... living with the tension between and within composition and disruption. It is a process of building, confirming, and affirming that is saturated with the tension that a person feels when growing and changing and the added stress when such work is done in an environment—the school—that works to avoid change and to perpetuate itself (knowingly or unknowingly).

Gibboney (1994) predicts we would feel this way:

> Conversation uses language to foster thinking to make schools more stimulating places in which to learn and to teach; and conversation may be a practical way to renew schools in educationally fundamental ways ...
> School reform efforts that rely on the play of powerful social dynamics [conversation] exact a cost. This cost is paid for in hard physical, emotional and intellectual dollars. The value of these dollars is created by the participants' willingness to deal with uncertainty within a dialogue process that demands both thought and practical action. These are tough demands, but any serious reform, whatever its mode of intervention, will require that this payment be made. Our seriousness about reform and our maturity as a profession will be determined by our willingness to undertake this work and make the payment. (p. 214)

Other teacher inquirers may anticipate a wide range of emotional and physical states as their groups organize and sustain themselves. They may also experience an increased desire to advocate for teachers and children as inquirers.

ADVOCACY AND TEACHER STUDY GROUPS

The teachers in our group initiated the "upgrading of the prestige of the teaching profession" that Bruner (1963) called for more than 30 years ago. Principals and other district and school administrators may expect that teachers will want input into many aspects of schools. Teachers will want time to think, to form thought collectives that have different arrangements than are traditional (not restricted to grade level), and to read and react within their collectives.

The work in thought collectives may result in action for children and for curriculum. The desire to compose schools that are sensitive to the "local settings" (Moll & Diaz, 1987) will be increasingly expressed as teachers create curriculum with children, indeed become coresearchers with the children in their classrooms as they work together to uncover the curricular and learning possibilities there. Increasingly, teachers will have evidence that demonstrates that inquiry supports lifelong learning. The teachers will show that inquiry addresses literacy learning as well as learning in the disciplines (math, art, music, science, etc.) and that it helps citizens compose themselves for participatory lives within a democracy. This emphasizes that inquiry is *for* something; it is life-changing for the self and for others.

I am not the first inquirer to suggest that research be *for* teachers and children. Edlesky (1994) calls for research that "aims to be transformative" (p. 69) because it is based in a distinct theoretical orientation. Transformative research works at addressing inequities and unfairness; it has the goal of helping us uncover untapped possibilities. Inquiry is partnerships that demand the mutually beneficial stance of research *with* and *for* rather than research *on* teachers, students, and community. Such inquiry leads to voice and advocacy *for* students, curriculum, particular forms of assessment, equity, and further inquiry. Others will invent things I haven't thought of yet because we can expect the unexpected when teachers and children are encouraged to think and express their interests and what they wonder about.

There may be, then, advocacy for self, relationships, curriculum, children, and, eventually, the very ethos of the school, the district, and the profession. If we are to honor this growth, we need to think of ways in which schools may be places for teachers to safely engage in systematic inquiry that will support sustained change. For schools to be safe for such activity, they must be "a place where you are able to tell the truth about yourself and not feel ashamed" (Paley, 1995, p. 130).

Teachers will want more control of their teaching lives, more democratic ways within the profession, and the support of groups willing to coadvocate with them. Teachers' unions may participate as coadvocates or teachers may need to find other ways to organize and advocate. Although it may be expected that teachers unions negotiate for salary, there is rarely an expectation that unions negotiate for the right to create curriculum; indeed, districts and the corporations that supply curriculum rely on teachers' unions not engaging in such work. It may be time to invent more functions for unions.

Teacher groups may want to study the ways in which voice and advocacy are addressed by other marginalized groups in order to understand how systems tend to perpetuate silence for certain groups. For example, Polakow (1993) wonders, as she considers the lives of disenfranchised poor single mothers:

> *What if* women were to strike, crippling the bureaucracy?
> *What if* squatting became an effective strategy for homeless people?
> *What if* poor women organized to take over buildings from abusive and neglectful landlords?
> *What if* evictions were resisted in the same way that segregated lunch counters once were?
> *What if* Head Start Teachers earning only $11,000 a year went on strike?
> *What if* poor, uninsured mothers marched on doctors' offices and clinics and hospitals that denied them services?
> All of these nonviolent strategies have been used as part of protest movements pushing for change against intractable judicial and legislative machinery. (p. 182)

And there are "*what ifs*" for teachers that suggest strategies they might use to advocate for themselves and a workplace that respects them and their students as learners:

> *What if* teachers negotiate for the freedom to inquire?
> *What if* they assume strong stances, risking court procedures, in facing irrelevant curricular expectations?
> *What if* they demand the time they need to create democratic and participatory curriculum?
> *What if* they march on the district offices that distribute mandated curriculum?
> *What if* they refuse to attend district staff development days because those inservice activities do not meet their or their students' needs?
> *What if,* instead, they engage in sustained servicing-in relationships?
> *What if* they become so well read (and well published) that they can present sound arguments to boards of education for the activities in which they want to engage with each other and their students?
> *What if* teachers' stories are heard?
> *What if* they write books, make learning bubbles, give presentations, have parents visit for project fairs and other learning celebrations, and make important connections with their colleagues in the teaching community and beyond?

These are some of the advocacy questions that linger and haunt. Silverstein, the poet, (1974) writes:

Everything seems swell, and then
The nighttime Whatifs strike again! (p. 90)

It is time to expect teachers to look at what appears to be out of their control, to examine what feels like someone else's view of what seems "swell," and to insert some "Whatifs". Teachers and others involved in education, reading the list above, might find themselves concerned, as does Polakow; she continues:

Such strategies, nevertheless, do create ominous risks, particularly for women with children. But the voices of the disenfranchised must be taken account of, and they must be heard. Their stories must be told so that they are given voice and space to become actors. (p. 182)

Inquiring teachers are growing in numbers and feeling the frustration of a system that disenfranchises them. Ridgeway was fortunate to be in a school system that was somewhat supportive, having hired Jane who worked to cut a path through some of the resistance and inertia that teachers can feel as forces that work against change. Jane is still composing her position and dealing with the conflicting messages sent by the district office. Advocacy is complex activity when it takes place in a school system that places multiple and mixed demands on teachers and students. Increasing our awareness of this complexity helped our group make decisions about what to advocate for and may explain to other groups why things do not always unfold as planned.

Consistent with servicing-in theory, advocacy may begin at a very local level. Children being supported in presenting a learning fair to their families and friends are involved in advocacy because a teacher, proactive about curriculum and inquiry, is engaging them in a public statement of their learning. This is advocacy, as the teacher clears the way for learning events to occur. It is advocacy when teachers change schedules to have big blocks of time with their students, meet regularly to plan and think, collect data to make a case for a child, or write a chapter in a book. It is advocacy when a teacher faces her team and says that she and her students are going to do something different from the rest of the team. And it is advocacy when teachers present thinking and action that is contrary to mandated curriculum. Advocacy that supports inquiring minds is advocacy that is rooted in rousing minds to life (Tharp & Gallimore, 1988), reminding us that inquiry is political work for children's and teachers' minds.

INQUIRY CAN'T BE DUPLICATED

Word traveled fast in this district. Jane, as the early childhood consultant, worked with all the schools within the district and lauded the success that the group was having as we supported students' ventures into inquiry. By February of our first year, teachers from other schools were visiting group members' classrooms, looking for a single answer, a single correct way to engage in inquiry. As Kim R. said:

> Well, that's why these guys shut us off as soon as they saw how we had our rooms, they shut us off. And I kept saying, "This is not the only way to do projects. Look at [other classrooms]. Talk to Kim Z. There's lots of different models of doing projects [inquiry]." (Transcript from a study group session)

As an increasing number of teachers visited the group's classrooms, the teachers in the group were faced with other teachers who believed that the district office was sending the message that all teachers in the district needed to look like the teachers at Ridgeway. Group members were uncomfortable with this for many reasons. They believed that each member of the group taught differently and that there was no pattern or template to follow. They became annoyed with visitors who wanted a guide for duplication.

It was at this point that I began to see the difference between composing and identifying. Teachers who *identify* a program that they want for their classrooms are often responding to outside pressures. They think that teachers who are receiving recognition are those doing things "the right way"; the teachers identify that "way" and then incorporate it into their classrooms. When these teachers visited Ridgeway, they became frustrated at the individuality and the differences across classrooms. Some of the visitors (as well as nongroup members at Ridgeway) were confused about the role of the teacher and did not understand that engaging in inquiry "does not mean that we relinquish our roles as teachers" (Thomas & Oldfather, 1995, p. 201). Identification is a strategy for accumulating classroom procedures and a response to having lived with mandated curriculum; it entails neither the reflection inherent in composing the self as an inquirer nor the learning of strategies for supporting inquiry. Identification is only superficially disruptive because the teachers are unsettled as they try to meet the demands that they believe are emanating from the district office. Identification rarely disrupts children's intuitive understanding of schools as places in which curriculum is teacher directed. Identification is the reification of composing.

Placing group members in high regard and promoting them as exemplary was considerable pressure for them to bear because the group was so new. They certainly had evidence of student learning, but were increasingly convinced that teachers needed to compose themselves as inquirers, rather than identify and adopt from this group (or anyone else's) particular areas of inquiry or ways of inquiring. Newly formed teacher study groups, as a cautionary, need to become and remain cognizant of their roles in their schools and districts to insure that things don't move so quickly that they undermine themselves or are overrun by others. If there is some tacit or explicit expectation that things should change quickly, it may still be possible to engage in inquiry, but the intensity that will probably be felt needs to be acknowledged, named, and confronted in some way so that the group is not overtly, covertly, intentionally, or unintentionally sabotaged.

HONORING A VARIETY OF SIGN SYSTEMS

Short et al. (1996) discuss the uses of a variety of sign systems for the expression of meaning. Although their "authoring cycle" was originally suggested as a way to create the writing curriculum in classrooms, they "experimented in our own college classrooms as well as talked and worked with other teachers and colleagues ... [and] ... came to see the authoring cycle as a metaphor for learning and a general framework for curriculum" (p. 39). They found, as our group did, that engaging in inquiry to learn to read, write, build, draw, or use some other sign systems also involves using that sign system to learn inquiry. To paraphrase Halliday, (1988), we learn inquiry, we learn through inquiry, we learn about inquiry (and the inquirers); similarly, we learn sign systems, we learn through sign systems, and we learn about sign systems.

We are still coming to terms with this issue because reading and writing are afforded high prestige in our society. As Kim L. explained (chapter 4) in her examples of children making models of cats out of clay, designing art centers about fish, and making models of sharks, the teachers honored their students' uses of many sign systems as ways in which the children would come to be readers and writers. There is evidence, as Berghoff (1994) has shown, that a student's literacy development may support and parallel his or her development in the use of other sign systems.

There is little doubt that literacy activity occurred as the students were encouraged to use a variety of systems for making meaning. They spoke more, wrote more, and read more. And something happened within our group, too, during the use of multiple ways of gathering and interpreting data. As teachers collected their students' growth by taking notes, gathering artifacts, audio taping, video taping, and taking still photos, they found themselves with data that was a window into conversations about their students' and their own growth as inquirers. We spoke more, wrote more, and read more, too. The use of other sign systems was not a focus for our group, but is something to which group members are giving greater attention now. The children and their teachers made meaning the way artists, researchers, scientists, mathematicians, sociologists, musicians, and more do. As members consider a broad spectrum of ways of knowing and making meaning, a teacher study group, becomes, "… a place where theories are remade in relation to the knowledge teachers bring with them" (Flannery, 1995, p. 33).

IMAGINE WHAT COMES NEXT

Our group was bonded by a deep sense of imagination. This sustained the group, along with:

Relationships.
Fear.
Love.
Anger.
Curiosity.
Thoughtfulness.
Reading.
Writing.
Discovery.
Eating grapes and popcorn.
Talk.
Tears.
Commitment.
Stubbornness.
Whining.
Vulnerability.
Margaritas (off school grounds!)
Plans.
Dreams.
Conference proposals.
Book proposals.
Jane dancing.
Kids.

Mostly, it was the students' and the teachers' willing imaginations that congealed the group. We found ourselves wandering and wondering (Short et al., 1996) quite a bit; we asked, "What if,… " and we were tenacious about finding out, only to ask, "What if …" again.

Groups must be committed to taking action that will change members' lives, change students' thinking, and change the school and its place in the district and the community. This will entail working towards demythifying, a process that supports connections to others around a sense of mutual responsibility to composing realities that are safe, productive, and committed to individuals' growth within a collective zone of proximal development. Groups need to work to imagine ways of facing fears as well as proceeding to disrupt aspects of traditional schools that hurt children, perpetuate racism and classism, and keep teachers from being thoughtful.

Maybe we were an imagination collective as much as we were a thought collective. Our group understands that you need to compose your own group in your own way, with your students at the center, and expect and deal with the disruption you create within yourself, within other teachers, within your students, and within your community.

Inquiry is thinking, questioning, working, wondering, writing, sharing, meditating, mediating, and planning. It has no strictly predictable sequence, and I suggest that we need to learn to delight in that as much as we are confused by it. It is the creation of self, the uncovering of self, and the intersections of self with children, language, learning, the school, the community, and more. To perpetuate this process demands the individual expression of each self within a school, wildly and passionately with imagination. It requires that we enter the "great conversations", indeed, disrupt these conversations, as Greene describes:

> Allowing myself to be carried along by the great conversation initiated by others (and, indeed, maintained by others), I would not have to disrupt. I would not have to begin anything; I would need only be swept along by what the great ones have said and remain partially submerged in them.
> But then I think of how much beginnings have to do with freedom, how much disruption has to do with consciousness and the awareness of possibility that has so much to do with teaching other human beings. And I think that if I and other teachers truly want to provoke our students to break though the limits of the conventional and the taken for granted, we ourselves have to experience breaks with what has been established in our lives; we have to keep arousing ourselves to begin again. (Greene, 1995, p. 109)

Teacher inquiry groups are about hope for discovering the possibilities, for ourselves, within and among and between ourselves, and with the children with whom we live our lives in schools. The groups are imagination forums, thought collectives, and safe harbors, and they support teachers in creating schools as places for thinking, growing, inquiring, learning, disrupting, and composing.

Appendix A

Elaboration of the Context of Our Work

¤ ¤ ¤

The study group formally began during the 1994-1995 school year when the teachers at Ridgeway Elementary School became involved in a districtwide initiative focused on changing the ways in which young children are educated. The district office offered the 34 elementary schools in the district the opportunity to have an additional $25,000 for one school year (1994–1995), provided the money was used to support staff development for teachers of young children; early childhood education in our district is defined as children through Grade 3 (from birth through age 8). The use of the funds was at the discretion of the selected sites because the district office was not adopting or implementing a preformulated curriculum. The selected sites were referred to as research and development (R & D) sites. Fourteen schools in the district submitted proposals to access the funding; 2 schools were selected because their comprehensive proposals were supported by their entire staffs; Ridgeway was one of the schools selected.

AN R & D ORIENTATION

The district office set the stage for inquiry, growth, and change by choosing to present teachers with an Early Childhood Philosophy Statement that was developed by teacher representatives and other interested community members, rather than a packaged curriculum. Since the 1994–1995 school year was designated by the director of instruction for the district as the year in which the district would implement an early childhood curriculum, an Early Childhood Study Committee was formed. The Committee was responsible for districtwide early childhood curriculum implementation. The district's early childhood consultant (Jane) wanted to help the teachers of children in prekindergarten through third grade adopt an attitude toward learning reflective of developmentally appropriate practice and consistent

214

with Fullan's (1991) ideas of mutually developed and supported change. Her goal was not to adopt a curriculum, but to develop a districtwide theoretical orientation to young children's learning.

The Early Childhood Study Committee developed the district's Early Childhood Philosophy as a brief statement of their understanding of developmentally appropriate practice (Bredekamp, 1987). The Philosophy Statement encouraged teachers to grow through staff development that would take place in teacher study groups. The idea for staff development as a way of increasing children's learning emerged at the district office where consultants employed by the district were searching for ways to support teacher change from the district level while allowing it to grow at the local level.

Members of the Early Childhood Study Committee were searching for a document that was more substantive than the brief Philosophy Statement. They knew they could generate a lengthy reading list for teachers, but wanted something self-contained. The State Department of Education had, at the same time, established a relationship with British Columbia, Canada, and was given access to their extensive document on primary education. British Columbia was receiving international acclaim for its work with young children. Eventually, because our neighboring state education department was also interested in the work in British Columbia, the two states formed a collaboration between their state education departments and developed their own document, *The Primary Program: Growing and Learning in the Heartland* (Nebraska Department of Education,1993), which relies heavily on the British Columbia Document. Bredekamp (1987), *The Primary Program: Growing and Learning in the Heartland*, and the district's early childhood philosophy statement became the foundation documents for early childhood education in the city's public schools.

The Primary Program: Growing and Learning in the Heartland is referred to throughout this book as *The Primary Program*. Basically, it is a learner-centered approach to school activity that suggests that curriculum emanates from children and needs to be created or negotiated with them. It is consistent with whole language and other inquiry-based approaches to teaching and learning. *The Primary Program* is written as a theoretical orientation to teaching and learning, not a prescribed set of curricular activities.

The Early Childhood Study Committee developed the proposal process in which schools submitted proposals for implementation plans describing how they might use the foundation documents in their schools. The committee honored every proposal by allotting small amounts of funding ($1,200 for the year) to the 12 schools that submitted less comprehensive proposals, submitted by individuals or small groups of teachers.

I was a new professor at a nearby university and offered to join the Early Childhood Study Committee as a researcher and resource, to help with selection of the R & D sites and, subsequently, with the year of work at each site. My commitment at Ridgeway, although initially to the whole school, became increasingly focused on our group. My relationship with the second school would take another book to describe.

THE SCHOOL IN WHICH THE TEACHERS WORKED

Ridgeway Elementary School is situated in a lower socioeconomic (SES) neighborhood in the capital city of a middle-America state. The city's population is approximately 200,000, consisting of generally White middle- and upper middle-class people. Most of the city's diverse and poor population is limited to the neighborhoods around 6 of its 34 elementary schools. There is an African-American area in the city, an international community of students that attend the university, a Native American population (less that 1%), and a growing Hispanic and Southeast Asian population, all within the neighborhoods of the lower socioeconomic status schools.

Ridgeway has one third of the English as a second language (ESL) children in the district. The principal, Mr. Z., calls the school an "international school" with 15 languages represented from the Mideast, Asia, Spanish-speaking countries, and Bosnia. "Anywhere there's been a war is represented at our school," he said. The school is quite diverse with 9.01% African-American, 16.5% Asian, 12.24% Hispanic, 1.7% Native American, and 60.54% White students. Twenty-six percent of the students are involved in the ESL program. With an enrollment of 600, the school has a large population of identified special education students (more than 110). Of the 75 sixth graders in attendance at Ridgeway, only 7 began their school lives in kindergarten at the school. Of the 590 names that could be included in the school directory, only 300 responded affirmatively and the rest asked not to be included. Mr. Z. suggests that this is because families do not want their addresses and phone numbers known publicly because of the possible access this would allow various agencies. In the 1994–1995 school year, there was a turnover of about 200 students, meaning that a student either left or enrolled in school while the overall school enrollment remained the same.

The school has an early childhood special education program for 4-year-olds, a Head Start Program, and a "Baby Eagles" (eagles are the school mascot) program for 2-year-old children in the neighborhood. The federally funded Transition Grant at Ridgeway supports the transition of students from Head Start to primary-grade classrooms by helping teachers via workshops, release time for home visits, and site visits by curriculum support staff.

Ridgeway goes through Grade six, with four classes of each grade from kindergarten through sixth grade. The school has what Mr. Z. refers to as "economic diversity," with about 75% of the children on free or reduced lunch. In 1996–1997, Ridgeway will become a Title I school because of its low scores on standardized tests and the low SES of the families that send their children there. Ridgeway scored the lowest in the district on standardized tests administered in spring, 1995.

Ridgeway's R & D plan called for an extension of work that had already been initiated at the school. The teachers, in the 1993–1994 school year, began the Ridgeway Institute. The Institute was designed by Mr. Z. in an effort to allow teachers to share ideas. Each month, one teacher was responsible for researching an area of interest and reporting his or her findings at the Institute's meeting, which took place in lieu of a faculty meeting. Attendance at the Institute was not mandatory, but typically more than 80% of the teachers showed up. Teachers learned from each other about portfolios, other alternative forms of assessment, issues of language and literacy, and more over the course of the school year. Ridgeway teachers, all of whom signed their proposal, wanted to have an Institute with pay, with access to external experts, and with release time for teachers to have larger chunks of time to learn and plan. Although the money was originally intended for teachers of young children, Ridgeway's comprehensive proposal for teachers through Grade 6 was accepted by the Early Childhood Study Committee because of its consistency with the Committee's goal of supporting the school site as the context for teacher growth.

Almost all of Ridgeway's teaching staff met for 1 week in June to initiate and outline goals for the R & D year. Teachers were paid to attend the summer session; many outside speakers were invited to participate. Teachers learned about assessment, literacy, and other issues they had identified on a survey of areas of interest. Many teachers continued to meet (on their own time) throughout the summer to plan for the coming year.

There was tension at the final sessions of the Institute in spring 1994, leading to Mr. Z.'s decision to have grade-level institutes (study teams) be the focus of the 1994–1995 school year. Teachers wanted to focus more on grade-level specific problems and issues, and they wanted to meet with adjacent grade levels periodically (e.g., second- and third-grade teachers met to discuss issues that cross the grades, such as instruction in math). The bulk of the $25,000 that was allotted to Ridgeway was spent on substitute teachers. Substitutes were hired for either mornings or afternoons so that each teacher received nine half-days out of their classroom. They used the time to study issues specific to their grade levels.

Quite often, the R & D release time was used to plan, as a team, the areas that students would next study. Initially, this frustrated Jane, the district's early childhood consultant, because she thought that teachers already had sufficient planning time and that support from her office should be reflected in activity less typical of what teachers usually do. Her frustration was not entirely quelled on a schoolwide basis because many teachers continued to engage in planning during their R & D release time. Eventually, the teachers and Jane came to appreciate the results of increased planning time because the children benefited from well-planned units of study.

OUR GROUP FORMS

By the middle of October, there were many areas of study being undertaken by various grade levels of teachers at Ridgeway. They were pursuing alternative assessment, literacy, children-as-inquirers, thematic planning, and more. I met with teachers from many of the groups, usually with groups of primary teachers (reflective of my interest in emerging literacy). Two first-grade teachers, one second-grade teacher, three third-grade teachers, the teacher of the Montessori (multiage) classroom, and the early childhood special education teacher continually raised issues in common, began talking increasingly among each other, and decided to meet together after school. As the first semester progressed, we met informally on the one day each week when I was at Ridgeway. By the beginning of the second semester, our group was meeting every Wednesday after school because our informal discussions whet our appetites but did not satisfy our needs for conversation.

Jane and I offered the teachers inservice staff development credit (for salary enhancement) or university credit (independent study) for their work. Some attended for personal/professional growth with no interest in gaining staff development or university credit. Although most would have attended regardless of credits toward salary enhancement, the contact hours required for credit helped structure the regularity of our meetings.

Most of the participants attended each week; Jane attended about every other meeting and Pam attended only a few. As discussed earlier, one teacher would be transferred out of her classroom for the coming school year and rarely attended when she knew this was the case.

The study group meetings were always announced on the public address system of the school, the doors were always open to newcomers, and the readings were available to any interested colleagues. We did not intend to create an isolated or elitist group; the teachers wanted to have a committed time for intensively exploring issues that were arising in their teaching lives. At one meeting, the computer teacher attended for about an hour. Aside from that, no other teacher attended our meetings.

Appendix B
Procedural Issues

¤ ¤ ¤

I anticipate that some readers may want to know more of the particulars of how we ran our group. As discussed in Appendix A, we met once each week, after school. Our meetings lasted from 1½ to 3 hours; folks came and went as they needed. In the following two sections I discuss the typical beginnings and endings of our meetings. I want others to know that we needed to spend time on personal issues and administrivial issues so that our minds would be clearer to focus on the more intense facets of the work that formed the substance of our sessions.

BEGINNING A SESSION

We met in one teacher's classroom, decided on at the previous meeting, and that teacher would supply a snack such as popcorn or fruit. We typically dealt with administrative issues first. Folks who registered with me for university independent study credit or those taking district staff development credit for salary enhancement wanted to know about schedules, time, number of credit units, cost of credit, salary advancement, grading policies, and the nature of the commitment required by the group. I also spent portions of the beginning few minutes of some sessions informally advising group members about advanced degree programs.

By the end of our third session, most of the issues of registration issues were finally settled. Only half of the group registered for any kind of credit. We dealt with the district policy that prohibited teachers from attending staff development courses before the school day officially ended at 3:30 p.m. This was a sensitive topic because the children were sent home 40 minutes prior to this time, and group members did not understand the district rationale for having us wait to begin staff development activity. We made the decision to start as soon as possible at the end of the school day. The fact that our own children would be in daycare for extended hours and that our families needed us were added pressures for the group.

We heard about ear infections, baby teeth, pregnancies, and other issues of living the life of a teacher and a mother or father and a wife or husband. We also shared in more intense tragedies. Kim L. was going through a very upsetting divorce and left a few times to meet with a lawyer. She missed days of school when she attended court. In early February, we learned that Linda's husband's cancer had returned. He had been in remission for the past 4 years, but by March he was in the final stages of liver cancer. He died before the school year was out. She returned to our group and immersed herself in her students, her own children, and her writing. Writing with her third-grade partner, Liz, helped her get through some hard times because those writing sessions were, they reported, rich in many conversations. The tensions in school, out of school, and between in-school lives and out-of-school lives were real and recognized and shared within our group. We supported each other across the many contexts of our lives.

As these issues wound down, a group member would typically ask about others' progress or begin to discuss her own progress on her writing, reading, thinking, and classroom activity. This evolved into a check-in reminiscent of Atwell's (1987) status of the class. We moved around the circle, and folks filled us in on their progress and experiences since our last meeting. Thus began our process of opening our collective zone of proximal development (Vygotsky, 1978), our thought collective. Individuals who wanted or needed more time to focus on their and their students' inquiry were afforded such time after everyone else, who wanted to, reported their status.

THE END OF A SESSION

Different administrative issues re-emerged near the end of many sessions as we looked forward to our next meeting. We planned how we would like to spend our time together in subsequent sessions and agreed that we might listen to a member read something that she wrote; present data that we were collecting as a way of initiating discussions about what the data showed or implied; share our writing by distributing copies at our meeting; read articles or chapters in common; subgroup for articles not read in common (this was never done); discuss the meaning and nature of curriculum; do book talks on books read by an individual within the group; respond to drafts of pieces we wrote and circulated prior to our meeting; and plan to use time to discuss life at the school and within the district. By the time we were ending, folks were anxious to leave, resulting in quick plans that often changed on meeting the next time.

One end-of-the-session activity was when Mona mentioned that she had completed her reading of Graves (1991); I requested that she do a book talk on that at our next meeting. Another week Liz and Linda described some work their children were doing in their study of our city. They requested some time that would focus on processes of finding information, grouping kids, and other pragmatic issues. Liz was insistent that we "not spend more than 10 minutes on this … just a quick sort of brainstorming." At another meeting, Kim Z. announced that she would report on her progress as she read chapters of Wells (1986) and related those to language and learning in her classroom.

Sometimes, as the session wound down, someone would comment on the writing style of one of the authors we had read. One evening, after we struggled to understand the implications of Dewey (1938) in classrooms, Liz asked, "Why did he write that way?" Others nodded and moaned in agreement; Dewey was hard to understand and teasing out the implications of his work for classrooms was difficult. We were debriefing from our time together.

Our sessions felt like we were immersed in something and I could sense a lightening up as time and energy wound down. Before leaving the room of the person who had sponsored our meeting, we'd help to clean up and confirm our next meeting. The end of session wrapups put some closure on the meeting.

THOSE LITTLE THINGS …

Our meetings took place in the school and were affected by that context. There were announcements paging staff because of phone calls, the assistant principal tracking down a child who didn't show up at home because he hadn't gotten on his bus, calls for the janitor to attend to something in the building, and brief visits by Mr. Z. or other teachers who needed to talk to the sponsor of the meeting but didn't know that our whole group was in her room. I mention these so that other groups trying to organize a study collective like ours will not become discouraged by these background incidents. They add some tension to getting focused, but holding our meeting in the school made it quite accessible to those interested in attending. We were also right at the site of teachers' changing thinking and practices and could view the teachers' contexts and other evidence within the classrooms.

References

□ □ □

Agar, M. (1980). *The professional stranger: An informal introduction to ethnography*. Orlando, FL: Academic Press.

Allende, I. (1989). *The stories of Eva Luna*. New York: Bantam.

Atwell, N. (1987). *In the middle: Writing, reading, and learning with adolescents*. Portsmouth, NH: Heinemann.

Avery, C. (1993). *... And with a light touch: Learning about reading, writing, and teaching with first graders*. Portsmouth, NH: Heinemann.

Bateson, M.C. (1989). *Composing a life*. New York: Plume.

Baumann, J. F. (1992). Organizing and managing a whole language classroom. *Reading Research and Instruction, 31*(3), 1–14.

Beane, J. (Ed.). (1995). *Toward a coherent curriculum: 1995 yearbook of the association for supervision and curriculum development*. Alexandria, VA: Association for Supervision & Curriculum Development.

Belenky, M., Clinchy, B., Goldberger, N., & Tarule, J. (1986). *Women's ways of knowing: The development of self, voice, and mind*. New York: Basic Books.

Berghoff, B. (1994). Multiple dimensions of literacy: A semiotic case study of a first-grade nonreader. In C. Kinzer & D. Leu (Eds.), *Multidimensional aspects of literacy research, theory and practice: Forty-third yearbook of the National Reading Conference* (pp. 200–216). Chicago: National Reading Conference.

Bloom, B. S. (1956). *Taxonomy of educational objectives Handbook 1: Cognitive domain*. New York: David McKay.

Boyd, C. (1993). Creating curriculum from children's lives. *Primary Voices K–6, 1*(1),

Boyer, E. (1990). *Scholarship reconsidered: Priorities of the professoriate*. Princeton, NJ: Carnegie Foundation for the Advancement of Teaching.

Brady, J. (1995). *Schooling young children: A feminist pedagogy for liberatory learning*. Albany: State University of New York Press.

Bredekamp, S. (Ed.). (1987). *Developmentally appropriate practice in early childhood programs serving children from birth through age 8*. Washington, DC: National Association for the Education of Young Children.

Bruner, J. (1963). *The process of education*. New York: Vantange/Random House.

Calkins, L. (1986). *The art of teaching writing*. Portsmouth, NH: Heinemann.

Calkins, L. (1994). *The art of teaching writing* . Portsmouth, NH: Heinemann.

Calkins, L. M., with Harwayne, S. (1991). *Living between the lines*. Portsmouth, NH: Heinemann.

Cambourne, B. (1995). Toward an educationally relevant theory of literacy learning: Twenty years of inquiry. *Reading Teacher, 49*(3), 182–190.

Cheney, S., & Duncan, I. (1969). *Art of dance* (S. Cheney, Ed.). New York: Theatre Art Books.

Clandinin, D. J. (1993). Teacher education as narrative inquiry. In D. J. Clandinin, A. Davies, P. Hogan, & B. Kennard (Eds.), *Learning to teach, teaching to learn: Stories of collaboration in teacher education* (pp. 1–15). New York: Teachers College Press.

Clandinin, D. J., Davies, A, Hogan, P., & Kennard, B. (Eds.). (1993). *Learning to teach, teaching to learn: Stories of collaboration in teacher education*. New York: Teachers College Press.

Clark, G. (1990). *Dialogue, dialectic, and conversation: A social perspective on the function of writing*. Carbondale: Southern Illinois University Press.

Cochran-Smith, M. (1991, August). Learning to teach against the grain. *Harvard Educational Review, 61* (3), 279–310.

Cochran-Smith, M., & Lytle, S. (1990, March). Research on teaching and teacher research: The issues that divide. *Educational Researcher, 19* (2), 2–11.

Cochran-Smith, M., & Lytle, S. (1993). *Inside outside: Teachers research and knowledge*. New York: Teachers College Press.

Cohen, D. (1995). What is the system in systemic reform? *Educational Researcher, 24*(2), 11–17, 31.

Cohen, D. (1996). *More democratic schools for the disadvantaged?* Symposium presented at the annual meeting of the American Educational Research Association, New York.

Corbett, D., & Wilson, B. (1995). Make a difference with, not for, students: Plea to researchers and reformers. *Educational Researcher, 24*(5), 12–17.

Crowell, C. (1993). Living through war vicariously with literature. In L. Patterson, C. Santa, K. Short, & K. Smith (Eds.), *Teachers are researchers: Reflection and action* (pp. 51–59). Newark, DE: International Reading Association.

Darling-Hammond, L. (1995). The quiet revolution: Rethinking teacher development. *Educational Leadership, 53*, 4–10.

Darling-Hammond, L., & McLaughlin, M. (1995). Policies that support professional development in an era of reform. *Phi Delta Kappan, 76*(8), 597–604.

Deal, T. (1990). Healing our schools: Restoring the heart. In A. Leiberman (Ed.), *Schools as collaborative cultures: Creating the future now* (pp. 127–149). New York: The Falmer Press.

DeStefano, J. (1981). Research update: Demonstrations, engagement, and sensitivity: A revised approach to language learning—Frank Smith. *Language Arts, 58*(2), 103–112.

Dewey, J. (1904). The relation of tehory to practice in education. In C. McMurry (Ed.), *The third yearbook of the National Society for the Scientific Study of Education* (pp. 9–30). Chicago: University of Chicago Press.

Dewey, J. (1938). *Experience and education*. New York: Collier Books, Macmillan.

Dillard, A. (1989). *The writing life*. New York: HarperCollins.

Doake, D. (1994). The myths and realities of whole language: An educational movement at risk. In A. Flurkey & R. Meyer (Eds.), *Many cultures many voices: Under the whole language umbrella* (pp. 125–157). Urbana IL/ Bloomington, IN: National Council of Teachers of English/ Whole Language Umbrella.

Dyson, A. (1993). *Social worlds of children learning to write in an urban primary school*. New York: Teachers College Press.

Edelsky, C. (1994). Research about whole language; research for whole language. In A. Flurkey & R. Meyer (Eds.), *Under the whole language umbrella: Many cultures, many voices* (pp. 64–84). Urbana, IL/Bloomington, IN: National Council of Teachers of English/Whole Language Umbrella.

Fine, M. (1987). Silencing in public schools. *Language Arts, 64*, 157–174.

Fisher, B. (1991). *Joyful learning: A whole language kindergarten*. Portsmouth, NH: Heinemann.

Fisher, B. (1995). *Thinking and learning together: Curriculum and community in a primary classroom*. Portsmouth, NH: Heinemann.

Flannery, K. (1995). "What does theory have to do with me?" Reading literacy theory in a teacher preparation program. *Reader: Essays in reader-oriented theory, criticism, and pedagogy*, (33/34), 13–37.

Fosnot, C. (1989). *Enquiring teachers, enquiring learners: A constructivist approach for teaching*. New York: Teachers College Press.

Freire, P. (1970a). *Pedagogy of the oppressed*. New York: Continuum.

Freire, P. (1970b, May). The adult literacy process as cultural action for freedom. *Harvard Educational Review*, 40(2), 205–225.

Fullan, M. (1991). *The new meaning of educational change*. New York: Teachers College Press.

Geertz, C. (1973). *The interpretation of cultures*. New York: Basic Books.

Gibboney, R. (1994). *The stone trumpet: A story of practical school reform 1960–1990*. Albany: State University of New York Press.

Giff, P. R. (1988). *Best friends*. New York: Bantam Doubleday Dell Books for Young Readers.

Gilligan, C. (1993). *In a different voice: Psychological theory and women's development*. Cambridge, MA: Harvard University Press.

Ginott, H. (1972). *Teacher & child: A book for parents and teachers*. New York: Macmillan.

Glaser, B., & Strauss, A. (1967). *The discovery of grounded theory*. Chicago: Aldine.

Glatthorn, A. A., (1990). *What is a teacher?* Canada: British Columbia Ministry of Education.

Glover, K. M. (1993). A bag of hair: American first graders experience Japan. *Primary Voices K–6, 1*(1),

Goldberg, N. (1986). *Writing down the bones: Freeing the writer within*. Boston: Shambala.

Goodlad, J. (1994). *Educational renewal: Better teachers, better schools*. San Francisco: Jossey-Bass.

Goodman, K. (1986). *What's whole in whole language?* Portsmouth, NH: Heinemann.

Goodman, K. (1996). *On reading*. Portsmouth, NH: Heinemann.

Goodman, Y. (1985). Kidwatching: Observing children in the classroom. In A. Jaggar & M. Smith-Burke (Eds.), *Observing the language learner* (pp. 9–18). Newark, DE /Urbana, IL: International Reading Association/National Council of Teachers of English.

Goswami, D., & Stillman, P. (1987). *Reclaiming the classroom: Teacher research as an agency for change*. Upper Montclair, NJ: Boynton/Cook.

Graves, D. (1983). *Writing: Teachers and children at work*. Portsmouth, NH: Heinemann.

Graves, D. (1986). Do you know what backstrung means? *The Reading Teacher, 39*, 807–812.

Graves, D. (1990). *The reading/writing teacher's companion: Discover your own literacy*. Portsmouth: Heinemann.

Graves, D. (1991). *The reading writing teacher's companion: Build a Literate classroom*. Portsmouth: Heinemann.

Graves, D., & Sunstein, B. (1993). *Portfolio portraits*. Portsmouth, NH: Heinemann.

Graves, J. (1994, June). Presentation at the summer workshop for the Research and Development Project of Lincoln Public Schools, Lincoln, NE.

Greene, M. (1995). *Releasing the imagination: Essays on education, the arts, and social change*. San Francisco: Jossey-Bass.

Griffin, G. (1983). The work of staff development. In G. Griffin (Ed.), *Staff development: Eighty-second Yearbook of the National Society for the Study of Education* (pp. 1–10). Chicago: University of Chicago Press.

Griffin, G. (1995). Influences of shared decision making on school and classroom activity: Conversations with five teachers. *The Elementary School Journal, 96*(1), 29–45.

Halliday, M. A. K. (1988). ¡There's still a long way to go ..." An interview with emeritus professor Michael Halliday. *Journal of the Australian Advisory Council on Languages and Multicultural Education, 1,* 35–39.

Hansen, J. (1987). *When writers read.* Portsmouth, NH: Heinemann.

Hargreaves, A. (1996). Revisiting voice. *Educational Researcher, 25*(1), 12–19.

Harste, J., Woodward, V., & Burke, C. (1984). *Language stories and literacy lessons.* Portsmouth: Heinemann.

Harste, J. C. (1993). Inquiry-based instruction. *Primary Voices K–6, 1*(1),

Hartman, J. A., & Eckerty, C. (1995). Projects in the early years. *Childhood Education,* 141–147.

Harwayne, S. (1992). *Lasting impressions: Weaving literature into the writing workshop.* Portsmouth, NH: Heinemann.

Hendricks-Lee, M., Soled, S., & Yinger, R. (1995). Sustaining reform through teacher learning. *Language Arts, 72*(4), 288–292.

Heath, S. (1983). *Ways with words: Language, life, and work in communities and classrooms.* Cambridge: Cambridge University Press.

Hogan, P., & Clandinin, J. (1993). Living the story of received knowledge: Constructing a story of connected knowing. In D. Clandinin, A. Davies, P. Hogan, & B. Kennard (Eds.), *Learning to teach, teaching to learn: Stories of collaboration in teacher education* (pp. 193–199). New York: Teachers College Press.

Hollingsworth, S. (1992). Learning to teach through collaborative conversation: A feminist approach. *American Educational Research Journal, 29*(2), 373–404.

Hollingsworth, S. (1994). *Teacher research and urban literacy education: Lessons and conversations in a feminist key.* New York: Teachers College Press.

Katz, L. (1994, April). *The project approach.* (ERIC Digest report No. EDO–PS–94–6).

Katz, L., & Chard, S. (1989). *Engaging children's minds: The project approach.* Norwood, NJ: Ablex.

Klassen, C., & Short, K. (1992). Collaborative research on study groups: Embraching the complexities. In C. Kinzer & D. Leu (Eds.), *Literacy research, theory, and practice: Views from Many perspectives. Forty-first yearbook of the National Reading Conference* (pp. 341–348). Chicago: The National Reading Conference.

Kohn, A. (1993, September). Choices for children: Why and how to let students decide. *Phi Delta Kappan, 75*(1), 8–16.

Kostelnik, M. (1992, May). Myths associated with developmentally appropriate programs. *Young Children, 47*(4), 17–23.

Langer, J., & Applebee, A. (1987). *How writing shapes thinking: A study of teaching and learning.* Urbana, IL: National Council of Teachers of English.

Lareau, A. (1989). *Home advantage: Social class and parental intervention in elementary education.* London: Falmer.

Larson, K. (1996). Writing revisited. *NEBLAB: The Nebraska Language Arts Bulletin, 8*(2), 27–28.

Lather, P. (1991). *Getting smart: Feminist research and pedagogy with/in the postmodern.* New York: Routledge.

LeFevre, K. (1987). *Invention as a social act.* Carbondale: Southern Illinois University Press.

Leiberman, A. (1995). Practices that support teacher development: Transforming conceptions of professional learning. *Phi Delta Kappan, 76*(8), 591–596.

Lester, N., & Onore, C. (1990). *Learning change: One school district meets language across the curriculum.* Portsmouth, NH: Boynton/Cook Heinemann.

Lortie, D. (1975). *Schoolteacher: A sociological study.* Chicago: University of Chicago Press.

MacLeod, J. (1995). *Ain't no makin' it: Aspirations and attainment in a low-income neighborhood.* Boulder: Westview Press.

McLaren, P. (1989). *Life in schools: An introduction to critical pedagogy in the foundations of education.* New York: Longman.

Mehan, H. (1982). The structure of classroom events and their consequences for student performance. In P. Gilmore & A. Glatthorn (Eds.), *Children in and out of school: Ethnography and education* (pp. 59–87). Washington, DC: Center for Applied Linguistics.

Merriam, E. (1991). *The wise woman and her secret.* New York: Simon & Schuster.

Meier, D. (1995). *The power of their ideas: Lessons for America form a small school in Harlem.* Boston: Beacon Press.

Meyer, R. (1995). Servicing-in: An approach to teacher and staff development. *Teacher Research, 2*(2), 1–17.

Meyer, R. (1996a). *Stories from the heart: Teachers and students researching their literacy lives.* Mahwah, NJ: Lawrence Erlbaum Associates.

Meyer, R. (1996b). *neblab: The Nebraska language arts bulletin, themed issues: Teacher change.* Lincoln: The Literacy Studies Group and the Nebraska Writing Project.

Meyer, R. (1996c). *Teachers and research: A study group engaged in liberatory activity.* Paper presented at the annual meeting of the National Reading Conference, Charleston, SC.

Meyer, R., & Ridder, K. (1996, November). *Stories from the heart: Our students, our lives, our research.* Paper presented at the annual meeting of the National Council of Teachers of English, Chicago, IL.

Meyer, R. with Ridder, K., Larsen, K., DeNino, L., Brown, L., MacKenzie, M., Filbrandt, T., & Kolbe, T. (1996, August). *Layers of inquiry: Children, teachers and teacher researchers learning from themselves and each other.* Presentation at the annual meeting of the Whole Language Umbrella, St. Paul, MN.

Moll, L., & Diaz, S. (1987). Change as the goal of educational research. *Anthropology and Education Quarterly, 18*(4), 300–311.

Momaday, N. S. (1976). *The way to rainy mountain.* Albuquerque: University of New Mexico Press.

Montessori, M. (1964). *The advanced Montessori method.* Cambridge, MA: Bentley

Montessori, M. (1966). *The secret of childhood.* (M. J. Costelloe, Trans.). Notre Dame, IN: Fides Publishers.

Montessori, M. (1967). *The absorbent mind.* New York: Dell.

Montessori, M. (1976). *From childhood to adolescence.* New York: Schocken Books.

Murray, D. (1982). *Learning by teaching: Selected articles on writing and teaching.* Portsmouth, NH: Heinemann.

Nebraska Department of Education, Iowa Department of Education, Iowa Area Education Agencies, & Head Start–State Collaboration Project. (1993). *The primary program: Growing and learning in the heartland.* Lincoln, NE: Office of Child Development, Nebraska Department of Education.

Newman, J. (1991). *Interwoven conversations: Learning and teaching through critical reflection.* Toronto: Ontario Institute for Studies in Education (OISE).

Noddings, N. (1984). *Caring: A feminine approach to ethics & moral education.* Berkeley: University of California Press.

O'laughlin, M., Bierwiler, B., & Serra, M. (1996, April). *The Possiblities of Literacy in an Urban School: Report of a Field Study.* Paper presented at the annual meeting of the American Educaional Research Association, New York.

Paley, V. (1995). *Kwanza and me: A teacher's story.* Cambridge: Harvard University Press.

Patterson, L., Santa, C., Short, K., & Smith, K. (Eds.). (1993). *Teachers are researchers: Reflection and action.* Newark, DE: International Reading Association.

Perrone, V. (1991). *A letter to teachers: Reflection on schooling and the art of teaching.* San Francisco: Jossey-Bass.

Philips, S. (1971). Participant structures and communicative competence: Warm Springs children in community and classroom. In C. Cazden, V. John, & D. Hymes (Eds.), *Functions of language in the classroom* (pp.   ). New York: Teachers College Press.

Polakow, V. (1993). *Lives on the edge: Single mothers and their children in the other America.* Chicago: University of Chicago Press.

Potok, C. (1967). *The chosen.* New York: Fawcett Crest.

Power, B. M. (1996). *Taking note: Improving your observational notetaking.* York, ME: Stenhouse.

Reimer, K., Stephens, D., & Smith, K. (Eds.). (1993). Asking questions/making meaning: Inquiry-based instruction. *PrimaryVoices K–6, 1*(1),   .

Richardson, V. (1994). Conducting research on practice. *Educational Researcher, 23*(5), 5–10.

Rief, L. (1991). Why can't we live like the monarch butterfly? In B.Miller & R. Hubbard (Eds.) *The Heinemann reader: Literacy in process* (pp. 244–256). Portsmouth, NH: Heinemann.

Rogers, C. (1969). *Freedom to learn.* Columbus, OH: Merrill.

Rosenblatt, L. (1978). *The reader, the text, and the poem: The transactional theory of the literary work.* Carbondale and Edwardsville: Southern Illinois University Press.

Sarason, S. (1971). *The culture of school and the problem of change.* New York: McGraw-Hill.

Sarason, S. (1990). *The predictable failure of educational reform: Can we change course before it's too late?* San Francisco: Jossey-Bass.

Schon, D. (1983). *The reflective practioner: How professionals think in action.* New York: Basic Books.

Schon, D. (1986). *Educating the reflective practitioner.* San Francisco: Jossey-Bass.

Shannon, P. (1989). *Broken promises: Reading instruction in twentieth-century America.* Granby, MA: Bergin & Garvey.

Shannon, S. (1990). *The struggle to continue: Progressive reading instruction in the United States.* Portsmouth, NH: Heinemann.

Shor, I. (1987). Educating the educators: A Freirean approach to the crisis in teacher education. In I. Shor (Ed.), *Freire for the classroom: A sourcebook for liberatory teaching* (pp. 7–32). Portsmouth, NH: Boynton/Cook Heinemann.

Short, K. (1993). Teacher research for teacher educators. In L. Patterson, C. Santa, K. Short, & K. Smith (Eds.), *Teachers are researchers: Reflection and action* (pp. 155–159). Newark, DE: International Reading Association.

Short, K., & Burke, C. (1991). *Creating curriculum: Teachers and students as a community of learners.* Portsmouth, NH: Heinemann.

Short, K., & Burke, C. (1996, February). Examining our beliefs and practices through inquiry. *Language Arts, 73,* 97–103.

Short, K., & Harste, J. with Burke, C. (1996). *Creating classrooms for authors and inquirers* (2nd ed.). Portsmouth, NH: Heinemann.

Short, K., Schroeder, J., Laird, J., Kauffman, G., Ferguson, M.,& Crawford, K. (1996). *Learning together through inquiry: From Columbus to integrated curriculum.* York, ME: Stenhouse.

Silverstein, S. (1974). *A light in the attic.* New York: Harper & Row

Sirotnik, K. A. (1983). What you see is what you get: Consistency, peristency and mediocrity in classrooms. *Harvard Educational Review, 53,* 16–31.

Smith, F. (1988). *Joining the literacy club: Further essays into education.* Portsmouth, NH: Heinemann.

Spradley, J. (1980). *Participant observation.* New York: Holt, Rinehart & Winston.

Stuckey, J. E. (1991). *The violence of literacy.* Portsmouth, NH: Boynton/Cook.

Sunstein, B. (1994). *Composing a culture: Inside a summer writing program with high school teachers.* Portsmouth, NH: Boynton/Cook Heinemann.

Tharp, R., & Gallimore, R. (1988). *Rousing minds to life: Teaching, learning, and schooling in social context.* Cambridge: Cambridge University Press.

Thomas, S., & Oldfather, P. (1995). Enhancing student and teacher engagement in literacy learning: A shared inquiry approach. *The Reading Teacher, 49*(3), 192–202.

Van Manen, M. (1986). *The tone of teaching.* Portsmouth, NH: Heinemann.

Van Manen, M. (1990). *Researching lived experience: Human science for an action sensitive pedagogy.* Albany: State University of New York Press.

Vygotsky, L. (1978). *Mind in society: The development of higher psychological processes* (M. Cole, V. John-Steiner, S. Scribner, & E. Souberman, Eds. and Trans.). Cambridge: Harvard University Press.

Walker, A. (1993). *Possessing the secret of joy.* New York: Pocket Star (Simon & Schuster).

Wasserman, S. (1988). *Serious players in the primary classroom.* New York: Teachers College Press.

Watson, D., Burke, C., & Harste, J. (1989). *Whole language: Inquiring voices.* New York: Scholastic.

Wells, G. (1986). *The meaning makers: Children learning language and using language to learn.* Portsmouth, NH: Heinemann.

Wells, G., & Chang-Wells, G. L. (1992). *Constructing knowledge together: Classrooms as centers of inquiry and literacy.* Portsmouth, NH: Heinemann.

Wells, G. with Bernard, L., Gianottic, M., Keating, C., Konjevic, C., Kowal, M., Maher, A., Mayer, C., Moscoe, T., Orzechowska, E., Smieja, A., & Swartz, L. (1993). *Changing schools from within: Creating communties of inquiry.* Ontario: OISE.

Wertsch, J. (1991). *Voices of the mind: A sociocultural approach to mediated action.* Cambridge: Harvard University Press.

Wideen, M. (1987). Perspectives on staff development. In M. Wideen & I . Andrews (Eds.), *Staff development for school improvement: A focus on the teacher* (pp. 1–17). New York: The Falmer Press.

Wilcox, K. (1988). Differential socialization in the classroom: Implications for equal opportunity. In G. Spindler (Ed.), *Doing the ethnography of schooling: Educational anthroplogy in action* (pp. 268–309). Prospect Heights, IL: Waveland Press.

Wolcott, H. (1973). *The man in the principal's office.* New York: Holt, Rinehart & Winston.

Wortman, R. (1996). *Administrators supporting school change.* York, ME: Stenhouse.

Yonemura, M. (1982). Teacher conversations: A potential source of their own professional growth. *Curriculum Inquiry, 12*(3), 239–256.

Author Index

¤ ¤ ¤

229

Subject Index

¤ ¤ ¤